To Body & Jack
fr Carla &
gene
11/92

THE ONEIDA LAND CLAIMS

Laurence M. Hauptman, *Series Editor*

Wilson Cornelius

THE ONEIDA
LAND CLAIMS

A Legal History

GEORGE C. SHATTUCK

 SYRACUSE UNIVERSITY PRESS

First Edition 1991
91 92 93 94 95 96 97 98 99   6 5 4 3 2 1

This book is published with the assistance of a grant from the John Ben Snow Foundation.

Frontispiece: Courtesy of Delia Waterman, daughter of Wilson Cornelius.

The paper used in this publication meets the minimum requirements of American National Standard for Information Sciences—Permanence of Paper for Printed Library Materials, ANSI Z39.48-1984. ∞™

Library of Congress Cataloging-in-Publication Data
Shattuck, George C.
    The Oneida land claims : a legal history / by George C. Shattuck.
  — 1st ed.
        p.   cm. — (The Iroquois and their neighbors)
    Includes bibliographical references and index.
    ISBN 0-8156-2524-3 (cloth : alk. paper). — ISBN 0-8156-2525-1
(pbk.)
        1. Oneida Indians—Claims—History.   2. Indians of North America—
New York (State)—Claims—History.   I. Title.   II. Series.
KF8228.O45A3   1991
346.7304'32'089975—dc20
[347.306432089975]   90-22625
                                                            CIP

Manufactured in the United States of America

To Mrs. Delia Waterman

GEORGE C. SHATTUCK is a tax lawyer with the firm of Bond, Schoeneck & King in Syracuse, New York. He received his J.D. degree from Syracuse University College of Law and has been practicing law in Syracuse since 1954. He is now completing a second book, *Owner's Guide to Succession Planning: For the Family Business.*

CONTENTS

MAP

FOREWORD

JACK CAMPISI

I MET GEORGE SHATTUCK for the first time at his business office on a glorious, sunny day in September of 1975. He had called a few weeks before to invite me to discuss some Oneida Indian research he was interested in. I had the previous year completed a dissertation on the Oneidas, and one of the leaders of the New York Oneida tribe, Jake Thompson, had brought my name to his attention.

Shattuck's interest in research was more than adacemic. The prior year the United States Supreme Court had overturned—by a unanimous eight-to-zero vote—both the federal district court and the court of appeals, ruling in favor of the Oneidas' right to have their claims settled in federal court. Shattuck and his colleagues had argued the case before the lower court and through the two appeals and had ultimately won in spite of the conventional legal wisdom that the case was hopeless. Having won the right to be heard in district court, Shattuck, and the Oneidas now faced the task of carrying the evidentiary burden at the subsequent trial. That trial was what motivated the call to me.

With my arrival at the offices of Bond, Schoeneck & King, on the top two floors of an office building in the center of Syracuse, I was ushered into a conference room, offered a cup of coffee, and introduced by Shattuck to the others present: John Freyer, another attorney in his firm; Thomas N. Tureen and Sharon Eads from the Native American Rights Fund; and Jake Thompson. I must confess that I was a bit bewildered by the ensuing conversation; it was like walking into the middle of a dialogue without the slightest notion as to what was going on and finding that at least a portion of the conversation was in another language, in this case legalese. Shattuck gave a brief résumé of the situation facing the tribe, and then he and the others began a polite but insistent probing of my knowledge of Oneida history, particularly the state treaty of 1795. Although I had a reasonable grasp of the tribe's history, I had to confess that that particular treaty had escaped my attention.

Somehow, this gap in my knowledge did not discourage Shattuck. He asked me if I would be willing to research the treaty and to present evidence at a trial set for that November. Naïveté and the prospect (unusual to an academic) of actually getting paid to do research led me to agree. We shook hands on the arrangement (there was never a formal contract), had lunch, and I went off to begin the search.

By the time of our meeting, Shattuck had fought for nearly a decade to get the Oneidas their day in court. He had propounded a legal theory that ultimately was to upset one hundred years of precedent and open the courts to the claims of a dozen or more eastern tribes. He had argued and upheld, first with his conservative partners, then with opposing counsels and jurists, and finally before the U.S. Supreme Court, the justice of the case. He had exhausted the avenues to compromise; the governors and state legislators had ignored the tribe's pleas, and both Congress and the executive branch had turned their backs on the Oneidas' appeals for justice.

But Shattuck had persisted. A tax lawyer by trade, he had mastered the essentials of a very different, arcane branch of law—Indian law. A political conservative, he had taken on a liberal cause for the most fundamental of reasons: it was right. He somehow convinced his equally conservative partners to support and finance the case as a speculative venture. And after all of that, he risked the success of the case on a handshake with a largely unknown scholar.

Fortunately for me, the lawyers, and the Oneidas, the research went well; and by the end of October it was completed. Again I traveled to Syracuse, on Halloween, to review the material with Shattuck and John Freyer. We spent the afternoon and evening reading and discussing the documents. The evidentiary problem was simple: Had there been a U.S. Indian commissioner present at the treaty negotiations and had the state treaty been ratified pursuant to the provisions of the Indian Trade and Intercourse Act of 1793? The evidence argued no. Shattuck went through each document, questioning its meaning and relevance.

I returned to Syracuse for the trial on Monday, November 10. Although Shattuck was conversant with every aspect of the case, from legal precept to particular fact, when it came time for the trial, Jack Freyer took over the presentation. For the next two days the three of us reviewed all the documents as Freyer organized his presentation and mine. Periodically he would go off to handle another trial, leaving me with a set of questions to answer, or maps and papers to peruse. On his return we would resume the preparation. The work continued well into the evening, and by the end of the second day I had been asked and had answered a dozen times every question I might possibly be asked during direct testimony. The remarkable thing about all of this to me, besides the time commitment and the intensity of the work, was the ease with which control of the case had been transferred to the trial lawyer. It was as though Shattuck had no ego involvement in a case that had consumed so much of his time and energy for ten years. As for Freyer, he took control, mastered the material, designed the trial strategy, and prepared the witnesses and documents, while managing several other cases simultaneously. I gained great respect for both of them.

Trial was set for Wednesday, November 12, in the ornate nineteenth-century courthouse in Auburn, New York. On Tuesday, the eleventh, Shattuck, Freyer, and I drove to Auburn for a pretrial session, at which time Freyer introduced some fifty exhibits that we planned to use. It was a beautiful day for golf, as one of the defense attorneys remarked, and they did seem anxious to end the hearing. The judge in the case was Edmund Port, a diminutive gentleman with, as I was to find out, a wry sense of humor and a sharp mind. After a few moments of courtroom pleasantries, the defense attor-

neys collected their copies of the documents and left, assuming the
materials were the same ones they had seen many times before, ones
included in a previous Indian Claims Commission case. The trial
lasted three days. The defense called no witnesses; they later complained that the counties had refused to provide funds for experts.
I felt a sense of smugness on their part, that although Shattuck had
won the jurisdictional battle at the Supreme Court, they believed
there was no real evidence to sustain such a radical remedy as a finding for the Oneidas.

Yet the plaintiff had some problems too. Because of a split in
the New York Oneida tribe, none of its leaders was called to testify.

Following the conclusion of the arguments at noon on Friday,
the mood was upbeat. The Oneidas, their attorneys, and witnesses
joined in a luncheon celebration at one of the local restaurants in
Auburn. A favorable decision had not yet been rendered, but we
thought a very strong case had been made. The legal wheels grind
slowly. It would take Judge Port the better part of two years to render a verdict, and it would take another ten years to proceed through
appeals, try the issue of damages, and initiate negotiations with the
state and federal governments to settle the claim. In fact, that negotiation is still in process.

The post-trial euphoria of that luncheon was soon past, to be
replaced by a doggedness to see the case to completion. In the interim Bond, Schoeneck & King felt obliged to withdraw from the
litigation. The Native American Rights Fund took over the case
and the issues were revisited by the U.S. Supreme Court. But through
it all, Shattuck remained involved.

I tell this story to provide the reader with background into the
case from the perspective of a witness, and to offer some insights
into the role George Shattuck played in this enterprise, a role he
modestly downplays. As a person closely involved in the litigation
for some fifteen years now, I can safely say that without Shattuck,
the case would not and could not have proceeded. He not only provided its intellectual core; he was its emotional leader. Affable and
gregarious, Shattuck kept the many aspects of the case in focus. He

worked patiently with the different tribal entities and cajoled members of Congress, governors, and presidents for an administrative solution. And when that strategy failed, he found the means to move the case through a series of courts and challenges toward a favorable legal resolution. This is a remarkable achievement for an upstate tax lawyer, with ramifications we are only beginning to see.

ACKNOWLEDGMENTS

I OFFER SINCERE THANKS to my wife, Carla Amussen, who encouraged and helped me to write this account of the Oneida land claims; to my secretary, Barbara Baker, who for twenty-five years has assembled, typed, edited, and materially contributed to countless documents and pleadings, and to this text; to Jan Jinske for typing countless drafts; to John Freyer, George Bond, and Charlie Schoeneck, and to twenty-seven other lawyers at Bond, Schoeneck & King who have counseled and helped and made this all possible; and to Norbert Hill, Irwin Chrisjohn, and Oscar Archiquette and the many Oneidas who helped me to understand.

Cazenovia, New York   GEORGE C. SHATTUCK
September 1990

A HISTORICAL INTRODUCTION

LAURENCE M. HAUPTMAN

THE ONEIDA INDIAN LAND CLAIMS CASES have had a long and cir-
cuitous history, which is summarized here to provide readers with
background to the personal memoir that follows. The Oneida Indians were part of the Iroquois Confederacy, which in colonial times
controlled most of New York State plus large areas south and west
of New York. Over the years, the millions of acres they originally
called their own have been reduced to several small reservations.
The land claim cases involve lands lost by the Oneida Indians both
before and since 1790.

The "post-1790 claim" covers approximately 260,000 acres of
land. The Oneidas in their legal arguments, as formulated principally by George Shattuck, claim that New York State violated fed-
eral-Indian treaties made in 1784, 1789, and 1794, as well as the
federal Indian Trade and Nonintercourse acts of 1790 and 1793.
The 1790 act regulated trade with the Indians and prohibited the
unauthorized purchase of Indian land on all land sales not approved
as treaties by the United States Senate. The 1793 act tightened federal control over Indian policy by adding a section requiring the
presence and approval of a federal commissioner. The second act
was in response to the states' intention to extinguish Indian land
rights.

Unable to convince the federal or state governments of the
seriousness of their claim, the Oneidas filed a test case in federal
court in 1970. They sued Oneida and Madison counties, New

York, challenging the validity of an Oneida–New York State "treaty" of 1795 and seeking trespass damages for a two-year period, 1968 and 1969. By suing the two counties and not New York State directly, the Oneidas attempted to circumvent the presumed federal constitutional legal restrictions against suing a state. Hence, the case initially revolved around whether the federal courts had jurisdiction in this matter.*

Oneida hopes were soon raised when the United States Supreme Court agreed to hear the case. In argument in November 1973 before the high court, George Shattuck, acting as attorney for the Oneidas, reiterated the long-held Oneida position that the 1795 New York State treaty was executed in violation of the Constitution, three federal treaties, and the Trade and Intercourse acts. Using the findings of anthropological, historical, and linguistic experts, Shattuck demonstrated that the Oneidas he represented were federally recognized successors in interest to the Oneidas of the 1790s, as well as to the Oneidas of the colonial period.

As Shattuck observed, the Oneidas were not complaining of mere technical failures to comply with the letter of the law. In his exhibits Shattuck showed that federal officials had always responded to the Oneidas by denying the merit of their claims and by discouraging legal action. The Oneidas were wrongly advised many times that they had no federal tribal status in New York; they were also wrongly advised that Congress would retroactively ratify any illegal land sales even if they won in court; and they were also told that they were under state jurisdiction, which precluded any federal action of redress. Because the Indian nations were also barred from New York State courts by the long-held principle that state courts cannot hear Indian land cases, the Oneidas were in effect denied a legal forum. Thus, Shattuck argued that the United States had constitutional responsibilities, treaty obligations, and a congressional

*Jack Campisi, "New York–Oneida Treaty of 1795: A Finding of Fact," *American Indian Law Review* 4 (Summer 1976): 71–82; and Campisi, "The Trade and Intercourse Acts: Land Claims on the Eastern Seaboard," in *Irredeemable America: The Indians' Estate and Land Claims,* ed. Imre Sutton (Albuquerque: Univ. of New Mexico Press, 1985), 337–42.

mandate to provide the Oneidas with their day in court by allowing them to sue for redress of wrongs done them by the state.*

In a unanimous decision rendered on January 21, 1974, with eight justices participating, the U.S. Supreme Court sustained the Oneidas' position and remanded the case back to the lower federal courts. In this landmark decision the Supreme Court held that the 1790 and 1793 Trade and Intercourse acts were applicable to the original thirteen states, including New York, and thus opened up the federal courts to the Oneidas as well as to all other Indians seeking to get back land in the original thirteen states. No longer need they be stymied by jurisdictional barriers. According to Justice Byron White's written opinion: "The rudimentary propositions that Indian title is a matter of federal law and can be extinguished only with federal consent apply in all of the States, including the original 13." White added that controversy arises under the laws of the United States sufficient to invoke the jurisdiction of federal courts, and he reversed the earlier federal court determinations, remanding the case for further proceedings to the federal District Court for the Northern District of New York.

On March 4, 1985, the Oneidas won on the merits of the 1970 claim in the U.S. Supreme Court. This phase of the 1970 test case, which involved fewer than 900 acres of the extensive Oneida tribal land claim, was argued by Arlinda Locklear, herself a Lumbee Indian, who was serving as the Native American Rights Fund attorney for the Oneidas. The Court in a five-to-four decision held that Oneida and Madison counties were liable for damages—fair rental value for two years, 1968 and 1969—for unlawful seizure of Indian ancestral lands. Associate Justice Lewis F. Powell, Jr., who wrote the majority opinion, insisted that the Indians' common-law right to sue is firmly established and that Congress did not intend to impose a deadline on the filing of such suits. This effectively nullified the counties' contention that the Indians had not made a timely effort

---

*Laurence M. Hauptman, *The Iroquois Struggle for Survival: World War II to Red Power* (Syracuse: Syracuse Univ. Press, 1986), 179–203.

to sue and thus had forfeited their legal rights. The decision thus erased the main argument against the Indians and opened the door for further Oneida litigation involving their lost lands.

The Court also suggested that, because of the tremendous economic implications of the case, Congress should help settle the New York Indian claims, as it had done in Connecticut, Maine, and Rhode Island. Despite this suggestion, neither Congress nor the New York State government subsequently has made much effort to resolve this claim, which is called the "post-1790" claim.

The far larger pre-1790 Oneida land claim covers approximately 5.7 million acres of land "acquired" by New York State in 1785 and 1788. The Oneidas have insisted that the 1788 land transaction was a lease; that the Fort Stanwix Treaty of 1784 between them and the federal government was violated by New York State in 1785 and 1788; that the Articles of Confederation barred states from making treaties and dealing with Indian lands; and that the United States Constitution, ratified by New York State before the 1788 Oneida–New York agreement, forbade states to make treaties. Recently, the federal courts have rejected the Oneida arguments for possessory rights over lands lost before 1790; nevertheless, the federal circuit court did leave the door open for "a claim for rent, not repossession of land."*

The litigation of the Oneida land claims appears far from over. But the efforts of George Shattuck and others representing the Oneidas have already helped to reshape the legal history of the United States by creating a new body of American Indian law. Although, sadly, the Oneidas have not tasted the final fruits of victory, their counsel's tenacity in this matter has led to major precedents that have aided other Native Americans. It is largely because of the Oneida cases that first Americans in Connecticut, Maine, Massachusetts, and Rhode Island have succeeded in their own quests to restore ownership of, or just compensation for, their ancient land.

---

*691 F. 2d 1096 (1982). The U.S. Supreme Court recently refused to overturn this decision (1989).

THE ONEIDA LAND CLAIMS

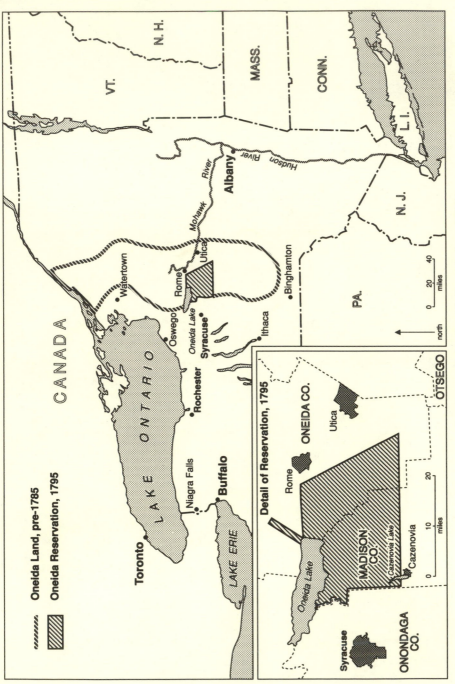

Oneida Land, 1788, and the Oneida Reservation, 1795.

1

Peter Smith's Legacy

The construction of the Indian Non-Intercourse Act by New York State for close to two hundred years, acquiesced in by both the Federal government and the Indians, should not be changed especially where change would result in an economic upheaval.*

IN THE SPRING of 1965, in the midst of President Lyndon B. Johnson's forging of a "Great Society," I was the tax specialist at Bond, Schoeneck & King, an upstate New York law firm. I had, in fact, just successfully completed a complex and important tax case. But my invention of a tax-computing slide rule languished, unsold, and my interest in filling out Form 706 estate tax returns had lost whatever bloom it once had. To a tax specialist, the tastiest morsel on the legal platter was the recent change in the rules on qualified stock options for executives of public companies. My fifth son had been born, and I had moved into a large old house in Syracuse. From a professional and personal perspective, life was very comfortable.

It was then that I was to meet two people who changed my life: Jacob (Jake) Thompson, president of the Oneida Indian Nation of New York, and his wife, Geralda. Jake is of medium height, with curly black hair and one unseeing eye, which I later learned had been hit with a white-hot rivet while he was working on a construction job. Geralda, with her olive skin and straight black hair, was a strikingly attractive woman, who, along with her husband,

*From brief of New York State, 1973.

3

was a key to the Oneida land claims case. Later, I was to meet Geralda's mother, Delia (or Dolly) Cornelius Waterman. Jake Thompson, at our first meeting, showed me a slim black book, the "Treaty Book," which contained old treaties between New York State and the Oneida Nation, along with a collection of maps. He also spun what seemed a wild yarn, namely, that the Oneida Indians still owned a large part of New York State! Yet owing to my own personal background, I was actually predisposed to believe his impassioned story.

In 1928, when I was one year old, my parents built a large summer home on the northwest shore of Cazenovia Lake, in Madison County, New York. For some reason, the "Indians" were very much present in my life. I remember the bedtime story of Hiawatha's canoe's being sunk in that lake—later I would learn that the story had some basis in fact. A ceremonial Iroquois canoe rests there now. Our gardener once found a tomahawk head and a grinding stone, which I still have. When I was about ten, I remember finding a flint arrowhead, which I subsequently lost. I learned that an ancient Indian village, the "McNab Site," was located about half a mile from our summer home. I remember hearing about John Lincklaen, agent for the Holland Land Company, which subdivided and developed much of the land south of Cazenovia. Growing older, I read the novel *Three Bags Full,* a story of the early settlement of Cazenovia. I heard family stories about my grandmother Eudora Day Shattuck's friendship with the Oneida Indians when, as a young bride, she lived near Oneida Castle, New York.

In the 1930s my parents were antique collectors, and I have a vivid memory of their going to an auction at the Gerrit Smith house in the Village of Peterboro, Town of Smithfield, about five or six miles east of Cazenovia. The auction lasted three full days, and at the end of each day my parents returned with a car, plus a pickup truck, full of antiques. I remember a full complement of old farm tools, a box of flint arrowheads, a cannonball lamp from a Civil War battle, wooden children's sleighs, furniture, chinaware, on and on. I still have a very old pine desk that came from that very Gerritt Smith residence.

I also remember Peter Smith's shoe box. Peter was the father of Gerritt Smith. When Peter Smith married in the early 1800s, he gave his bride a wooden shoe box, about 20 × 20 × 12 inches, with a beaded needlepoint cover. That came from the auction too, and I now have it. In the 1790s Peter Smith acquired large tracts of land near what is now Cazenovia and subdivided it for sale to settlers from the East. The land my parents owned was originally part of this New Peterburg Tract, and the legal description on the deed refers to that tract. In the Village of Cazenovia, the Lincklaen House was named after John Lincklaen, who founded Cazenovia. For many, both Peter Smith and John Lincklaen were great men. They opened up great areas for development and settlement. At age twelve or fourteen, I saw these pioneers as heroes who moved westward over this land.

The question I did not ask was how did Peter Smith, John Lincklaen, and the Holland Land Company obtain the land? It never occurred to me to wonder what the Native American owners thought about the settlement of their land by the pioneers. Despite my awareness of the "Indians," I never made the connection.

About thirty years after the auction at the Gerritt Smith residence, Jake and Geralda Thompson came into my life and answered the questions I had not raised. They were not preaching to the already saved, but they did find an open mind, one prepared by personal history—perhaps by growing up with Peter Smith's shoe box—to hear and appreciate their story. Later, Jake and I reviewed the account books of the Holland Land Company in John Lincklaen's house, "Lorenzo," in Cazenovia. They record the transactions in land that, a few years before, had been inhabited by the Oneida Indians.

Even in the spring of 1965, Jake Thompson's maps still showed landmarks and bore names familiar to me. Jake's black treaty book was intelligible to me because I lived at the heart of the land it dealt with and knew generally the history of how New York State developed after the initial treaties were made. At age thirty-eight I began to ask the questions I perhaps should have asked in my teens. After extensive legal research, what happened became clear to me. My heroes, Peter Smith and John Lincklaen, knowingly or not, had dealt in land that the state had illegally acquired from the Oneida Indians. Perhaps Peter Smith paid for the shoe box with the profits of sales of land belonging to the Oneidas? I will never know. But to me that shoe box is now more than an antique. It has become a symbol of misplaced American legal history.

Jake Thompson had been introduced to my law firm in April 1965 by attorney Al Coughlin, a friend of George Bond, one of our senior partners. Coughlin was a member of another local law firm. At that time I was an associate attorney with Bond, Schoeneck & King. Coughlin thought that the Oneida case might have merit, but he did not have the time or resources to investigate or prosecute it himself. The initial meeting on the case, held in April 1965 as I recall, was a meeting of me, Bond, and two other partners in the firm along with Coughlin, Robert Rayback, a professor of history at Syracuse University, and Jake Thompson, then president of the New York Oneidas. In that first meeting Thompson gave a very general description of the Oneida claim. The thrust of his desired legal remedy was to enforce payment by New York State of promised rents and annuities. He did not envision a suit for return of the land. Thompson, with the book of old treaties in hand, had a fairly clear concept of the other historical facts involved in the loss of the land. As we later learned, his knowledge was the result of oral tradition maintained by the Oneidas from generation to generation.

I was assigned by the firm the job of investigating the Oneida claim and coming up with a recommendation about whether to take the case. Right from the start, the firm properly took the case on a contingent fee basis, not as a charity or pro bono case. Robert Wildridge, then an attorney at Bond, Schoeneck & King and now district attorney of Onondaga County, and I made an extensive survey of the merit of the Oneida claims as described by Thompson. Mainly on the basis of the then recent federal court holdings in *Tuscarora Indians* v. *New York State Power Authority* (257 F.2d 885 [2d Cir. 1958], 80 S.Ct. 543 [1960]), we came to the tentative conclusion that the Oneida Nation did indeed have a valid claim to most of its former lands.

The *Tuscarora* case was the key that helped me see the legal issues in the correct perspective. The Tuscarora Indians claimed that New York State could not condemn their reservation land without complying with federal law. The state, in defense, contended that the federal laws protecting Indian land do not apply to New York and the other original thirteen states. Its briefs made this the central point in the case. Then the Second Circuit Court of Appeals held that New York is bound by the federal law that protects Indian land, the Nonintercourse Act. The U.S. Supreme Court agreed on this point but concluded on another basis that the condemnation was valid. Thus the Tuscaroras lost their case but established a very important point: that the Nonintercourse Act does apply to such cases. When I started reviewing the law pertaining to the Oneidas, in 1965, the *Tuscarora* decision, 1960, was fairly recent and seemed most important.

Jake Thompson showed me an artifact that made a vivid impression: a bolt of muslin cloth delivered to Delia Waterman early in 1965 by the Bureau of Indian Affairs. This cloth represented fulfillment by the United States of one of the provisions of the federal treaty of 1794. Another provision of that same treaty promised to keep the Oneidas secure in their reservation land. Every spring the Oneidas of New York received the cloth as evidence of the United States' obligations to them. How strange, I felt, that the United States saw fit to keep the promise to supply cloth for 180 years and yet to ignore the promise to protect their land.

In our report to the firm Bob Wildridge and I concluded that the state land "treaties" with the Oneidas in the period 1785–1840 were all invalid. There remained, however, a serious question regarding what could be done 200 years later. Our report stated in part:

> The above statements indicate that many lawyers over the years have considered the validity of the treaties . . . and have decided that the treaties were illegal and invalid. Then why didn't they

bring suit? It may be that they couldn't find a court with jurisdiction. Or it may be that they were afraid to take on such a
case on a contingent fee basis. Or it may be that the implications of the suit invalidating the treaties were so fantastic that
the lawyers were just afraid to come to grips with it.

Before the *Tuscarora* case we might have backed away for
one or more of the above reasons.

But on the basis of *Tuscarora,* we concluded there was a good legal
case to be made that all of New York's land acquisitions from the
Oneidas were illegal and void.

In 1965 we did not see a clear way to recover on what I thought
was a valid claim. My plan was to write a formal demand to the
attorney general in Washington, citing the U.S. treaties that created
the Oneida Reservation and requesting the action of the United States
under Section 175 of the Federal Indian Law, which requires the
U.S. attorney to represent Indian nations in litigation. The report
to the firm concluded that we should take the case on a contingent
fee basis and that the main thrust should be a plea to the United
States to take action: "It has been explained to Mr. Thompson, and
he understands, that the only way in which taking the case can be
justified is if the potential fee to be earned is large enough to compensate for the risky investment of a large amount of our time."

The firm decided to take the case on a contingent fee basis.
It was recognized that the prospects of success were remote and were
balanced only by a potentially large fee. I recall that Howard Can-
non, one of the senior partners, reluctantly approved taking the case,
saying in effect: "We may get paid on this, but I'll be in my grave
a long time before that." Howard was right, as usual.

The next step was to negotiate a contingent fee contract. That
was not difficult as far as the Oneidas were concerned. Their only
problem was one of disbelief that a reputable law firm was really
serious about the claim against New York State. The Oneidas, and
other members of the Iroquois Confederacy, had been cheated and
misled so many times in the past that they were understandably sus-

picious of another new set of lawyers. Our law firm always made clear to the Oneidas that it was not taking the case on a charitable basis. I remember a meeting with the Oneidas of New York at the Onondaga Long House about that time, where I explained we were not trying to "do good" for them; rather, we proposed to work for them on a businesslike basis and earn a fee if we were successful. At another meeting held in Syracuse on January 15, 1966, I explained the firm's position to representatives of the three Oneida communities: New York, Wisconsin, and Canada. At that meeting the Oneidas made the crucial decision to retain my law firm. I remember how a very old Canadian chief, Amos Elijah, spoke only Oneida at the meeting and had to have all the dialogue translated for him. After the formal meeting was over Elijah gave me a charming smile and said in perfect English: "Well now, Mr. Shattuck, that was certainly an excellent meeting." He knew English perfectly well, but would conduct important discussions only in Oneida.

As it happened, the January 15, 1966, meeting was the first occasion since the early 1800s that representatives of the three branches of the Oneidas had met together. The ancestors of Wisconsin and Canadian Oneidas had been driven out of the state more than 150 years before. The New York Oneidas are descendants of the few who remained. At the meeting were Norbert Hill of Oneida, Wisconsin; Ray Elm, Delia Waterman, and Jake Thompson of Syracuse, New York; Venus Walker, Amos Elijah, William Charles, a Mr. and Mrs. Cornelius, and a Mr. and Mrs. Hill, all from the Oneidas of the Thames, Canada. Some of the Canadians represented the elective and some the hereditary governmental systems. Professor Robert Rayback, Lee Elm (a daughter of Ray Elm), Bob Wildridge, and I were also present. Lee Elm took detailed minutes of the meeting.

From the outset we made it clear to the Oneida representatives that, because of conflicts of interest, Bond, Schoeneck & King could never sue individual landowners because we were already representing many clients in the claims area on other legal matters. The potential for conflict of interest was always recognized, and our retainer contract was deliberately structured to contemplate only recoveries from the state or its municipal subdivisions.

The New York Oneidas, who initiated the current claims, numbered about 500 individuals and had no reservation, except the thirty-two-acre "Boylan" area on Route 46, near Oneida, New York. The Wisconsin Oneidas numbered about 10,000 and have a large reservation near Green Bay, Wisconsin. Those in the Canadian branch, numbering about 2,500, live on a reservation near London, Ontario.

The parties to the contract were the Oneida Indians of New York as represented by its elective system, the Oneida Indians of Wisconsin, Inc., and the Oneidas of the Thames, Canada. Both the hereditary and the elective leaders signed on behalf of the Canadian Oneidas, including their five hereditary clan mothers. It was our understanding that this agreement thus covered all Oneidas, including the so-called Marble Hill group of Oneidas residing near the City of Oneida, New York. Throughout the case we have viewed all enrolled Oneidas, everywhere, as being our clients, whether active in tribal affairs or not and whether living on a reservation or not.

Thompson advised us from the outset that the Oneidas were already represented in the United States Indian Claims Commission with respect to a similar claim against the United States for damages, and that their attorneys in that case were the firm of Aaron, Aaron, Schimberg & Hess, of Chicago.

Before the retainer contract was signed, we conducted correspondence and discussions with Marvin Chapman of Aaron, Aaron, Schimberg & Hess. It was agreed that Bond, Schoeneck & King would press the Oneidas' claim against the state and that Chapman's firm would proceed against the United States in the Indian Claims Commission. We thus proceeded along different paths. But despite some element of competition, Chapman always worked in a cooperative and helpful manner, showing great professional dedication to the Oneidas. By statute, recovery against the United States in the Indian Claims Commission was limited to the value of the land at the time of the illegal taking, without interest. Eventually, this proved to have a limit of just over $3 million. Potentially the claim against New York State, the actual taker of the Oneidas' land, was many times that.

It took a very long time to secure federal approval of the retainer contract, and it was not until 1967 that we had final approval to represent the Oneidas.

Thus in 1965 the Oneida Indians and the law firm of Bond, Schoeneck & King began a course that was to transform the basic law on Indian land claims. I cannot emphasize too strongly that, at first, Jake Thompson and I had to persuade the other Oneidas to press the claims. Some current leaders of the Oneidas regard the claim as a birthright, and properly so. But it was not a birthright in 1965. Rather, the claim was a legend, and recovery a wild surmise.

To understand the Oneida land claims case from 1965 onward, one must preface the discussion by mentioning the case of *U.S.* v. *Boylan* (265 F. 165 [2d Cir. 1920]). A thirty-two-acre tract of land on Route 46, near Oneida, New York, was the subject of litigation in *Boylan,* which reached the U.S. Second Circuit Court of Appeals. The *Boylan* case, decided in 1920, confirmed that the thirty-two acres were part of the aboriginal Oneida lands and could not be alienated. The land was an Indian reservation. Nevertheless, Jake Thompson advised us that New York Telephone Company had poles on the land, that Niagara Mohawk Corporation had power lines on the land, and that Consolidated Gas Corporation had a huge trunk gas line underground across the land.

We entered into an additional retainer agreement with the New York Oneidas, which was also approved by the Interior Department. Notices were sent to the three companies, and satisfactory settlements were negotiated with New York Telephone Company and Niagara Mohawk. Consolidated Gas refused to settle, and in 1969 we commenced a suit in federal court, on the basis of diversity of citizenship, the defendant being an out-of-state corporation. In a letter to Consolidated Gas I had told them to remove the pipeline "at your earliest convenience." Ultimately that case was settled, too, for $6,000, which was in part used to help pay for the printing of our briefs in the case against the counties.

With regard to the main thrust against New York State, I concluded that the key legal basis for a claim against the state was the federal Indian Nonintercourse Act, which was enacted in 1790. It is now Section 177 of the Federal Indian Law. This law specifically states that land cannot be acquired from Indians except by a treaty ratified by the U.S. Senate. Moreover, a party cannot even negotiate to acquire Indian land without the presence of a U.S. commissioner.

Yet the State of New York always contended, from 1790 down to the present, that the Nonintercourse Act did not apply to it. In the *Tuscarora* case, which I mentioned above, the state claimed the right to condemn Tuscarora land for a power dam and reservoir at Niagara Falls. Among other arguments, the state contended that the Nonintercourse Act did not apply to it and that "titles to large areas of the State would be invalidated" if it were held to apply to the state. When I read the *Tuscarora* case, holding that the Nonintercourse Act did apply to New York State, I "knew" in some intuitive way that the Oneidas had a perfectly valid legal claim, if only a way could be found to assert it. My research also disclosed that the Oneidas had repeatedly been cheated as to land value on sales to the state. Thus, conviction of the validity of the Oneidas' moral claim for justice grew stronger in my mind at the same time that I was evolving and creating an unprecedented legal strategy for asserting the legal claim. For me, Peter Smith's and John Lincklaen's legacy of landholdings in the part of central New York I knew so well was growing increasingly tarnished and questionable.

2

Petitions to All Agencies

The General Government will never consent to your being defrauded but it will protect you in all your just rights.[*]

A T THE OUTSET, neither the Oneidas nor I had any idea of suing any individual landowner to recover land, a process legally termed a suit for "ejectment." This was not just because we felt that the law firm could not be involved in ejectment suits against landowners, given our potential conflicts of interest. I also believed, along with the Oneida leaders of the time, that such ejectment suits would be both risky and unnecessary. I was also well aware of decisions that the Eleventh Amendment to the U.S. Constitution bars federal court jurisdiction on suits against a state for damages. These realizations and exigencies played a large part in determining our initial strategy.

My goal was to get the United States to fulfill its treaty and legal obligations and help force the state to make a fair settlement. As I saw it, litigation was a last resort, a tactical move to get the strategic plan in motion. I advised the Oneidas that their best approach was to petition to the proper state governmental agencies for a settlement and, failing that, request a suit by the United States against the state in the Oneidas' behalf. Jake Thompson had, in fact, already embarked on this course. In the early 1960s he had

*From a speech of President George Washington to the Seneca Indians. The same speech was later repeated to the Oneidas by Secretary of War Timothy Pickering.

13

contacted Louis Lefkowitz, the New York State attorney general, and John Hathorn, the director of New York State Indian Services, requesting a settlement of the long-standing claims. These requests came to nothing. In early 1965 he also wrote to Congressman James M. Hanley of central New York about obtaining federal help. On March 24, 1965, Hanley sent Thompson a letter that he had received from the U.S. Bureau of Indian Affairs, which stated that the Oneida treaties with New York "were not available to this Bureau." The letter added, "Neither this Bureau nor the Department of Interior employs attorneys to provide legal services to individual Indians or Indian tribes in the prosecution of claims which they believe they have against others; nor do we have any funds which we could give or lend to the tribe for this purpose."

The Bureau of Indian Affairs is the federal agency whose prime mission is to protect the interests of Native Americans. The bureau has vast regulatory and governance powers that stem from treaty relationships and the large group of statutes codified as the Federal Indian Law, volume 25 of the U.S. Code (25 USCA).

Yet the bureau's letter of March 24, 1965, quoted in part above, bypasses Section 175 of the Federal Indian Law, which reads as follows: "In all States and Territories where there are reservations or allotted Indians, the United States Attorney *shall represent them* in all suits at law or in equity" (emphasis mine). The Bureau of Indian Affairs interprets *shall* as being an optional directive.

The letter states that the bureau did not have in its file copies of the basic instruments, the "state treaties," by which the Oneida had lost 6 million acres of land. Incredible as it may seem, I do believe that the agency in 1965 actually did not wish to have these documents relating to the objects of its protection.

This earlier treatment of Jake Thompson by federal and state authorities was an augury of what would happen during the period from 1967 to 1970, when I filed petitions to various state and federal agencies in behalf of the Oneidas. Although I subsequently realized my petitions were doomed to failure, I played out the reasonable, fair, and friendly petitions route. I learned that in these matters the United States of America does not keep its word.

In early 1967 I prepared a letter to Nelson Rockefeller, then governor of New York, seeking a settlement for the Oneida land claims. In response, the governor suggested that an appropriate approach was to petition the forthcoming Constitutional Convention of New York State. Naïvely I thought that this seemed fair enough. Working with Jake Thompson and Syracuse University professor Robert Rayback, who provided valuable help, we prepared a petition to the Constitutional Convention (see appendix A). Thompson delivered the Oneidas' statement, which is a distillation of the Oneidas' tradition of friendship for the people of the United States and of their conviction that someday the treaty obligations and the laws of the United States would be observed. I prepared an extensive legal and historical statement on the illegal taking of the Oneida land by the state. This petition and statement served as the basis both of later petitions and of the federal court complaints filed by the Oneidas.

The petition, consisting of Thompson's statement and my extensive brief of law and facts, was presented to the 1967 Constitutional Convention via a public hearing held in Syracuse by one of the subcommittees. There, Jake and I described the history of the Oneida claim in some detail and asked the convention to change the jurisdiction of the New York Court of Claims to permit the claim to be heard. Later, at the request of the subcommittee, I went to Albany and gave a further statement. Julius Sackman, an assistant New York State attorney general, appeared at the Albany hearing to oppose the Oneida petition. His message, in effect, was "do not open the courts to the Oneidas." The attorney general's memorandum contended that the Indian Nonintercourse Act did not apply to New York, and the New York attorney general pointed out that the potential damage claim might range up to $858 million in 1967 dollars. This $858 million, the state's figure, would be approximately $2 billion dollars today after adjusting for inflation and interest.

The Constitutional Convention decided not to grant the requested jurisdiction to the New York Court of Claims, and in any event the proposed new constitution did not pass the voters' approval. Thus, the Oneidas had sought but failed to get relief from the state executive officer, Governor Rockefeller, and the state Constitutional Convention.

We then shifted the focus of our efforts. In 1970 the Oneidas appealed to the New York State Legislature, to the Assembly's Subcommittee on Indian Affairs. In a statement Thompson and I asked the Legislature either to negotiate with the Oneida Nation concerning their claims or to grant them the right to sue the state. As we should have expected, nothing came of this tactic either. The Oneidas had thus pursued their claim with all appropriate state agencies. New York State and its courts took the position that federal rules regarding Indian did not apply to it and that all the acquisitions of Oneida land were legal.

On June 20, 1967, I sent a copy of the Constitutional Convention petition and brief to the New York attorney general, receipt of which was later acknowledged by the New York solicitor general. I then wrote to the state solicitor general suggesting a meeting. Again, no response ever came. How much better it would have been for all concerned if the New York attorney general and solicitor general had agreed to meet with us in 1967 to discuss the Oneida claim.

Thompson and I also pursued a course of petitions to the federal government. Under the Federal Indian Law, Native Americans are wards of the U.S. government, which is supposed to protect them and to obtain redress for wrongs against them. These duties were further guaranteed by three federal treaties with the Oneida made in 1784, 1789, and 1794, and by the Federal Indian Law. In mid-1967 I had several meetings with personnel in the Interior Department to advise them of the Oneida claims and to obtain as much information as possible. Although they were courteous and helpful with information, they held out no hope whatever that the United States would ever initiate legal action for the Oneidas.

One 1968 meeting with federal officials stands out in particular. I met with Duard Barnes, other officials of the Bureau of Indian Affairs, and a Justice Department representative to discuss the Oneida case. The man from the Justice Department was very courteous and asked many questions. Several years later I discovered that the same man was representing the United States *against the Oneidas* in their case before the Indian claims commission.

In June 1967 I wrote a long, detailed letter to the Department of Interior describing the basis of the Oneida claim and pointing out the implications of the *Tuscarora* case, which were becoming ever clearer to me as I studied the law and history involved. In *Tuscarora* the holding was clear, but so large it was hard to see: Under U.S. law the post-1790 sales to New York State were all illegal and void. In the latter part of 1967 I started to prepare a formal petition to the president of the United States, Lyndon B. Johnson, on behalf of the Oneidas (see appendix B). This petition, to which was attached a detailed legal and factual brief prepared by me, was delivered to the White House on February 9, 1968. The answer was, atypically, not long in coming. Robert Bennett, himself an Oneida and then the U.S. commissioner of Indian affairs, replied on March 15 in essence as follows: "Since the United States has provided a forum for determining whether the Oneidas should be compensated for injuries sustained as a result of their eighteenth and nineteenth century dealings with the State of New York, no further government action on these claims seems necessary." The basic position of the United States was that it had no duty to help the Oneidas since they had filed a claim against the United States in the Indian Claims Commission, the "forum" referred to in the letter. Yet, as I have explained, the damages available in the Indian Claims Commission are minimal because recovery is limited to historic land values, without interest or recompense for 200 years of use by others.

When I called Geralda Thompson about the denial, she broke down and sobbed over the telephone. Once more the federal bureaucracy had spoken. Once more the Oneidas, who had always been the friendly allies of the United States, were denied what had been promised in solemn treaties. Once again, no one would listen. Characteristically, Geralda quickly rallied with her usual courage and spunk and told me to get on the job and appeal further. Without the courage, determination, ability, and strength of both Geralda and Jake Thompson, there would be no Oneida case today. Without the persistence and help of the Thompsons, I think I might somewhere have fallen by the wayside.

Later, in 1968, we wrote again to President Johnson, asking for a review of the decision not to help the Oneidas. Our letter quoted from a 1790 speech from George Washington to the Seneca Indians about the meaning of the Nonintercourse Act, in which Washington had said: "The General Government will never consent to your being defrauded but it will protect you in all your just rights." Our letter also received a negative response, signed by Stewart L. Udall, secretary of the interior, which was an affirmation of the federal position that the United States owed no duty to the Oneidas (despite three federal treaties), and that the Oneidas' claim against the United States in the Indian Claim Commission prevented the United States from doing anything further.

In May 1968, Jake Thompson and I met with Harry R. Anderson, assistant secretary of the interior, to press the claim for federal help. We restated the history and legal basis of the claim, but the answer was still negative. At that time the Oneidas' suit against the United States in the Indian Claims Commission was thought by U.S. officials to preclude any action by the United States in behalf of the Oneidas. Anderson's response reflected what was then thought to be the law (see appendix C). Once again, the Interior and Justice departments rejected intervention on the Oneidas' behalf.

All through this period the Oneidas simply sought justice and some form of fair recompense. They never tried to evict persons or governmental units from their land. If anyone had been listening, if anyone in federal or state government really cared about the treaty obligations of the United States, the Oneidas would never have proceeded to file suit against landowners, as they finally did in 1974 and 1979.

After being turned down by the federal executive branch, the

Oneidas continued their appeals at other levels. We formally petitioned Congress under the provisions of the U.S. Constitution that grant the right to peaceably assemble and petition for redress of grievances. Our petition was referred to a congressional committee, whose response was predictable: We can't help you. We then followed with a further petition to President Nixon when he took office, as well as a letter and petition to Senator Edward Kennedy. The answer was the same in all cases: The laws and treaties notwithstanding, the United States would not help pursue the claim against New York State.

The Oneida policy of friendly and reasonable conduct was a failure from 1784 down to 1974. The articulation by the Oneidas of their legal rights and claims was not always clear, but their factual statements were accurate and could leave no doubt as to the injustices done. The reason for inaction was not ignorance on the part of New York and the United States, nor lack of merit; the totality of the Oneida claim is a matter of historical public record. The real reason, I was forced to conclude, was that the Native American peoples were regarded as second-class peoples at best and nonpersons at worst. Bureaucrats at the state and federal levels did not take the Oneida claim seriously because they did not believe the Oneidas could effectively pursue the claim themselves. No court was thought to have jurisdiction over such a claim. The only reason the state is now discussing the claim with the Oneidas is that they ultimately succeeded in "shooting their way into the country club." They found a way to escape the legal roadblocks and get the claim into a federal court. I am pleased to have had a role in this accomplishment. After our case, *Oneida Indian Nation* v. *County of Madison*, was decided by the U.S. Supreme Court in 1974, everything began to fall into place.

3

The Test Case

An old problem will soon be solved.[*]

B Y EARLY 1970 it was apparent that all our efforts to secure justice by various administrative appeals would come to nothing. It was either abandon ship — and join the ranks of the other
persons unsuccessful in pressing the Oneida and Iroquois land
claims — or defy all legal precedent and charge ahead with a suit in
federal court. By this time I knew that any appeal to New York courts
would not succeed, but I felt that the law would be on our side in
federal court if we could just crack the jurisdiction barrier. Perhaps
because of our previously successful negotiations with Niagara Mohawk, New York Telephone, and Consolidated Natural Gas, in
which we prevailed in our claim of Oneida ownership, I was a bit
overconfident. In any event, I plunged ahead, fortunately relying on
my instincts rather than on legal precedent.

I designed a course of action and did enough historical and
legal research to see a way to eliminate likely defenses on grounds
of laches, the statute of limitations, abandonment, and others. (The
defense of laches refers to undue delay by plaintiff, and the statute
of limitations is a legal limit to elapsed time before a suit is commenced.) My chief comfort was the decision of the courts in *Tuscarora* v. *N.Y. Power Authority*.

In the *Tuscarora* case, the plaintiff Tuscaroras sought a federal

*From a Chinese fortune cookie, November 6, 1973.

20

court injunction against the taking of reservation land by the New York State Power Authority. They contended that the federal Nonintercourse Act forbade the state to condemn reservation land without federal consent. In its defense the state made the broad argument that the Nonintercourse Act did not apply to New York—the same argument it had been making since 1784. Ultimately, the state won because the Supreme Court found that Congress had sanctioned the condemnation; however, the Supreme Court and the lower federal courts held clearly that the Nonintercourse Act does apply to New York. Ironically, the state's briefs in the *Tuscarora* case, along with an excellent law review article about it written by Stanford University professor of law Gerald Gunther, gave me my first real understanding of how the Nonintercourse Act worked and how it might be used to press the Oneida claim. Even then, in 1970, I surmised that this could be a case of huge dimensions—if only a court could be found to hear it.

The chief obstacle to a federal court proceeding was the perceived lack of jurisdiction. To be heard in federal court, a case has to present a "Federal Question." Federal Question jurisdiction has always been constitutionally permissible, but it was not made a matter of statutory grant until about a hundred years ago. The courts then developed a very restrictive set of rules, based on obscure pleading technicalities, with the purpose of narrowing the boundaries of a Federal Question, the key to being heard in court. One of these rules, the "well-pleaded complaint" rule, held that if a cause of action could initially be brought under state law, it is never a Federal Question. This has kept many Native American land claims out of the federal courts because an action to recover land, an "ejectment" action, may be heard in state courts.

As for Native American land claims, if a Native American or a tribe was wrongfully ousted from its land, any suit to get the land back would necessarily be an ejectment action, one to obtain possession of the land. Since ejectment is a state cause of action, it does not and cannot raise a Federal Question. Thus, a federal court cannot hear the case. So the reasoning went. The fact that the land was taken illegally, or fraudulently, or forcefully, from treaty-protected Native Americans did not matter.

The classic case on this point was initiated by former New York State Assemblyman Edward Everett in behalf of a group of Mohawk Indians around the time I was born. Everett's case, *Deere v. St. Lawrence River Power Co., et al.,* was decided by the Second Circuit Court of Appeals in 1929 (32 F.2d 558 [2d Cir. 1929]). In it, James Deere, a Mohawk, brought suit on behalf of himself and other Iroquois Indians to recover possession of reservation land that had been in non-Native American hands for a century. The complaint cited federal treaties guaranteeing to these Indians the continued possession of their reservation — clearly a forerunner of the 1970 Oneida complaint.

The federal district court dismissed the suit, and, on appeal, the Second Circuit Court of Appeals held that the suit was essentially one for ejectment. Thus, it was a state and not a federal cause of action, hence no Federal Question, and no federal court jurisdiction. The court held that allegations of federal treaties were not essential where the cause of action was to gain possession of land by ejecting the other party from the land: "A guaranty of the right of possession by a treaty of the United States does not render an action in ejectment to recover possession of the property a case arising under a treaty of the United States, insofar as the jurisdictional statute is concerned." The court also referred to the Nonintercourse Act but discarded that as a Federal Question, because the *construction* of that federal statute was not in issue, only its enforcement. The court concluded:

> In this action for ejectment, if the appellant is right in his claim to possession, he must establish it without the construction of the law or treaty of the United States and the defenses which the appellees may interpose, if by chance they controvert the construction of treaties or laws under which the appellant claims or asserts rights. They cannot confer original jurisdiction upon the District Court. *Taylor v. Anderson, supra.* Because there

is no jurisdiction in the District Court, the court below properly dismissed this suit.

Decree affirmed.

These days, a lawyer imbued with the lore of the land claim cases of the 1970s and 1980s might think the *Deere* decision to be pettifogging. I think so, too—now. But it was a big obstacle in 1970, and I did not know any clear way around it. The pattern of the *Oneida* complaint was essentially the same as the complaint in *Deere*. In fact, as we will see below, the initial outcome of the *Oneida* case was also the same in U.S. district court and in the Second Circuit Court of Appeals.

The long and short of it was that, if a Native American tribe out of possession of land sued to get it back, that was a state cause of action and not one raising a Federal Question. Therefore jurisdiction in federal court was barred no matter what federal treaties or laws had been broken. In the context of Native American land rights guaranteed by law, the rule was unreasonable by any standard. It said: "You can sue in federal court to construe the Non-Intercourse Act, but you cannot sue to enforce it."

In 1975, when I read the Bureau of Indian Affairs files described in chapter 4, I realized in what detail history had repeated itself. In the 1920s the appellate counsel for Deere and the Mohawks, the New York City firm of Wise, Whitney & Parker, asked the Justice Department to intervene in the case and help Deere. They were advised on March 5, 1926, "that intervention—(by the U.S.)—is not advisable." Wise, Whitney & Parker pursued this further. The bureau files contain a memorandum of law from the law firm to the bureau dated December 7, 1926. They did much the same thing I did forty-six years later, with the same result. I thought I was novel and original but, come to find out, Wise, Whitney & Parker in the 1920s went through the same minuet with the Bureau of Indian Affairs in the *Deere* case that I had in the 1960s with the *Oneida* case.

To fully understand the impact of the *Deere* case and of the decision of the Second Circuit in the *Oneida* case, one must review *state* law too. The Federal Question rule, the well-pleaded complaint rule, was that a suit by a Native American tribe to recover land is not a federal case for jurisdictional purposes. One might say, "Well then, let's sue in New York State courts." But there is a catch here, too. There is a long-standing *federal* rule that state courts cannot hear Native American land cases, because such cases are exclusively a federal matter.

Thus the federal rule always had a double thrust: Federal courts cannot hear Indian land claims because there is no Federal Question jurisdiction, and state courts cannot hear Indian land claims because they are a federal matter, which state courts are barred from hearing.

For most states, that would be enough, but New York had to go further, because historically New York claimed jurisdiction over Native Americans in that state, ignoring all federal rules to the contrary. Thus, New York could not logically rely on the federal rules to protect its conquests and its illegal titles. The courts of New York had to evolve a different excuse to deny justice. They said that Native Americans and Native American tribes are not "persons" entitled to commence an action in New York courts. If you are not a "person," you cannot start a lawsuit.

The refusal of New York courts to hear Indian land claims is well illustrated by the efforts of the Montauk Indians to recover their reservation lands on Long Island. In the late 1800s a group of Montauk Indians brought an action in state court to recover land on Long Island. The New York Court of Appeals, in *Johnson* v. *Long Island Railroad Co.* (162 N.Y. 462 [1900]), held: "A decision holding that this action could be maintained either by the tribe or an individual member thereof . . . would be contrary to the policy and practice which have long been established in our treatment of the Indian tribe. They are regarded as wards of the State, and generally speaking possessed of only such rights to appear and litigate in courts of justice as are conferred on them by statute." In other words, Native Americans cannot sue to get their land back unless a law is passed to enable them to do so. The court suggested that the Montauks could apply to the Legislature for an enabling act, allowing them to sue. The Montauks *did* obtain an enabling act and *did* sue again in *Pharaoh* v. *Benson* (164 App. Div. 51, affd. 222 N.Y. 665 [1918]). Thus, the Montauk claim went back to the Court of Appeals, eighteen years after the *Johnson* decision.

Nevertheless, in the suit under the enabling statute, the trial court again held against the Montauks. The New York State Appellate Division, in 1914, held that the plaintiffs were not living as a tribe of Indians, thus not entitled to a remedy. Among the findings in the Montauk case was:

> . . . the purity of [Indian] blood was greatly impaired by miscegenation, particularly with the negro race. . . .
> . . . We are convinced that the present condition of the —
> [Montauks] — is far better than if they were allowed to return to their former dwelling place in Indian Field.

The Montauk case shows the judicial mindset that we had to overcome even in 1970 in order to open the federal courts to Indian land claims. It was similar to the bureaucratic mindset of the Bureau of Indian Affairs, of which I will have more to say. This decision of the Appellate Division was affirmed without opinion by the New York Court of Appeals in 1918.

In a more recent case, *St. Regis Tribe* v. *State* (5 N.Y.2d 24 [1958]), New York again affirmed its position that Native Americans could not sue in state courts. In that case the Indians sued to recover an island in the St. Lawrence river that was part of their reservation. The state contended that the St. Regis tribe, Mohawk Indians, had no capacity to sue in state courts. In an affidavit in support of the state's motion to dismiss the St. Regis complaint, a state assistant attorney general made this sworn statement:

> Assuming, but not conceding, that the American St. Regis Tribe
> of Indians had any independent interest in Barnhart's Island,

which was appropriated by the State of New York, such interest belonged to the Tribe collectively. *In the absence of specific statutory authority, an Indian Tribe does not have capacity to sue since it is not a recognized legal entity.* Similarly, an action involving tribal property cannot be maintained by the Chiefs or members of the Tribe, suing in their individual capacity and also for the benefit of all other tribal members, because the interest is tribal, not individual. *Only the Legislature may permit bringing of a suit pertaining to a tribal interest in real property;* but neither the general provisions of the Indian Law, nor Article eight thereof which specifically deals with the St. Regis Tribe, authorize claimants to prosecute the instant claim.

Since there is no enabling act which would allow this suit, claimants lack legal capacity to sue and the claim must be dismissed. [Emphasis added.]

The twists and turns of legalistic reasoning in federal and state courts always came out with the same answer: Native Americans cannot sue to recover land—an excellent legal device to protect the title to millions of acres of stolen land.

By early 1970 I generally knew the jurisdictional rules as described above. Though the odds against successful litigation seemed astronomically high, I decided to proceed anyway. After securing permission from the New York and Wisconsin Oneidas (the Canadians at that point did not want to become involved), I filed a lawsuit in Federal Court, Northern District of New York.

Our retainer agreement contemplated suit only against the state or its municipal subdivisions or both. Because the Eleventh Amendment was then thought to bar suits against a state for damages, I eliminated a suit against the state and selected a county as the next best defendant. Instead of outright ejectment, which would create a firestorm, I decided to sue only for the current rental value of the land. The premise was that the Oneidas still owned the land and were entitled to rent from the current occupants. Next came the questions: "What counties?" "What state acquisition to challenge?" It seemed to me best to select just one state treaty and a couple years' rent as an objective in order to keep a low profile.

Then I think the Great Spirit intervened and helped me select the best land purchase to challenge out of about twenty-five New York purchases from 1785 to 1840. I eliminated the state purchases of 1785 and 1788, which involved about 5.7 million acres of land (see map), because they preceded enactment of the Nonintercourse Act of 1790 and presented a different kind of case. I eliminated the purchase of 1798 and several thereafter because they gave some indication that a federal agent might have been present. This brought me back to the 1795 New York–Oneida "treaty" purchase, which involved about 100,000 acres of land in Madison and Oneida counties (see map).

I am not a trial lawyer, and drafting a complaint in federal court was new to me. I knew that I had to demonstrate jurisdiction on the face of the complaint, and I initially selected "diversity of citizenship"—plaintiff resides in one state, defendant in another—as my basis. I reasoned that the Oneidas of Wisconsin resided there, and Madison and Oneida counties were in New York. I had used this approach in the *Consolidated Gas* case. I soon realized this was not going to work and thus amended the complaint also to claim Federal Question jurisdiction and "violation of due process" jurisdiction.

The defendant counties made a motion to dismiss for lack of jurisdiction, as the defendants had in the *Deere* case. Before the argument on the motion to dismiss, I wrote to John N. Mitchell, then attorney general of the United States, asking for federal intervention and help. The request was denied on November 25, 1970. In his decision District Court Judge Edmund Port held that my reading of the law on diversity was "myopic." Predictably, citing the *Deere* case among others, he held that a Federal Question was lacking because the well-pleaded complaint rule bars suits to recover land. He dismissed the complaint for lack of jurisdiction.

I emphasize at this point that Bond, Schoeneck & King was still working on a purely contingent fee basis and that, in appealing further, I was devoting a great deal of my own and the firm's time to the case. However, we had told Jake and Geralda Thompson, Delia Waterman, Ray Elm, Norbert Hill, Amos Elijah, Bemas Elm,

George Hill, and other Oneidas that we would take a good shot at their case. They retained us in good faith, and we represented them in good faith. We kept our word when things looked bad and all economic considerations were discouraging. Undeterred by Judge Port's decision, I filed an appeal with the Second Circuit Court of Appeals. A further request for U.S. assistance on the appeal was again denied. The United States resolutely refused to help its "wards."

The Second Circuit made a good analysis of the case, expressed some sympathy for the Oneidas' position but basically hewed to the line of the *Deere* case forty-three years before. In its decision the court concluded, "Although on the surface the controversy seems highly appropriate for federal cognizance, that claim shatters on the rock of the 'well-pleaded complaint' rule for determining federal question jurisdiction, and we find no other basis that would permit a federal court to entertain the action." There was one dissent. Judge Lombard held that there should be federal jurisdiction but was outvoted. He said, in part, "the federal interest in seeing that the rights of Indian tribes are heard and adjudicated is so great that they should be controlled by federal law." The court also dismissed our diversity claim and said the civil rights claim was "impossible to fathom." The basis of the civil rights claim was that the Oneidas were being deprived of property, their own land, without due process because both federal and state courts had always refused to hear the claim. If that was not deprivation of due process, I do not know what is.

After the decision of the Second Circuit, the last opportunity to litigate the Oneida claim for land was an appeal to the U.S. Supreme Court. Encouraged somewhat by Judge Lombard's dissent in the Second Circuit decision, I decided to go the one last step. There was, however, no ground for automatic appeal to the U.S. Supreme Court. Rather, we had to proceed to ask them to hear the appeal and to issue what is called a certiorari order. There was no assurance that the Court would issue a certiorari order because the Supreme Court grants only about one in one hundred petitions for certiorari. Essentially the court has to be persuaded that the case is of enough national importance and legal merit to justify a further hearing.

In December 1972, I filed a petition for certiorari, outlining the jurisdictional question and stating why the Supreme Court should hear the case. The petition argued: "Because so many Indian tribal and land rights are founded on federal treaties, the decision will be of significance to many generations to come." Both Oneida and Madison counties, the defendants, filed briefs in opposition to the petition, and the Native American Rights Fund filed a brief in support of our petition. Though I sought the assistance of other civil rights and Indian rights organizations, they all refused to help in the belief that the case was hopeless.

The Oneidas had long sought the help of the federal government in pressing their land claims. Instead, consistent with its long-standing policy of protecting Native Americans by suppressing them, the U.S. government, through its solicitor general, now filed a brief *opposing* the Oneidas. This happened despite a conference I had with the U.S. solicitor general, Erwin Griswold, to persuade him to support the Oneidas' position. Although Griswold received me most courteously and discussed the case fully with me, his conclusion was adverse. His opposing brief was filed in May 1973. In part, the solicitor general's brief said:

> 1. Insofar as ordinary claims are concerned, it is long and well established that the "well pleaded complaint" rule is applicable in determining the existence of a federal question under the general federal question statute, 28 U.S.C. 1331. Thus it is established that a complaint in an action basically in ejectment presents no federal question even though a plaintiff's claim or right of title is founded on a federal statute, patent or treaty.

The solicitor's brief went on to apply this rule to Native American land claims and concluded: "The petition for a writ of certiorari should be denied." Thus, the hand of the United States was officially set against the Oneida cause.

Under the well-pleaded complaint rule, the basis for federal court jurisdiction had to appear as a necessary positive allegation in the plaintiff's complaint. Otherwise, the case was held to be proper only for state courts. If one was suing under specific authority given by a federal statute, that was a well-pleaded complaint, but if the suit was one like ejectment, which could be brought in a state court, there was no federal jurisdiction. If the plaintiff sued for ejectment on the ground that a federal treaty gave a right of possession, that was not a well-pleaded complaint.

Thus, the solicitor general, knowing full well the federal guarantees of possession, nevertheless contended that the well-pleaded complaint rule applied to deny federal jurisdiction.

I filed a reply to the U.S. solicitor general's brief on May 18, 1973. This reply was not normal procedure on the part of a Supreme Court petitioner. I figured a reply could not hurt and might help. I was given much help at that time by Graeme Bell, then an attorney for the Native American Rights Fund. When I sent him a first draft of my certiorari petition, he gently and tactfully pointed out that it was four or five times too long. The judges would never read it. Graeme's advice was sound; I condensed my draft to workable size, concentrating more on impact than on a complete history of the Oneida land claims.

Much to everyone's surprise, the Supreme Court did grant certiorari on the sole issue of Federal Question jurisdiction by the Federal courts. That did not win the case, but it was a threshold that had to be crossed. We at least had a chance to present the jurisdiction issue for a further hearing.

After certiorari was granted, a lot of work had to be done to research and prepare the detailed briefs needed. The stumbling block was the well-pleaded complaint rule, as previously explained. Taking it on its own terms, there was no way we could win. It was a contrived, artificial rule as applied to Native American land cases, and the *Deere* decision of the Second Circuit would be used as a precedent. What had to be done was to leap right over the rule as though it never existed, as though it was beneath the Supreme Court's dignity even to consider. Our brief did pay lip service to the rule by trying to distinguish and discuss some old cases, but our main thrust had to be that the *Deere* decision was unsound, that an Indian tribe could sue to get back possession of land.

The issue I presented was whether the United States was going to keep its own laws and treaties or not. One of the judges hearing our argument before the Second Circuit had laughed at me when I quoted Justice Hugo Black, reminding the court that "great nations, like great men, should keep their word." He said, "G'wan; all the lawyers in Indian cases say that." Fortunately, in the final analysis, the U.S. Supreme Court did not laugh, and after 180 years the United States did finally keep its word.

The formulation of our brief, the selection of what was to be the crucial issue, was the key to our winning. I realized that the key issue of legal tactics that had to be resolved was whether to emphasize 28 U.S.C. 1331, the historic Federal Question section, not the new 28 U.S.C. 1362, which on the surface seemed to provide a jurisdictional avenue for the Oneidas. Judge Lombard, in his dissent in the Second Circuit, held that 1362, the special statute, not 1331, provided jurisdiction. Graeme Bell of the Native American Rights Fund, who was of great assistance to me throughout, believed we should emphasize 1362 because the burden of showing jurisdiction and overturning years of precedent regarding Section 1331 was too great. Section 1362 reads, "The district courts shall have original jurisdiction of all civil actions, brought by any Indian tribe or band with a governing body duly recognized by the Secretary of Interior, wherein the matter in controversy arises under the Constitution, laws or treaties of the United States."

In a letter to the U.S. Justice Department dated December 21, 1972, Graeme urged, "I think the Second Circuit's opinion is reversible. The legislative history of 28 U.S.C. § 1362, enacted in 1966, indicates that Congress intended to have such land cases included within the ambit of this jurisdictional grant. (See my argument in the Fund's amicus brief to the Second Circuit, urging a rehearing of the case, pp. 4–5.) I hope that the Justice Department can support this contention."

In a further letter to me dated June 4, 1973, Graeme stated, "I personally think that § 1362 presents the strongest argument for the Oneidas and that it should be briefed by you." I, however, felt that Section 1362 really did not help because it, too, contained the wording "arises under the Constitution, laws or treaties of the United States" and was, therefore, subject to the same well-pleaded complaint problem as 1361. I believed strongly that a frontal attack on the precedent under 1361 was the only way to win.

After certiorari was granted, Graeme again wrote me, on June 19, 1973, recommending that the brief should make the argument "based on 28 U.S.C. §1362; the argument founded on 25 U.S.C. §233; and an argument attacking Judge Friendly's apparent assumption that any action in ejectment falls within the 'well-pleaded complaint rule.'"

Using Section 1362 was tempting, but I researched its legislative history and concluded that Section 1362 was not intended to confer any new jurisdiction, except that it dropped the $10,000 requirement for damages. Right there, I made a command decision that became the key to the case. I decided to go for broke and put the real issue right up in front for the Supreme Court. As I saw it, the real issue was the integrity of the United States, and not some legalistic quibble about whether I had a well-pleaded complaint. I made it very plain and very simple. The central argument took three-fourths of a page, fewer than 200 words.

ARGUMENT

I.

THE OVERRIDING LEGAL PREMISE FOR JURISDICTION IS THAT THE UNITED STATES GOVERNMENT, NO LESS THAN ANY INDIVIDUAL CITIZEN, MUST OBEY ITS OWN TREATIES, LAWS, AND PROMISES.

The cases under 28 U.S.C. 1331 and the legislative history of 1362 should be considered with the above premise in mind. The dignity of the treaties herein involved is exemplified in the opinion of this Court in *Federal Power Comm'n. v. Tuscarora Indian Nation.* 362 U.S. 99, 121–25 (1960) especially footnote 18 at 121–22.

In the *Tuscarora* case, the Supreme Court held that the taking of land for a reservoir: ". . . did not breach the faith of the

United States, or any treaty or other contractual agreement . . . in respect to these lands for the *conclusive reason that there is* none." *Id.* at 124. (Emphasis added.) In other words, no treaty or agreement concerning the lands near Niagara Falls taken from the Tuscaroras was before the Court. Footnote 18, *Id.* at 121–22 held that the treaty invoked by the Tuscaroras referred only to ". . . lands in central New York about 200 miles east of the lands in Question. . . ." These lands "200 miles east" are the very Reservation lands involved in the Oneidas' case.

In the Oneidas' case, now before this Court, there are *three treaties* promising the Oneidas "possession" of their Reservation.

Therefore, the failure of the United States to take action with respect to the Oneidas' Reservation would constitute a breach of treaties and laws of the United States.

I saw the full meaning of the *Tuscarora* case in 1965, and I wrote it down for the Supreme Court in 1973, never wavering from my conviction that the law had to be as I stated it. A court of lesser individuals than the then Supreme Court might have been displeased with that formulation and might have found a way to "beat" me, to best the Oneidas once again. A lesser court might have preferred 28 U.S.C.A. 1362 and might have carved out some narrow exception for the Oneidas, or worse yet, used 1362 for a further quibble.

In addition to my filing a brief to the Supreme Court, the Native American Rights Fund filed a brief on behalf of the Oneidas. Opposing briefs were, of course, filed by the defendant counties, and an opposing brief was also filed by New York State. The state's brief continued the position held in 1795 by New York governor George Clinton that the state of New York is not bound by the Nonintercourse Act and that the land transactions were and are legal. It further stated, "the petitioners have capacity to sue in New York State Courts." Now, in 1973, at argument, the state's solicitor general stated to the Court that the New York Court of Claims would be open to the Oneidas if they sued there. That, it had been repeatedly shown, was just not so. Under both federal and state law the

Oneidas could not sue in the courts of New York State; nor, if they could, would they get a fair deal. Case after dreary case had proved that.

The state's brief also raised the same old defense that, under the well-pleaded complaint rule, an Indian tribe out of possession of its land cannot sue in federal court to get it back because that is a state court matter. It is easy to call this a petty legal quibble now, but in 1973 it was not easy because the quibble was generally believed to be the law of the land.

After the briefs were filed, the date for argument was set for November 6–7, 1973. I went to Washington the day before and spent a long evening at the Hay Adams Hotel reviewing briefs and preparing an argument. At dinner that evening, I had a fortune cookie with my ice cream; it contained a slip of paper with the prophetic words, "An old problem will soon be solved." I am not superstitious enough to believe in such omens, but this particular fortune cookie offered a curious form of reassurance, so I decided to keep the slip of paper. I still have it.

The only Oneidas at the Supreme Court argument were Jake and Geralda Thompson. I sat alone at the left-hand counsel's table, and they were with the spectators. I am not a trial lawyer and felt a little lonely when I first answered the bailiff's call of the case and sat alone at the large table; however, the loneliness vanished when my sense of combat took over.

My recollection, after seventeen years, is of a large, wood-paneled courtroom, the justices' podium being set up high. The chief justice sat at the center, and the seven others flanked him. I remember especially Justices Brennan and Marshall for their sharp and penetrating questions. The lawyers for the counties, plus New York's solicitor general, sat at a table on my right. A green light flashed to let me know when to walk up to start my argument. I knew that another amber light would flash when I had five minutes left. Finally, a red light would blink when the allotted time was used up.

I do not recall any feeling of awe or nervousness—I think my main feeling was that of indignation that the Native Americans had to go to such lengths just to establish their right to be heard in court.

I started to present our case to the Court but soon was interrupted by many questions. Justice Brennan asked about the effect of the Indians claims case then pending against the United States. I replied that the Indian Claims Commission case had nothing to do with the jurisdictional issue and went on to say:

> I think what we are into, the way I see the case, is three treaties that promise the Oneida's possession of the land, and the federal law promises them possession. On a strictly jurisdictional issue, the Second Circuit has held that non-possession is what keeps us out of court, so that which the treaties and promises of the United States guarantee, possession, is what keeps us from getting equity or some kind of relief. This seems to be a very contradictory situation.

> As I read those cases, and there are certainly many of them decided by this Court, in every case there was an alternate state remedy, and we contend that both under the state law up to 1958 and the federal law down to this date there is no way that the Oneida Indians or any other Indian tribe can bring an action in a court, a state court of New York State, for a question dealing with land claims. It seems pretty clear to me that under the law, the legislation giving civil jurisdiction to state courts, that Congress in the questions submitted in the debates intended or thought that a case involving Indian land claims belonged in federal court.

> The Tuscarora case, which we cited to the Second Circuit, involved Indians who were at least under the state law not legally in possession of the land because a condemnation map had been filed, and under the condemnation law the state immediately became entitled to possession. Well, the courts took jurisdiction there and went on in the Tuscarora case, with which I am sure you are familiar.

The New York solicitor general carried the main argument for the state, reading the state's argument from a prepared text. At one point the state's solicitor general asserted:

We have almost 200 years that have gone by, and a practical construction such as we had here, which the parties have undertaken for such a long period of time, should not be changed even if there is an equally tenable interpretation the other way. In the instant case, I say this is very necessary because if we follow through to the fruits of a decision against us, we would really have an economic upheaval in all of the preemption states where deals were made for the purchase of land approximately about 200 years ago and it would be upsetting titles all over the eastern part of the country.

I had reserved time for a final summary and had the last word to the Court, as follows:

As I listened to my brothers here, and as I listened to the questions of the Court, that the Court directed to me yesterday, I have this to say, that when you boil this case all down, the only question for this court to decide is whether lack of possession will bar the Oneida Indians and other Indians throughout the United States from federal court.

Three treaties, federal statutes and the specific words of President George Washington to the six nations have promised possession to the Oneidas and the other six nations. The first President, in 1790, said to the Senecas, in behalf of the six nations, the general government will never consent to your being defrauded but it will protect you in all your just rights. And further on, in the same speech, President Washington, in a slightly different context, I must admit, but he did say to the Senecas, that the federal courts will be open to you for your just claims, or words to that effect. This speech is printed in our brief.

Now, all the Oneidas want is a fair hearing and to me, under the very singular facts, treaties and laws present in this case, a hearing should be available to them even under the most restrictive interpretation of section 1331 and certainly under the broader meaning given to section 1362 in Congress in 1966.

After the argument, waiting for the plane back to Syracuse, I met and chatted with the attorneys for the defendant counties. I remember clearly the barren waiting room of the ground-level ramp at Washington National Airport. I asked them how it happened that the State of New York had appeared in our case as an amicus (friend of the court) in opposition to the Oneidas' complaint. One of them told me that a judge of the Second Circuit had called the New York attorney general and suggested the state appear in the Supreme Court hearing because the case was very dangerous, or something to that effect.

After the argument on November 7, 1973, nothing happened for two long months, during which I could only wonder about the outcome. Then, on the afternoon of January 21, 1974, just as I returned from lunch, my secretary, Barbara Baker, ran out and jubilantly told me we had won the case. Someone from the Native American Rights Fund had heard of the opinion issued that day and had called me. It did not take long for me to call the Court and verify the message. We had won! The Oneidas had won! All Native Americans had won!

In their opinion, the Supreme Court totally rejected the Second Circuit's reasoning that the Oneidas' jurisdiction claim "shatters on the rock of the 'well-pleaded complaint' rule." It held, "Accepting the premise of the Court of Appeals that the case was essentially a possessory action, we are of the view that the complaint asserted a current right to possession conferred by federal law, wholly independent of state law."

The court plainly overturned the *Deere* case and a century of similar precedent. It said that this is a federal claim and a proper subject for Federal Question jurisdiction. The holding was not based on 28 U.S.C. 1362; in fact, that section was mentioned only in a footnote of the decision. The correctness of my decision to rely on Section 1331 instead of 1362 was later graciously confirmed by Graeme Bell of the Native American Rights Fund in a letter dated January 23, 1974. The whole fortune of the Oneida land claims, and other eastern land claims, turned on this presentation to the

U.S. Supreme Court in November 1973. A wrong decision on how to present the case would have been fatal. The Court dressed it up a bit, but the central theme of our brief comes through clearly in the decision. (For the Supreme Court's decision, see appendix E.)

The Supreme Court, in the ruling, went far beyond the narrow jurisdictional issue. It made it clear that, "Federal courts do have basic Federal Question jurisdiction to hear Indian land claims, even though the Indians are not in possession of the land. The Nonintercourse Act always forbade states, including New York, to acquire Indian land without federal consent. A cause of action exists to recover such land. Indian tribes or nations may bring such actions." When the New York attorney general and solicitor general saw this decision, they should have read the handwriting on the wall. New York State's position on inapplicability of the Nonintercourse Act—maintained since 1790—was totally repudiated. The prophecy of the 1960 *Tuscarora* case became reality in 1974.

After more than a decade, "the dust has settled" now in regard to the 1974 Supreme Court decision. Its historic legal precedents are taken for granted. Articles are written about the land claims of the eastern Indians without a word on how the cases reached the court in the first place. That's natural of course; time goes on. To me, however, a warm glow still pervades, the satisfaction of having thought out and practically invented a new body of law that has now been adopted and confirmed by numerous courts of this nation.

4

The Trial

After this transaction, the voice of the birds from every quarter cried out, you have lost your country—you have lost your country—you've lost your country! *

IN NOVEMBER 1975, one hundred eighty years and two months after the 1795 treaty by which the state illegally took the Oneidas' land, my partner John M. Freyer presented the Oneidas' case in court.

Before the case could be presented, we had to seek an extension of our retainer contract. The New York Oneidas agreed immediately, but it took some persuasion before the Wisconsin Oneidas agreed to extend our retainer contract and take part in the 1975 trial; the Canadian Oneidas had declined even to take part in the case in 1970. In 1975 I was somewhat puzzled by their reluctance to participate in what I regarded as an historic event. Now, looking back, I do not blame them for being a bit skeptical about what was happening. Two centuries of rejection and deceit by government agencies had made them cynical about the possibility of a recovery. When they did decide to participate, they sent superb representatives (Norbert Hill from Wisconsin; Ray George, Edward Nicholas, and Irvin Chrisjohn from Canada) who were of great help to us lawyers in the many crucial judgment calls that had to be made. I now

*Speech of Oneida Chief Good Peter, 1792, describing the results of a 1788 lease transaction with John Livingston.

39

count those men among my friends, persons who have enriched my life.

At the trial Judge Edmund Port, who initially dismissed the Oneida complaint for lack of federal jurisdiction, to his credit took the Supreme Court's reversal in stride. He kept a completely fair stance at all times. I am sure that his moral sympathies were always with the Oneidas, but his initial decision was to him sound legal policy. I remember seeing him at a dinner party while the appeal was pending before the Second Circuit. He said something to me about the Oneida case, to the effect that legal principles had to be maintained, but that I had done a good job. I told him—with some bravado—that one day I would be back in his courtroom. He just smiled.

In terms of legal precedents, Judge Port had been right, of course. At the time he wrote his initial 1971 opinion, all of the preceding cases had held that a claim by Indians for possession of land did not belong in federal court. The Second Circuit Court of Appeals had squarely held this in 1928 in the *Deere* case.

In early 1975, as we prepared for trial, another perplexing series of events began to evolve. I received a letter from Gloria Halbritter, who had been the secretary of the New York Oneidas under their elective system. Mrs. Halbritter is the daughter of Mary Winder, niece of Delia Cornelius Waterman, and a cousin of Geralda Thompson. She informed me that all "letters addressed to the President of the Oneida Indian Nation, will likewise be addressed to the Vice-President," who was an Oneida named David Honyoust. She added that all "correspondence from the Oneida Indian Nation now requires the signature of both the President and the Vice-President." Then I received the following letter dated August 11, 1975:

On August 10, 1975, at a duly organized Oneida Indian Nation meeting, constitutional quorum being present, Jacob Thompson was removed as President of the Oneida Indian Nation of New York. This was passed by majority vote of the people. David Honyoust, Vice-President, will be acting President until a duly organized meeting on September 7, 1975, when we will nominate and elect a new President. Until that date, all correspondence, documents, or business letters usually sent to the Nation President as pertains to the Oneida Indian Nation will be sent to David Honyoust—Acting President, at the above address. This letter will be followed by another, containing executive board member signatures.

Dated August 11, 1975   BY AUTHORITY OF THE ONEIDA
                               INDIAN NATION EXECUTIVE BOARD
                               DELORES NORTHINGTON,

                               S/DELORES NORTHINGTON
                               Oneida Indian Nation Treasurer,
                               and Acting Chief Administrative
                               Officer

Neither of these letters struck me as being unusual. I knew that the Oneidas of New York were an elective system and that leadership might change. I subsequently wrote Dave Honyoust as follows:

We received notice of your designation as Acting President of the Oneida Indian Nation of New York. Pursuant to the notice, we will of course send all further correspondence and notices to you until we have notice of the election of the new President. This is a period when many things may be happening in relation to the trial of your case against Oneida and Madison Counties, which will probably be held in early November. At some point I think we should meet, so that I can explain the case to you and answer any questions you may have concerning it or concerning our retainer arrangement. If you would like to make an appointment, please call me at the above address. If I am not here, ask for my Secretary, Mrs. Baker, and she will set up a meeting for a mutually agreeable time.

On August 25, 1975, I received a copy of a telegram to Mrs. Halbritter from Harry Rainbolt of the Bureau of Indian Affairs raising questions about the August 10 action of the Executive Board removing Thompson from office. Again, I was mildly surprised, but it did not seem much out of the ordinary. My concept then, as now, was that Bond, Schoeneck & King represented all persons enrolled as Oneida Indians in New York, Wisconsin, Canada, or elsewhere. I did not feel it was any of my business to determine who was running the Oneida branches. Later, I met with Honyoust and several persons he brought with him. I explained the case to them as best I could on short notice. Soon after, I received a further letter from Jacob Thompson advising me that another election had been held and that the original group was back in power, once again. This quick reversal was also surprising, but it did not alter the legal status of anyone or impede the case in any way. I felt that the leadership changes resulted from a natural increase in interest by the Oneidas as a land claim trial proceeded from a dream to a reality.

Another portent, which I did not then see as such, was a visit from several Oneidas who described themselves as the "Marble Hill" group. They were very concerned that they might be left out of the case. I assured them that I considered the Marble Hill Oneidas to be our clients, and they had an interest in the case, as did all other Oneidas. Early on, I had been told by Thompson of a group of New York Oneidas residing at Marble Hill, Oneida, New York. He indicated that they were Oneida Indians for all purposes and would participate in any recovery. My own research later confirmed this, and I concluded that the Marble Hill Oneidas were descendants of one of the groups of New York Oneidas who retained their original allotments of the reservation and did not move to Wisconsin.

In the summer of 1975, while these leadership changes were going on, we were preparing for trial. John M. Freyer, one of our firm's ablest trial lawyers, reviewed the evidence available. He decided that we needed a better factual underpinning for the case. The facts were all there in the treaties, in the New York State Legislative Report of 1888–1889 (known as the Whipple Report), and in the history books; nevertheless, John believed that more evidence was needed in the form of actual documents and reports, to bring the case to life and make it more believable to a trier of fact. To this end, we did two things: we hired Dr. Jack Campisi, an ethnohistorian, at Bond, Schoeneck & King's expense, to research the Indian Claims Commission files and other archives relative to the 1795 treaty, and we enlisted the additional help of the Native American Rights Fund.

Jack Campisi, our expert, and Sharon Eads, an attorney at the fund, each did extensive work and produced very valuable evidence. Campisi found evidence surrounding the 1795 transaction and also the repeated Oneida requests for justice through the years. These we felt would conclusively eliminate the laches issue (the contention that Oneidas waited too long to bring suit) if it ever arose. He discovered so many Oneida petitions to various federal and state agencies over the years asking for help that we decided to present only a representative sampling to the Court. Meanwhile, Sharon Eads spent days in the National Archives gleaning a whole file of Bureau of Indian Affairs documents. Preparation for the trial, under Freyer's leadership, took many days. During this time we were in contact with Native American Rights Fund attorneys, Tom Tureen as well as Sharon Eads, who rendered great assistance throughout this period.

The Bureau of Indian Affairs correspondence file, which was introduced in evidence at trial, commenced in 1910 and ended about 1946. The correspondence clearly negated any claim that the Oneidas had not pursued their rights. It also displayed the trusting nature of the Oneidas and the cynical violation of that trust by the bureau. No person familiar with the general outline of the Oneidas' case could fail to be outraged on reading this 1910–1946 correspondence. In some letters the bureau advised the Oneidas that they had no meritorious cause of action on land claims and discouraged them from taking legal action. In others the bureau told the Oneidas that they had no tribal status in New York that would entitle them to do anything. The Oneidas were also told that Congress would ratify any illegal land sales, even if they won in court. The Bureau of Indian Affairs told the Oneidas that they were under the jurisdiction of New York State and that the federal government was powerless to help.

Many of these letters were addressed to Wilson Cornelius,* father of Delia ("Dolly") Cornelius Waterman and grandfather of Geralda Thompson. When Sharon Eads produced this correspondence from the archives, we met with Jake and Geralda Thompson to review it in detail. Sitting in the firm's conference room, we read with interest the repeated efforts of Wilson Cornelius to pursue the land claims and the evasive replies to his letters. At one point, an interoffice bureau memo of 1909 indicated that Cornelius either had found some old treaties or was "mentally unbalanced." We non-Indian lawyers laughed at this because it was clear that Cornelius was, in fact, right on target and that the Bureau of Indian Affairs was evading and deluding him. It amused us that the bureau official was calling him "unbalanced" when he was so right about the old treaties.

When we laughed, Geralda Thompson became very indignant, saying, "That is my grandfather they're talking about!" We had not connected Wilson Cornelius with Geralda Thompson until then. Picture a lady in 1975 reading letters, recently uncovered from the dust of Washington archives, from and to her grandfather sixty years before, seeing how he was first deceived and then referred to by a bureau official as crazy. As I studied the file of letters, I became as indignant as Geralda. It became clear to me that over a long span of years the bureau officials had misled the Oneidas and tried in all possible ways to thwart their pleas for justice in regard to their land.

The existence of this deliberate policy of deception and discouragement is well illustrated by the *Boylan* case. (*U.S.* v. *Boylan* 265 F. 165 [1920]). As mentioned above in chapter 1, *U.S.* v. *Boylan* dealt with a thirty-two-acre parcel of the former reservation near the City of Oneida, New York. (You can locate the tract now, on N.Y. Route 46, just south of Route 5.) In 1915 the local U.S. attorney, on directions from officials in Washington, commenced an

*See frontispiece.

action in Federal District Court, Northern District of New York, to recover possession of the thirty-two acres of land that had been illegally foreclosed and taken from an Oneida family. The thirty-two acres was one of a few parcels of the original Oneida Reservation that had not been acquired by the state with illegal "treaties." This case was in the courts for several years. The federal district court, in 1919, held:

> The United States has steadily and uniformly asserted its jurisdiction over the Indians of the "Six Nations," which, as stated, included the Oneida Indians and other New York tribes. . . .

> Thus far we have dealt almost exclusively on the theory that the Indians are wards of the nation, and that the United States has full jurisdiction over them and the disposition of their lands, notwithstanding that such lands were part of the domain of one of the original states of the Union. . . .

> This brings us to the consideration of the all-important question in the case, whether or not the United States can maintain this action for the protection of these Indians. . . . the fact remains that the United States government has and shows an interest in these Indians and aids in their support and maintenance. The United States has an interest in their protection.

The court, in its analysis, quoted from the three federal treaties with the Oneidas:

> The Oneidas . . . shall be secured in the possession of the lands on which they are settled. Treaty of 1784.

> The Oneida and Tuscarora Nations are also again secured and confirmed in the possession of their respective lands. Treaty of 1789.

> . . . the said reservations shall remain theirs until they choose to sell the same to the people of the United States who have the right to purchase. Treaty of 1794.

The court stated: "I am of the opinion and conclude . . . the United States has such an interest as enables it to maintain this action and restore to these wards of the nation, for whom this action is brought, the possession of the lands." The person who had obtained the thirty-two acres by foreclosure was ordered to vacate it. The land was declared to be federally protected reservation land.

On appeal, this decision was affirmed in 1920 by the Second Circuit Court of Appeals. The Second Circuit held that the United States has the right to bring the action; that the Oneidas of New York still existed as a tribe of Indians; that the United States has the sole power to act as guardian of the Indians of a given state; and that the thirty-two acres were owned by the Oneida Indians.

The personnel of the Bureau of Indian Affairs were well aware of the *Boylan* case. The archives contain correspondence about the case. Yet, when in 1916 Frank Cregg, assistant U.S. attorney, Northern District of New York, had written to the Department of Interior asking for confirmation of authority to commence what became the *Boylan* case, E. B. Meritt of the bureau replied, saying that no record of the Boylan matter "is found in this office or in the Department of Interior." But later in 1916 Cregg reported to the commissioner of Indian affairs that the case had been tried. A reply was sent by E. B. Meritt. Meritt thus knew of the *Boylan* case at that point. In 1919 a copy of the district court's decision was sent by the Department of Justice to the secretary of interior. As stated, the Second Circuit affirmed the district court a year later. There is just no way that the personnel at the Bureau of Indian Affairs could have failed to know of the *Boylan* case and its holdings and implications. The bureau correspondence described here has to be read with this in mind. At least since 1919 the Bureau of Indian Affairs and the Interior Department *knew* of this major federal court decision. Yet subsequently bureau personnel repeatedly advised Wilson Cornelius and other Oneidas that the United States would not protect them, that they were not a recognized tribe, that they had no reservation land in New York. This advice was totally untrue and completely contradicts the holding of the *Boylan* decision.

I now see that my petitions, conferences, and other efforts in the 1966 and 1977 era were just a continuation of the whole process plaintively expressed in 1792 by Oneida Chief Good Peter. "After this transaction the voice of the birds from every quarter cried out you have lost your country—you have lost your country—you've lost your country." No one listened to Good Peter then. No one listened to the countless pleas for justice from 1790 onward. Instead, federal and state bureaucracy misled the Oneidas and stifled every attempt to get justice, or even to get information.

In the months before the 1975 trial I wrote to the Oneidas of the Thames in Canada, who in 1970 had declined to become parties to the initial suit. I advised them that it was in their best interest now to become parties. The elected government of the Oneidas of the Thames finally decided to send two delegates to attend the trial, but as observers, not as parties to the suit. I wrote several times to the hereditary chiefs in Canada asking them to become parties, but they never responded. I think I now understand how the heritage of bad treatment by federal and state authorities would render them unwilling to participate.

Then, just before the trial, I received the following letter from Jake Thompson:

To the Members of the Oneida Indian Nation (NY):

I, Jacob Thompson, to avoid violence and hostilities among the members of the Oneida Indian Nation, I therefore resign as the President of this Nation (OIN) effective immediately; my only concern and goal was to unite the Oneida people. Therefore, I do hope that the members call for a Nation meeting for peace and unity.

As we prepared for trial, I heard more and more about a power struggle among the New York Oneidas. One group led by Jake Thompson was pitted against another group, both contending that they were the real representatives of the Oneidas of New York. The culmination was Thompson's decision to keep away from the trial lest the case be damaged by fallout from the disunity of the local Oneidas.

Just before the trial, counsel for the parties met with Judge Port. John Freyer and I represented the Oneidas; Bill Burke, Jim O'Rourke, and Rocco Mascaro represented Oneida and Madison counties, respectively. By this time, the counties had brought in the state as a codefendant, but the state, which had butted in to the Supreme Court hearing, decided to butt out of the trial. Following its long-standing head-in-the-sand policy, the state sought to ignore the problem and stayed away from the trial. At the initial meeting it was agreed to "bifurcate" the trial, as the judge put it, and first try the issue of liability: "Do the defendants occupy land owned by the Oneidas?" If the defendants were held liable, if the land belonged to the Oneidas, a second trial would be held on the issue of the amount of damages. Remember, the case was initially brought to recover rent for 1968 and 1969 on land used by the counties and located within the Oneida Reservation. It was also formally stipulated by the parties that the trial was a test case, to govern other similar Oneida claims. A favorable decision here would govern Oneida claims to the whole 260,000-acre reservation.

The mid-November days were cool and crisp. John Freyer, Robert Meisenhelder (then an associate lawyer with our firm), and I, together with my secretary, Barbara Baker, met at our office in Syracuse each day before the half-hour drive to Auburn. Working with us at the trial were Tom Tureen and Sharon Eads of the Native American Rights Fund. John Freyer had been trying major cases for years, but this was the first full-scale trial which I—a tax and business lawyer—had ever attended. The federal courtroom in Auburn, which was Judge Port's hometown, was small, with classic dignified design. Only a few spectators attended, mostly Oneidas, plus a reporter or two. The fact that such a trial was being held at all was an historic event in New York State, but it proceeded quietly, with no fanfare. One would never have guessed that a central tenet underlining the state's land title foundation and geographic extent was being challenged.

At the time of the opening statements Judge Port made it clear that he had been instructed in the law by the Supreme Court's decision and was ready to apply it.

In his opening statement Freyer promised factual evidence that New York State deliberately violated the federal Nonintercourse Act.

> We believe that the proof will show that the State of New York did not act out of ignorance but in direct contradiction of advice received from the Federal government.
>
> The proof will further show that the Treaty of September 15, 1795 was never ratified or approved by the Federal government—
>
> THE COURT: (Interrupting) I am not sure I heard correctly. Did you just say that the State of New York acted not out of ignorance, but in direct contradiction to it?
>
> MR. FREYER: That is correct.
>
> THE COURT: To the instructions of the Federal authorities?
>
> MR. FREYER: We will prove, your Honor, through documentary evidence that there were communications between the State of New York and the Federal government, particularly between Mr. Pickering, who was then Secretary of War, under whose jurisdiction [was] Indian Affairs, and that the opinion of the Attorney General of the United States was sent to Governor Jay of New York, prior to this session, and that New York was advised that to proceed in this matter would contradict Federal law.

There was a clear judicial double take. Judge Port was incredulous that New York State deliberately violated federal instructions. The very respect for order and precedent that caused the judge initially to dismiss the case for lack of federal jurisdiction had now turned in our favor. The counties' attorneys, having no rebutting facts to present, started to talk about legal defenses in their opening statement, but Judge Port cut this short. He said he wanted first to find out what the facts were, and then the defendants would have ample opportunity to present their defenses.

Our first witness was Leslie Gay of the Bureau of Indian Affairs. He testified as to the existence of the New York and Wisconsin Oneidas as federally recognized Indian nations. The defendants sought to discredit the New York Oneidas by getting Gay to say that Jake Thompson was no longer the president of the New York Oneidas. This point was shown to be irrelevant since the New York Oneidas are a legal entity that does not depend on any one person for status.

After the warmup with Gay, Freyer called our key expert witness. Jack Campisi was the best choice we could possibly have made to establish that the New York, Wisconsin and Canadian Oneidas were the direct descendants of the 1795 Oneidas and that tribal entities had always remained intact. He had made a lifetime study of just that subject. His research into records of the Indian Claims Commission case and other activities uncovered the documentary evidence that made the Oneidas' legal case incontrovertible. At the end of the first morning of the trial, November 12, 1975, he had established that the Oneida lands in question were part of the reservation guaranteed by New York State in 1788, and by federal treaties in 1784 and 1789.

After the lunch break Campisi identified the Nonintercourse Act of 1790 and 1793, which forbade purchase of Indian land without the presence of a U.S. commissioner and without consent of the U.S. Senate. He also described the 1794 federal treaty promising the Oneidas they would be secure in the possession of their lands. Campisi then described the events immediately following the 1794 federal treaty, a treaty in which the United States pledged to protect the Oneida land. In April 1795 the state legislature appointed a commission to meet with and purchase land from the Oneidas and other Iroquois. Learning of this, the U.S. secretary of war asked U.S. Attorney General Bradford for an opinion as to whether the Nonintercourse Act applied to purchases by New York State. The secretary of war did this because he was charged with enforcement of federal protection of Indians. The decisive response, a letter from Bradford dated June 15, 1795, states that the New York Indians' claim to their lands "cannot be extinguished but by a treaty holden under the authority of the United States, and in the manner prescribed by the laws of Congress," referring to the Nonintercourse Act. Documentary evidence in the form of official correspondence also brought out that this opinion was transmitted to the governor of New York, John Jay, by the U.S. secretary of war. Thus the governor of New York was specifically advised that the proposed purchase from the Oneidas was illegal. (The legal meaning of Attorney General Bradford's opinion was surely clear to Governor John Jay; he had just resigned as chief justice of the U.S. Supreme Court in order to become governor of New York.)

As further proof, we also showed that the state knew of the impact of the Nonintercourse Act, in that it contemporaneously followed the correct federal procedures in purchases of land from the Senecas and other Iroquois. In the case of the Oneidas, the state ignored the federal procedures because officials knew the United States would not grant permission to purchase part of the Oneida Reservation for a pittance, even though it could cheat the other Iroquois with impunity.

At the same time, a letter from Secretary of War Timothy Pickering informed Israel Chapin, the federal superintendent to the Oneidas, that the federal law applied to New York, and that any sale by the Oneidas to the state would be illegal.

The July 27, 1795, letter from President George Washington to Secretary Pickering, quoted in chapter 2, showed his agreement that the state's proposed dealings with the Oneidas were illegal. A letter dated August 19, 1795, from the federal superintendent, Israel Chapin, to Secretary Pickering proved that Chapin told both the Oneidas and the state commissioners that the state had no right to purchase Oneida land. The commissioners went ahead anyway and continued to negotiate at Oneida Castle with the Oneida leaders. Ultimately these negotiations broke down. No land was purchased from the proper and duly authorized Oneida leaders. After the Oneida leaders voted against the sale, the council at Oneida Castle disbanded.

The state's next step was to assemble a group of Oneidas in Albany and have them put their marks on a treaty selling about 100,000 acres of their reservation. But the key point is that the ones who did put their marks on the treaty, which they could not read, were not authorized to do so.

After the 1795 treaty was signed, however illegally, the federal government felt powerless to stop the state. On August 26, 1795, Secretary Pickering wrote to Israel Chapin as follows:

> I received your letter informing of the treaty held at Scipio where the Commissioners of New York purchased the land of the Onondagas and Cayugas; and that you proposed to go to Oneida where you supposed that tribe might be influenced to avoid a sale. Seeing the Commissioners were acting in defiance of the law of the United States, it was entirely proper not to give them any countenance; and as that law declares such purchases of the Indians as those commissioners were attempting to make, invalid, it was also right to inform the Indians of the law and of the illegality of such purchase. But having done this much, the business might there be left. The negotiation is probably finished by now, if not, you may content yourself with giving the Oneida the information above proposed, and there to leave the matter.

Thus, our presentation of the official documents established that the 1795 sale was illegal and that the state officials, including Governor John Jay, former chief justice of the U.S. Supreme Court, knew it was illegal. At the end of the direct examination by Freyer, James O'Rourke, attorney for Oneida County, cross-examined Campisi. O'Rourke's intention was to show that the federal government had in fact sent an agent for the September 15, 1795, treaty with the state and had ratified the transaction. But Campisi demonstrated, in response to many questions, that no U.S. commissioner was present and that the U.S. Senate had never ratified the so-called treaty. At this point Judge Port adjourned the trial for the day. Thus, in a few hours, legal history had been made. In 1974 the Supreme Court had reversed legal history by granting federal jurisdiction to a Native American land suit. In November 1975 the first trial of its kind was under way.

Before and during the trial we had been meeting with Ray George and Irvin Chrisjohn, delegates from the elective government of the Oneidas of the Thames, Canada. They now advised us that the Canadian Oneidas had decided to join the lawsuit as party plaintiffs after all. The next morning, November 13, 1975, Freyer moved that the Oneidas of the Thames, Canada, be admitted as a party to the suit. O'Rourke made no objection but asked for time to consider the possible impact of a new party. His request was denied. Dr. Campisi, called as a witness, then testified about the lineage of the Canadian Oneidas. The judge granted our motion to admit them as a party.

O'Rourke then resumed cross-examination of Campisi on his testimony about the 1795 treaty. Unintentionally, his further questions emphasized an important historical point: The deed to the area that formed part of the test case was executed by some Oneidas at Albany, New York, on September 15, 1795, but not by the Oneida leaders, who in a council in August at Oneida Castle had voted to reject a sale. Campisi then testified that the Oneidas who put their marks on the 1795 treaty were not the sachems who were traditionally authorized to negotiate and transact business for the Oneidas. In modern terminology, the proper officials did not sign.

Q. When the land was bought by the State of New York, the State did not deal with the main body of illiterate Indians, did it? It dealt with the Chiefs and through the interpreters and the Agents?

A. Well, that is a question which hasn't been touched on. The Oneida Indian Tribe consisted of a number of leaders, both Sachems, and there are also a number of leaders who are War Chiefs, and prominent people, and also prominent citizens of the tribe. The basic principle upon which the Oneidas and other Iroquois operated were the principles of unanimity and consensus, and agreements were not made unless they had attained unity and the consensus in the community.

If you look at the first attempt of the State of New York in 1795 you see it was held in Oneida, where the entire tribe was meeting. You see that they have rejected, and then you see if you look at the 1795 instrument, a very interesting part to it. In that part, a number of individuals, Oneidas, half of them women, signed an instrument giving the power of attorney to another group of individuals, as far as I can see, none of whom are Sachems, civil chiefs of the tribe, hereditary chiefs of the tribe, and gives an instrument to them to go to Albany to negotiate a treaty for the sale of the land on which at least part of the tribe was objecting. So when you say to me did the Chiefs of the Oneidas sign it, the answer is that it doesn't—

Q. (Interrupting) I didn't ask you that question.

A. I thought that that was what you said; who signed the instrument?

Q. I said who did they deal with?

A. They dealt with anybody that they could get to sign a treaty.

Q. But they went through the interpreters and the agents?

A. Right.

Q. Who presumably explained the contents of these treaties?

A. That is true, but you also see in the treaties that the agents, like Kirkland and Dean, received sections of land from the Indians, so that to argue that they are impartial—

Q. (Interrupting) I don't want you to read anything into my questions. I would just like you to answer it.

A. I did answer it.

MR. O'ROURKE: I have no further questions.

With all due respect to O'Rourke, a fine attorney, Campisi saw an important point that had not risen before and took the opportunity to bring it out. He showed that the 1795 state treaty had not been executed by the proper authorities. O'Rourke obviously did not want to pursue that line of questions any further and terminated the cross-examination; however, the question of the authority of Oneida signatories did not die. In his redirect examination Freyer pounced on the point raised by Campisi:

REDIRECT EXAMINATION

BY MR. FREYER:

Q. In those last few questions of counsel, and your answers, the women at that time, and you said that women signed this, and let's call it the power of attorney, and were the women allowed to speak in tribal council at that time?

A. No, the custom was (not) for the women to have women speakers. They could have their opinions voiced, but through a man.

Q. And as I understand it, you are familiar with the traditional names of the Oneida Chiefs?

A. Yes, right, and they are on the instrument of December 2nd, 1795. (Referring to an unrelated, but authentic document.)

Q. There are not the signatures of any traditional Chiefs on the instrument of September 15th, 1795?

A. Not as far as I can tell.

THE COURT: Isn't there another addendum, or sort of a power of attorney attached to that instrument that at least appears to be a power of attorney going from the Sachems and the women to these negotiators?

THE WITNESS: Yes. But when you take—you see the names of the Sachems, the nine Sachems of the Oneidas are fixed names, and they continue through time. So, the number—if you take one of the Sachem names and—those names should appear on that instrument, and I haven't been able to determine that they—I can't show that those names are on the instrument.

THE COURT: What you are saying is that the power of attorney that is recited there, the Sachems, the warriors and the women of the Oneida Indians or the Oneida Nation of Indians in full council assembled, in fact, is not signed by those people.

THE WITNESS: Yes, using the names, the traditional names that we have of the Oneida Sachems, I cannot find that list of men, nine in number, signed that instrument.

THE COURT: What you are saying is that you are equating some document that started out, "I, Dr. Campisi, a District Court Judge in and for the Northern District of New York—", and then you sign it?

THE WITNESS: Yes.

THE COURT: All right.

We, of course, were delighted that the judge had been so impressed with the importance of the improper execution of the 1795 treaty with the state.

The 1795 state treaty, transferring title to more than 100,000 acres of land, was thus a nullity. It was as though a few citizens of Syracuse sold city land without the concurrence or knowledge of the mayor and Common Council. Clearly, the state had been determined to get the land for development by any means. After the Sachems, the proper leaders, had rejected a sale, the state apparently gathered a few Oneidas, brought them to Albany, and had them put their marks on a treaty.

The essential legal point in the case was that in 1795 New York acquired the land in a transaction that violated federal law: it was not negotiated with a U.S. commissioner present, and it was not ratified by the U.S. Senate. The above-quoted questions by O'Rourke and answers from Campisi also brought out the lack of proper execution of the treaty.

After Campisi's testimony was complete, I was called to testify to authenticate certain documents. These were the Oneida petitions to the state and federal governments that I had prepared in the period 1967–1973. These petitions were introduced to show that the Oneidas had pursued every possible administrative appeal before starting a lawsuit.

The next witness was Norbert Hill, the delegate from the Oneidas of Wisconsin. Norbert testified as to the poverty and illiteracy that had prevailed among the Oneidas, frustrating their efforts to obtain justice, and also to the authorization by the Wisconsin Oneidas to commence the lawsuit. Dr. Robert Venables, then a history professor at SUNY-Oswego and our next witness, testified to the continued efforts of the Oneidas to obtain justice from state and federal authorities. This testimony, like mine, was to disprove the contention that the Oneidas had "slept on their rights" and lost the right now to complain.

After Dr. Venables testified, the judge declared a short recess, during which Jack Freyer met with the judge to discuss the introduction of new evidence. After the recess Freyer advised the court and the counties' counsel that a mass of new evidence had just arrived and that to introduce it properly required a postponement of the trial until the next day. This delay was granted.

On the next day, November 14, 1975, we introduced evidence, provided by Sharon Eads, that was superbly telling proof that the Oneidas had not "slept on their rights" but, rather, had persevered in asserting them. This evidence was the file of Bureau of Indian Affairs correspondence described above. The evidence also showed the bureau in a poor light, not as protector of Native Americans but as the defender of those whose interests are adverse.

After the introduction of this additional evidence, the Oneidas' case was complete, and O'Rourke promptly moved to dismiss the Oneidas' case. Freyer presented counterarguments and Judge Port declined to rule at that point. It is instructive to note that both counties rested their cases without calling witnesses or submitting any proof of their position. Essentially, they conceded the facts we presented but asserted that, even so, the Oneidas should lose because they had waited too long to press their claim and had abandoned the land.

The judge directed the exchange of briefs at the proper time and recessed the trial. Ultimately, the decision of Judge Port did not come out until July 12, 1977, nineteen months later. When it did, it substantiated our entire position. In an exhaustive opinion he held that the 1795 sale to the state was void and that the Oneidas still own the land:

> This case tests the consequences of the failure of the State of New York to comply with the provisions of the Indian Nonintercourse Act, enacted by the first Congress in 1790 and re-enacted in substance by subsequent Congresses to the present date. 25 U.S.C. § 177. Familiarity with the prior opinions in the case is assumed. . . .
>
> The plaintiffs have established a claim for violation of the Nonintercourse Act. Unless the act is to be rendered nugatory, it must be concluded that the plaintiffs' right of occupancy and possession to the land in question was not alienated. By the deed of 1795, the State acquired no rights against the plaintiffs; consequently, its successors, the defendant counties, are in no better position.
>
> This Memorandum-Decision and Order shall constitute the court's findings of fact and conclusions of law. Fed.R. Civ. P. 52(a).
>
> The court having jurisdiction of the subject matter and the parties hereto, for the reasons herein, it is
>
> ORDERED, that the issue of liability be and it hereby is decided in favor of the plaintiffs and against the defendants; and it is further
>
> ORDERED, ADJUDGED AND DECREED that the defendants be and they hereby are held liable to the plaintiffs by reason of said defendants' occupancy of the land in question during the years 1968 and 1969, all other issues to be determined in a subsequent trial.

Judge Port had obviously done a great deal of further research in arriving at his decision. I could then see why he took so long to decide this momentous issue. Appendix F provides a full copy of his decision, which sets forth the facts and law in detail. I remember how delighted I was to read Judge Port's exhaustive opinion, which seemed complete vindication of our theory of the case from the very beginning.

The decision was appealed and wound its way through the court system, until it ultimately was affirmed on the merits by the U.S. Supreme Court in 1985, almost ten years after the trial was held. Starting in 1978, Arlinda Locklear and other lawyers from the Native American Rights Fund, representing the Oneida Indians of Wisconsin, Inc., and Bert Hirsch, representing the Oneida Indians of New York, did an excellent job in the further proceedings, culminating in the Supreme Court's 1985 decision that affirmed Judge Port's July 12, 1977, ruling in favor of the Oneidas (see appendix H).

Although this is a legal case, the moral overlay is crucially important to me. What has morality got to do with it? Everything! The Oneidas are now seeking a very large recovery in land and funds. Many people say that it is not fair to do so after almost 200 years. If the Oneidas were relying on some legal technicality or trick, then I might feel constrained to agree; however, the tricks were all played by New York State. Judges have used the technicalities over the past 200 years to deny fairness and justice to the Oneidas. The land was taken illegally and unfairly by a fully knowing state government.

What I am talking about here is not treaties and legalities but, rather, a transfer of wealth. In 1788 and the years that followed, the state violated the federal Constitution and law by trickery, duress, and deceit. It forcibly transferred wealth from the illiterate Native Americans to invading bands of grasping land speculators. If this transfer of wealth had not occurred, New York would still be the Empire State, but different persons over 200 years would have enjoyed the wealth. One group, dispossessed of their inland empire, lived in poverty for 200 years while the other group prospered. This case is all about a restoration of at least some of the wealth from the now prosperous state back to the Oneidas in recompense for what was done.

5

Genesis of the Pre-1790 Claim

*—the Governor of New York said to us;—"you have now leased to me all your territory, exclusive of the reservation, as long as the grass shall grow and the rivers run." He did not say "I buy your country." Nor did we say "we sell it to you."**

THE 1975 TRIAL was a test case involving only a relatively small amount of the original Oneida land acquired by the state in the period 1785–1840. I was, of course, well aware that the greater part of acreage of the aboriginal Oneida land had been acquired by New York State before 1790, and thus before the Nonintercourse Act. Jake Thompson over the years repeatedly asserted that the Oneida claim involved the pre-1790 land, too. I always told him that Article 4 of the 1794 federal treaty of Canandaigua seemed to cancel any rights to land ceded prior to 1794.

> Article 4. The United States having thus described and acknowledged what lands belong to the Oneidas . . . now the Six Nations, and each of them, hereby engage that they will never claim any other lands within the boundaries of the United States.

*Statement of Oneida Chief Good Peter, 1792, concerning the 1788 treaty with New York State.

I had discussed this claim with the Native American Rights Fund lawyers, and we all mistakenly took this to mean that the Oneidas had thereby relinquished all land sold before 1790.

At the close of the revolutionary war in 1783, the Oneida Indian Nation possessed land in two tracts: the 6 million acres of land in what is now the central part of New York State, and an interest in the huge Iroquois domain in Pennsylvania and the Ohio River Valley, extending hundreds of miles west and south of Buffalo.

In 1783 New York State's western boundary was located where the Oneidas' 6 million acres began, a north-south border line, roughly at Utica. The Oneida land was not in New York State. But even then, the state was planning to grant bounties of Iroquois land to its war veterans, land situated on the west side of the Oneida land. Thus, the white settlers would have to cross over Oneida land to get to their bounty land. The Oneidas did not know their lands were to be used as a passageway, nor did the other Iroquois to the west know that the state was planning to grant part of their land to war veterans.

In the fall of 1784 representatives of the United States met with the Six Nations of the Iroquois at Fort Stanwix (now the City of Rome), New York. There they exacted a treaty of peace wherein the Onondagas, Mohawks, Cayugas, and Senecas (who had sided with England in the war) were forced to surrender all of their Ohio Valley land, their land to the south and west of what is now New York State. This cession was part of the spoils of war, surrendered by these four Iroquois nations who had fought on the side of the English. In another part of the same treaty the United States promised to the Oneidas and Tuscaroras (who had sided with the colonies) that they would always be secured in the possession of their land, which would of course include their interest in the Ohio River Valley lands to the west of Buffalo.

Yet the 1784 treaty had a crucial ambiguity. It could be construed to mean that the Oneidas and Tuscaroras, too, were ceding to the United States their interest in the Ohio River Valley lands. Since they had been valuable allies of the United States, there was no reason for them to give up such land; however, ringed by federal soldiers and unable to read, write, or even speak English, the Oneida leaders put their marks on the treaty. All they saw was that the United States promised to protect their land. They could not see the ambiguity by which they lost their interest in the land in the West, the Ohio River Valley.

Despite the promise of the United States in 1784, the land hunger of New York State was not to be constrained by a federal treaty, nor by the Articles of Confederation, which forbade the state to acquire Indian land. In June 1785, using deception and threats, the state exacted a deed to about 300,000 acres of land, near the present Binghamton, New York, for a total consideration of $11,500, or four cents per acre. In September 1788 the Oneidas ceded about 5.5 million acres to the state with the understanding that the state was to pay them an adjustable rent, starting at $600 per year: Six hundred dollars a year for the whole 5.5 million acres! Subsequently the state repudiated the lease agreement, treated the 1788 transaction as a sale, and deeded the Oneidas' leased land outright to speculators and developers. Unfortunately, the provision about adjustable rent was not included in the state's written version of the treaty.

Ironically, the 1788 transaction was consummated *after* New York had joined the union of states by ratifying the U.S. Constitution—a constitution that forbade states to make treaties and placed all Indian commerce under federal control. New York's pact with the other states was thus broken within two months after it became effective. As I view it, the 1788 transaction directly violated the United States Constitution.

In 1789 another federal treaty guaranteed the Oneidas the possession of their lands, and in 1790 the Nonintercourse Act became law. Still, there was unrest among the Iroquois, much of it growing out of the ambiguities inherent in the 1784 federal treaty of Fort Stanwix. One large remaining problem was that the Oneidas, who fought on the side of the colonies, had seemingly lost their land in the Ohio River Valley as spoils of war to their former ally, but in fact still claimed it.

Therefore, in 1794 another federal treaty was executed to try to clear up the Ohio Valley issue and to assure the Oneidas of the continued protection of the United States in regard to their remaining 5.7 million acres of land in New York, part of which was leased to the state in 1788. The true meaning of the 1794 federal treaty was at first not clear to me because I did not understand its historical context, nor the ambiguity of the 1784 treaty.

I did not know the pre-1790 facts correctly until I read the March 19, 1976, decision of the Indian Claims Commission on the Oneidas' pre-1790 case. But when I read the findings of fact in that decision, sent to me by attorney Marvin Chapman, I saw at once that the Oneidas had an excellent pre-1790 case because the 1788 transaction was really a lease, and not a sale, as I had previously thought. The implications of a lease finding by the Indian Claims Commission were twofold: the pre-1790 transactions violated the pre-1788 Articles of Confederation, law, and treaties, and the 1788 transaction did not effect a transfer of beneficial title to the state but, rather, created a form of lease or trust for the benefit of the Oneidas. It was like a light switch being turned on. I visualized a claim for the pre-1790 land as soon as I saw the commission's findings. We were dealing with a claim for 6 million acres, instead of 260,000 acres.

At this time in 1976, remember, we had already tried the 1795 test case against the counties, and the legal principles seemed clear. My revision of opinion about the pre-1790 case used the same principles applied to newly understood facts. I started immediately to convey my change of mind to the clients and to do the further factual and legal research needed to confirm the flash of intuition. I reasoned that the Eleventh Amendment barred monetary damage suits against a state in federal court (as I then thought), but not an ejectment suit. Therefore, the Oneidas could sue the state for recovery of land held by it, and sue counties and other subdivisions for both land and money damages. I concluded that a suit should be commenced as soon as possible to increase the Oneidas' claim by upping the size from 260,000 acres to 6 million acres. After considerable further research on the pre-1790 era, I prepared a draft complaint against New York and its subdivisions in respect to the whole 6 million acres.

At about this time we were told that the Interior Department had advised the Justice Department to bring a suit in respect to the reservation confirmed to the Oneidas by the 1794 federal treaty, the post-1790 case. On November 6, 1976, I informed my clients of this development and enclosed a copy of a draft complaint to be filed by the Oneidas for the entire 6-million-acre claim. The Interior Department's letter covered only the post-1790 claims for 260,000 acres. Our efforts had generated considerable momentum, and I now wanted to go for the 6 million acres.

Not untypically, some of the Oneidas were conservative and careful and seemed unwilling to file the pre-1790 claim. As before, I had to persuade the Oneidas to take action on the pre-1790 claim. Thus, I concluded that I had to firm up the pre-1790 claim with further research and to get the clients accustomed to a many-fold increase in the acreage under claim. With regard to the pre-1790 claim, I had to pull the Oneidas and the Native American Rights Fund along with me, as Jake Thompson had previously pulled me along. I had a sense of urgency about the claims because, stemming from land claims in Maine and other New England states, a bill had been filed in Congress to cancel forthwith all Native American land claims. I wanted to get all possible Oneida claims filed before such a bill became effective.

By spring 1977 the pre-1790 claim had been developed further, and I clearly outlined it in a March 21, 1977, petition to President Jimmy Carter. Wishing to get more factual backing, my law firm again retained Dr. Jack Campisi, at our cost, to do preliminary historical research confirming the historical validity of the pre-1790 claim.

The pre-1790 claim still had one conceptual flaw so far as ejectment was concerned: how to get around Article 4 of the 1794 federal treaty in which the Oneidas seemingly had promised to claim no land but that which was reserved for them by agreement with

New York. Jack Campisi had the answer. He found that Article 4 was never intended to apply to land in New York but, rather, to the land farther west, the Ohio River Valley, which had been taken from the Oneidas without their knowledge in the 1784 federal treaty.

It was in the summer of 1977, when Campisi and I were meeting with the Litigation Committee of the Oneidas of Wisconsin, that a real breakthrough occurred. The meeting was held in a former seminary that the Oneidas were using for their offices. Before the meeting I was having breakfast in the cafeteria with Campisi, discussing the 1794 treaty problem. Crunching on his toast, Campisi came up with a great realization: If the 1788 treaty with New York really created a trust or lease relationship whereby the Oneidas continued as owners of the land, then that ownership was protected by the 1789 federal treaty and the 1790 Nonintercourse Act. This meant that the Oneidas had not lost title to the land in 1788; they still owned it as lessors in 1790, and the state merely managed it for them. Therefore, in 1790, it came under the protection of the Nonintercourse Act. Furthermore, the 1788 treaty land was part of the "reservation" carved out by the state and guaranteed under Article 2 of the 1794 treaty. This realization completed the circle and provided a firm conceptual basis for the suit for present and back rent on the entire 6 million acres.

The pre-1790 treaties were not transactions in which the parties bargained as equals. Using threats, New York dictated the terms of the agreements, and the Oneida had no choice but to accept them. The so-called treaties were written in the English language; in fact, the Oneidas had no written language whatever. Few of them spoke English, and none could read. They executed the instruments with their marks. Their white interpreters were paid with large tracts of land set aside in the treaty, a true conflict of interest.

Assuming the transactions were viewed as sales, the total consideration paid the Oneida Nation by New York State for the Oneida land acquired in 1785 and 1788 amounted to approximately one-half cent per acre. In contemporaneous transactions involving large areas of less desirable land, the title was sold for much larger sums.

(See the data incorporated in appendix B.) Thus the sum provided to the Oneida Nation by New York State in 1785 and 1788 was grossly inadequate, and the representatives of New York State at the time knew that this was so. The extent of underpayment at that time was on the order of millions in 1788 dollars, before allowance for statutory interest or inflation.

The Oneida land was of exceptional strategic value because it lay across the historic water-level route from the northerly colonies to their manifest and logical expansion westward. The water-level route started at Albany and proceeded west on the Mohawk River to present Rome, New York (formerly Fort Stanwix), and then continued along the southerly shore of Oneida Lake. It was the site of the Erie Canal and all early roads and railroads to the West. It now is occupied by U.S. Route 5, the East-West Conrail and Amtrak railway tracks, the Erie-Barge Canal, and the New York State Thruway. The next good water-level route from the East to the West was hundreds of miles to the south. This land was literally the gateway to the American West. The Oneidas could have grown to be a wealthy nation had not possession of this land been illegally taken from them by the state in the 1785–1840 era.

Such land also had exceptional and unique value because it lay between the then western border of New York, approximately at Utica, and the so-called Military Tracts to the west, which were composed of land that was purchased from the Onondagas, Cayugas, and other Iroquois and given to revolutionary war soldiers. Without the Oneida lands, the veterans and the developers would have had no access to the lands farther west. The patents issued to pay war debts would have been almost valueless. Intact, as promised by U.S. treaties, the Oneida land could have been a dam stemming America's access to and development of western New York, the Ohio River Valley, and points west.

Instead of paying for the access, New York State, with federal acquiescence, took the dam. In any arm's-length transaction between equals, the state would have had to pay very dearly for the right to use the only water-level east-west corridor in the northern United

States. Instead, it paid a pittance of about $28,000 for the whole 5.5 million acres of land sold before 1790.

Unfortunately, these arguments have not been vindicated in court. A suit on the pre-1790 claim was filed against the state and its subdivisions by Jake Thompson and a group of New York Oneidas in late 1978. In 1979 Native American Rights Fund attorneys filed a similar suit in behalf of the remaining Oneidas, but this suit additionally claimed the possession of the land of some 60,000 private landowners in the pre-1790 area reaching from Pennsylvania to the St. Lawrence River.

On October 31, 1988, the U.S. Second Circuit Court of Appeals dismissed the pre-1790 complaints as a matter of law and held they did not state a legal cause of action. The Supreme Court, on October 2, 1989, decided not to allow an appeal on certiorari. Hence, the Oneida Nation may never have a trial on the merits of the pre-1790 claim. But who knows for sure?

My concept had always been to sue for the current and past rental value of the land claimed, not to eject current occupants. The Second Circuit Court of Appeals dismissed the Oneidas' claim for ejectment, but seemed to leave open still a claim for the rental value of the 5.5 million acres allegedly leased to the state in 1788 (see 691 F. 2d, p. 1096).

History can be suppressed, but it does not go away.

6

Further Petitions
and Alternative Strategies

*If there is no office in the United States to come to
our aid as we were promised in the treaties, we shall
have to defend ourselves with our bear hand.**

S TARTING IN 1965, our basic strategy and objective in the Oneida
case was simply that the United States should be made to
keep its word, obey its own laws, and represent the Oneidas
against New York State. It was only when I became convinced that
the United States would not keep its word that the test case against
Madison and Oneida counties was commenced in 1970. In fact, after
the 1974 Supreme Court decision delineated the Oneidas' rights,
we redoubled our efforts to enlist the aid of the United States. We
wanted to avoid the costs and delays of further litigation and achieve
an equitable settlement for the Oneidas.

The response was always negative. The United States clearly
did not want to get mixed up — at least on the side of the Oneidas —
in the land claims battles. This was a political decision, and the
same attitude prevailed in the administrations of Presidents Johnson, Nixon, Ford, and Carter. We petitioned to all of them, and the
response was always negative.

Before the trial, in February 1975, we had written to Rogers
C. B. Morton, secretary of the interior, requesting federal aid in a
suit against New York. In prior requests to the United States for

---

*William Rockwell, secretary and treasurer, Oneida Nation (New York).

help, the response always was that the Oneidas were suing the United States in the Indian Claims Commission, and "conflict of interest" prevented the U.S. attorney general from helping the Oneidas against the state. We pointed out that if there ever was a "conflict of interest" problem arising from the Indian Claims Commission case, it was now resolved, because (1) the commission had already found in favor of the Oneidas, and (2) the U.S. solicitor general, in his brief to the U.S. Supreme Court opposing the Oneidas' position on jurisdiction, had said there was no conflict of interest.

When it suited the political position of the United States, it claimed there was a conflict of interest stemming from the case against the United States in the Indian Claims Commission; when the wind blew the other way, the federal officials found no trouble saying there was not a conflict of interest. Thus, the United States again found a reason to decline to take action.

Later, in May 1975, I wrote to Edward H. Levi, attorney general of the United States, again asking for federal help to achieve negotiations and a settlement with the state. I pointed out that the Oneidas' policy at that time was "of an equitable recovery, rather than ousting non-Indians occupying the Reservation" and I suggested how such a policy could be implemented without disturbing land titles. Finally, our petitions bore some fruit, and the United States did take up serious study of the Oneida case. There was some encouragement that the United States might intervene. But in view of past experience, we proceeded on two fronts: We asked for United States help against the State of New York, which would avert title problems, and we proceeded to get ready for trial in case the federal officials continued to refuse to help.

In June of 1975 we were advised by the U.S. attorney general that legal action could not be taken without a specific request from the Department of the Interior. This bucked the case back to where we had started in the February 1975 letter to Rogers C. B. Morton. At this point it became perfectly clear that a trial *challenging the counties' land titles* was needed, even though the Supreme Court had spoken so clearly in the Oneidas' favor.

Long after the initial trial, in October 1976, we were advised that the Department of the Interior had requested the U.S. attorney general to "bring an action on behalf of the Oneida Nation of New York to have treaties which it entered into with New York State without the consent of the United States declared void, to recover those lands occupied by the State for nonvital public purposes, and for damages for trespass." This was basically a confirmation of all that we had sought over the years: The United States would help the Oneidas achieve resolution of their land claims.

At this point, in response to the Department of Interior, the U.S. attorney general once again raised the issue of conflict of interest in regard to the Indian Claims Commission case, again despite the fact that the U.S. solicitor general, in 1973, had said he saw no conflict. Efforts were made to settle the Oneidas' Indian Claims Commission case so as to eliminate the conflict once and for all.

In early 1977 the settlement problem became acute because there was concern that a period of limitations on certain aspects of the claim might expire on July 18, 1977. If so, any legal action by the federal government in the Oneidas' behalf had to begin by that date. However, the United States again said that the issue of conflict raised by the Indian Claims Commission case still barred the United States from commencing an action in behalf of the Oneidas unless the claims case were settled before July 18. Thus, the United States used this "whipsaw" situation to try to pressure the Oneidas into a favorable settlement. This was yet another example of the continuing U.S. policy of unfairness and duplicity in regard to the Oneidas.

In early 1977 a petition was prepared and submitted to the newly elected President Carter (see appendix H). This petition was signed by the Oneidas of New York and Canada. The Wisconsin Oneidas did not sign the petition but did later indicate their approval. This petition is significant because it laid out publicly for the first time the elements of a cause of action in regard to pre-1790 transactions. On March 25, 1977, following the filing of this petition, we wrote to the new U.S. attorney general to request a conference to discuss the claim.

At about that same time we learned that legislation might be introduced in Congress to cancel the claim of the Maine Indians and all other similar claims. Congressmen from Maine and other areas were becoming increasingly concerned about the threat posed by the *Oneida* and similar cases. I prepared a draft "emergency complaint" against the State of New York to be filed in the event passage of such legislation seemed imminent. In response to the petition to President Carter, we were invited to a meeting with Leo Krulitz, solicitor of the U.S. Department of Interior. I prepared a detailed memorandum for him describing the Oneida claims and the litigation to date. The memorandum contained a complete description of the pre-1790 claim as then envisioned. At the meeting on April 7, 1977, we did have a meaningful discussion. For the first time, I felt we were being listened to and not brushed off. I remember expressing great indignation at the way the United States was treating the July 18, 1977, limitations on the Oneida claims, using it as a whipsaw to get a favorable settlement of the Oneida claims against the United States in the Indian Claims Commission. The meeting bore fruit because on April 23, 1977, we received a letter from William Gershuny, acting associate solicitor:

> This is to advise you that the Solicitor will recommend to the Department of Justice that an action be brought before July 18, 1977, on behalf of the Oneida Nations seeking ejectment and damages against those persons claiming an interest in the lands confirmed to the Oneida Nation in the Treaty with the Six Nations, 7 Stat. 44 (1794). These are the lands involved in claims 3–8 in the Indian Claims Commission Docket 301 proceeding and consist of about 246,000 acres; Findings of Fact dated August 18, 1971. We also are requesting that the Department of Justice consult with tribal representatives prior to the institution of suit.
>
> Our theory of the case is that the approximately 25 subsequent dispositions of the lands were in violation of the Indian Nonintercourse Act, 25 U.S.C. § 177.

Because of the impending statute of limitations deadline, we invite your assistance in identifying potential defendants in the action.

Later, in June, we received a copy of a further letter from Krulitz to James W. Moorman of the Department of Justice requesting preparation of a suit in regard to the 231,000 acres of reservation land before July 18, 1977:

> The involved lands were reserved to the Oneida Tribe of Indians in the Treaty of September 22, 1788, with New York State. They consist of a contiguous tract of 231,310.81 acres. In the Treaty with the Six Nations of November 11, 1794, 7 Stat. 44, the United States confirmed three of the tribes of the Iroquois confederacy, including the Oneida, in the lands that had been reserved to them in their treaties with the State. In 25 subsequent treaties all of the reserved lands, except for 757.42 acres, were ceded to the State. It is our position that the conveyances made in 23 of those treaties were in violation of the Indian Non-intercourse Act and Indian title today is paramount with respect to those lands. . . .
>
> We recommend that litigation be initiated on behalf of the Oneida Nation of Indians. There are these constituent groups of Oneidas located in New York, Wisconsin and Ontario, Canada. We are unsure whether the Oneida of the Thames at Southwold, Ontario have a legal claim to the United States lands as do the other groups. However, we think it is adequate for present purposes to identify the beneficiary of our trust responsibilities as the "Oneida Nation of Indians."

It became clear, in June 1977, that the United States was at last prepared to act—at least in regard to the post-1790 claim. This, I should note, was *before* Judge Port rendered his decision in the suit against the counties. What we had set out to do in 1965 had come to pass. We had finally prevailed on the United States to obey its own laws and treaties and come to the aid of the Oneida Nation.

Although we had learned a lot since 1965 about the facts and the law involved, the framework envisioned in 1965—and incorporated in our retainer agreement—was intact.

Because of the 1974 *Oneida* decision of the Supreme Court, other Native American groups became able to bring suit to recover land, and several such cases were now filed in New England and elsewhere. A new force, a new strategy seemed to be evolving, one that was incompatible with Bond, Schoeneck & King's continued representation of the Oneidas.

Assuming the United States could not be prevailed on to help the Oneidas, my plan since 1965 was to get the Oneida land back piece by piece. According to an Oneida legend told to me by Jake Thompson, the remaining Oneida lands, those not sold to the state, were lost at the rate of two plow furrows a year. Each year at plowing time, the non-Indian neighbor of an Oneida farmer would plow two more furrows on the Indian's land. The Indian, having no civil rights, was unable to fight back. With three feet a year lopped off each property line, the Oneida acreage inevitably shrank over time.

My plan was to reverse the flow of those two furrows a year. I sought to get the Oneidas' land back, or to receive recompensation for it, chunk by chunk, and to let each recovery finance the next initiative. In a time of great social revolution—the 1960s—I did not want to provoke more revolutionary strife. I wanted a tide that advances almost imperceptibly, yet sweeps all before it. That is why the initial suit against Madison and Oneida counties for 1795 treaty land was for the rental value of the land owned by the counties for just two years.

The plan was: We have a good case. We should take our time, move step by step, furrow by furrow. Establish the point and eventually things will fall into place. Do not raise the alarm level too high, or they will send in the cavalry. Back the state slowly into a corner, and eventually we can settle by negotiation.

Our strategy was also dictated by the legal and ethical realities. Bond, Schoeneck & King is a law firm with partners and many clients living in areas that could be affected by the claim. We had made it clear to the Oneidas from the first that we would not sue to eject private landowners; we would seek recovery only from the state and its political subdivisions. Moreover, the prospect for recovery of land in 1965 seemed farfetched; only our later success made that possible. We were also concerned that Congress would become alarmed and simply retroactively ratify the New York treaties. The Oneida leaders agreed with the furrow-by-furrow strategy. In this vein Irwin Chrisjohn of the Oneidas of the Thames wrote me on May 1, 1977:

> 1. I must acknowledge first that the strategy and actions up to this point by you and the Bond, Schoeneck and King law firm have been effective and above reproach. As "Partners", we have a great deal to be proud of, so far.
>
> 2. It has been our contention that our "Diplomatic" approach has made us and our actions less than newsworthy, but this approach in itself has led to us having public opinion with us rather than against us, since we are not thought of as frightening to the general public.
>
> 3. As a "Public Relations" type of individual I would prefer to continue the Diplomatic Strategy with PUBLICITY EMPHASIS on the possibility of us joining in with the Mass Ejectment Movement, only if necessary.

Perception of potential conflict of interest arose because of a classic feedback situation: "You can never do merely one thing." If the 1974 jurisdictional decision of the Supreme Court had been confined only to the narrow facts of the *Oneida* case, that would have been perfect for my low-profile approach; no person's or company's title would have been challenged, and land owned by government entities would have been the only target. What happened was that other Native American groups used the 1974 decision as the basis for their own lawsuits. In the other lawsuits, an ejectment strategy was adopted involving mass claims against landowners in a given area. I was not in favor of that strategy, but in fact in many of these cases that approach seemed to be working.

Given the apparent success of other Native American groups in court, the impulse to use the mass-ejectment strategy for the Oneidas was hard to resist. At one point in early 1977 I was pointedly warned by one of the Native American Rights Fund attorneys that Bond, Schoeneck & King had a major conflict problem because the Oneidas should be suing landowners. Where legal ethics are concerned, we have to avoid even the appearance of conflict. And it became clear that potential conflict might have prevented our clients from electing to adopt a more aggressive strategy for the future.

The potential conflict was apparent to us from the first and carefully explained to our clients at an initial meeting and many times thereafter. Ray George, of Canada, used to joke with me about pasturing his race horses on my lawn at Cazenovia Lake when the case was won. Jake Thompson used to joke with George Bond about using George's large home in Cazenovia as the Oneidas' "Presidential Palace." As jokes usually do, these remarks held a measure of basic truth, well known to all.

I viewed the conflict problem, not as one of suing myself and clients of the firm; we never even remotely entertained doing that. Nor was there a conflict problem if the United States took up the claim against New York State, as we had long urged, because we would then withdraw entirely, having then earned our fee. The conflict was as to the choice of the best strategy if the United States did not bring suit. One choice would leave us, with the clients' knowledge and consent, as active attorneys with a claim against New York, which is where we started in 1965 using the furrow-by-furrow approach to get land back or recompense for it. The first "furrow" was the county land involved in the 1970 suit. The Thruway, where it passes through Oneida land, might be a later "furrow," and so on. My concept was a rifle shot that would hit only the state.

The other strategy choice, mass ejectment suits, was a shotgun blast at all who were nearby and would force us to withdraw in favor of other counsel who had no conflict. While I still believe the furrow-by-furrow strategy, including litigation initiated by the United States, was the correct one, that is just clear hindsight now.

With these considerations in mind, how could we ethically advise the clients on the pros and cons of the choice of approach? We could not. My law firm, Bond, Schoeneck & King, thus decided to withdraw from active participation in the case. We would still help where we could, but we would disqualify ourselves from responsibility for choice of strategy or from implementation of an ejectment strategy if that was adopted.

I decided to recommend the Native American Rights Fund as substitute counsel. They could provide objective strategic advice, and they had repeatedly demonstrated to me their dedication and their expertise. I gave some consideration to private law firms specializing in Indian matters, but it was hard to recommend a commercial firm when the fund's attorneys would do an excellent job at no charge. The Native American Rights Fund was then retained on a no-fee basis by the Wisconsin, Canadian, and New York Oneidas.

Arlinda Locklear, an attorney at the fund assigned to the Oneida case, has done superb work in the further proceedings in the post-1790 test case. This included a trial on the issue of damages, a further appeal to the Second Circuit Court of Appeals, and finally the victory in 1985 when the U.S. Supreme Court rendered final judgment in favor of the Oneidas in the post-1790 test case. Locklear, aided by Bert Hirsch, attorney for the New York Oneidas, has also done a fine job in the prosecution of the pre-1790 claim, which was in court ten years before it was dismissed without a trial.

I never did learn what happened to the decision of the United States authorities to bring suit against the state on behalf of the Oneidas.

7

"Circle the Wagons"

for as long as the grass grows and the rivers run.[*]

W HEN I THINK ABOUT WHAT HAPPENED after the 1974 decision of the U.S. Supreme Court, I am torn between disbelief and cynicism. When I learned about the avarice and treachery of the State of New York in the 1788–1795 treaties, I was indignant enough, but that after all was history that reflected a mindset about Native American people 200 years removed from our more "enlightened" times. In 1975, when I studied the Bureau of Indian Affairs file from 1909 onward, I was again indignant— and this time astounded—at the duplicity and the condescending attitudes of the bureau officials. A lot of the events in the file occurred during my own lifetime, and it was harder to believe that it could happen— but I adjusted to that, too, on the basis that Washington, D.C., is far away and the letters were written by bureaucrats in the sunset of a former era.

In contrast, when I studied the January 21, 1974, decision of the U.S. Supreme Court, I was astounded at its breadth and gratified that the legal philosophy I had assembled turned out to be just the right combination. My first instinct was to think that a meeting with representatives of New York State might now be arranged to quickly settle the case and put an end to legal costs and title issues. I thought that surely the state officials would comprehend the rami-

*Governor George Clinton, 1788.

77

fications of the Supreme Court decision and want to get the problem solved once and for all time.

But this is where the officials of New York State once again disregarded the portents and blew their chance. Despite the fact that New York itself had filed a brief and had sent its solicitor general to argue in the Supreme Court, the state seemed not to comprehend the significance of the January 21, 1974, decision. The state's officials should have sat down at once with the Oneidas and their representatives to negotiate a resolution of the land claims. Since then, in an effort to flog a dead horse, the state has expended, and caused the counties to expend, millions of dollars in further legal defense fees. Another decade of legal gyrations had to take place before the Supreme Court again held against the state in January 1985. Though the game was up in January 1974, the state apparently decided to pursue its policy of asserting state supremacy over federal law.

One fallout of the state's decision was a challenge to the title of several farmers living on Route 46, just north of Oneida, New York. After the Supreme Court decision, the New York Oneidas considered suing these farmers. I tried to talk the Oneidas of New York out of suing private landowners and assured them that the state would soon start to negotiate. I was wrong. I tried several times to contact the state about negotiations but received no response. Only after my attempts were unsuccessful did the New York Oneidas retain the Native American Rights Fund to bring suit for return of the balance of the 800 acres in the *Boylan* case. Their purpose was not to hurt the farmers, but to get the state to the bargaining table. It did not work. The state preferred to ignore the whole thing and let the landowners bear the burden.

For example, a week after the Supreme Court's decision, on January 29, 1974, I wrote to the New York attorney general, Louis Lefkowitz, as follows: "On January 21, 1974 the Supreme Court held unanimously in favor of the Oneida Indians on the question of federal court jurisdiction on land claims. I would very much like to discuss this case with you. Would you please let me know when it would be convenient for you." I received no response.

On February 14, 1974, I wrote to the attorney for Oneida

County in part, "I have received no acknowledgement of my letter to the Attorney General. I am a little concerned at this, since the public interest law firm in Washington is champing at the bit to bring a lawsuit against some of the individual landowners. This would certainly be a regrettable development."

Again, on March 4, 1974, I wrote to the attorney for Madison County: "Enclosed is a copy of the Supreme Court's letter on costs. I propose that we forget about costs in this suit assuming that is O.K. with you and Mr. Mascaro. The attorney for the Native American Rights Fund called me about the suit against the individual land owners, and I wonder if you have heard from Mr. Lefkowitz." This refers to the fact that I had persuaded the New York Oneidas and the fund to delay the ejectment suit against the landowners by assuring the Oneidas that the state would respond to my letters and sit down to negotiate an overall settlement. I asked them to hold off until I tried once more. On March 6, 1974, I again wrote to Lefkowitz about a negotiating session. I once again received no response. On March 13, 1974, I received the following letter from the attorney for Madison County:

Dear George:
Representatives of the Oneida County Attorney's office and myself will go to Albany on Thursday, April 11, 1974, at 1:00 P.M. for a conference with the Assistant Attorney General, Jeremiah Jochnowitz and the Solicitor General, Ruth Kessler Toch.
At that time we will get together and decide what the position of the State will be and the contents of our answer to the complaint.
Very truly yours,

On March 18, 1974, as a last step before an ejectment suit, Graeme Bell of the Native American Rights Fund wrote to the Corporation Counsel of the City of Oneida, advising of the potential suit, "in the hope that this matter can be discussed and perhaps resolved without litigation."

The local authorities followed the state's example. On March 11,

1975, the Corporation Counsel of the City of Oneida wrote to me, "The City of Oneida does not acknowledge the existence of an Oneida Indian Nation, and much less, Jacob Thompson as the, so-called, President thereof." This was written more than a year after the Supreme Court's 1974 decision and more than fifty years after the decision of the Second Circuit Court of Appeals in *U.S.* v. *Boylan*.

In 1977 we again attempted to initiate settlement discussions with the state. In March 1977 I sent to the counsel to the governor of New York a copy of the petition filed with President Carter earlier that year. Then the Oneidas of New York sought to give the governor a petition to the state. The governor refused to accept it and directed that it should be sent to Mario M. Cuomo, then New York secretary of state. I then sent two Oneida petitions, on March 14 and 25, 1977, to the governor and to his counsel, Judah Gribetz. No one from the state ever replied. Just as in 1974, the state refused to meet or to discuss the case. The government officials had never been able to face up to the Oneida case. It is simply too big. Yet, despite these rebuffs, we did not end our attempts to resolve the case before it escalated into suits against landowners. In early 1977 Charles Schoeneck made an appointment with a Mr. Redmond, one of the governor's counsel, to discuss the case. First, Charles and I flew to Wisconsin to discuss the case with the leaders there. Then, with several Oneida representatives, we went to Washington to discuss intervention in the case by the United States.

After the Washington meeting Charles and I flew directly to Albany to meet with Redmond. Of course, we had told the clients about the proposed meeting and its purpose. We were received most hospitably by Redmond and, at length, we described the Oneidas' claim, the Supreme Court decision, the trial in 1975, and the general nature of the pre-1790 claim. Redmond, a very able lawyer, questioned us closely and seemed to have a very good comprehension of the case and its implications.

What happened then? Nothing. The "test case" strategy had failed to stir the state to action, and the Oneidas had no recourse except further litigation, the filing of the 1979 suit. The state's failure to respond to our early petitions is regrettable, but understandable. But after the 1974 U.S. Supreme Court decision, the state failed to even respond to settlement overtures. The state government officials have always pursued a policy of "circle the wagons and fight to the end."

Now, under a different Governor, representatives of the state are meeting with Oneida delegates to effect a resolution of the Oneida claims. It is my hope that the final settlement will be one that confers immediate benefits on the present Oneida people and also preserves their land and capital base intact for future generations.

My vision of what the Oneidas should obtain, going back to the filing of the original suit for rent in 1970, is recognized sovereign title to their land, coupled with lease payments from the State "for as long as the grass grows and the rivers run." The rent would be based on the current unimproved value of the land and would be adjusted periodically to account for inflation. The underlying title to the land would have all the protection accorded to a federal Indian Reservation. All future generations of Oneidas would thus have a secure land base.

In addition, there would have to be a feasible and reasonable cash and land settlement from the state to account for the past loss of use of the land since the dates of the state treaties: 1788, 1795, and so on. In other words, the state would have to live up to Governor George Clinton's promise made in 1788 for a perpetual lease with adjustable rent. The cash and land part of the recovery would enable the Oneida people to settle and live in their ancestral homeland.

This may seem a farfetched vision, but it is not nearly as staggering as our effort to overturn nearly two hundred years of precedent and open the federal courts to jurisdiction over the Oneida Land Claim.

APPENDIXES

INDEX

ONEIDA INDIAN NATION PETITION TO THE
CONSTITUTIONAL CONVENTION OF
NEW YORK STATE, JUNE 12, 1967

I AM JACOB THOMPSON, President of the Oneida Indian Nation here in New York State. This is a plea for justice addressed to the Delegates to the Constitutional Convention and, through the Delegates, to the people of New York. My people were among the original organizers of the Ho do no sau ne, or the League of the Five Nations. So you might know me as an Iroquois Indian.

As a nation, we Oneidas date our history within today's New York State boundaries back to an era when most of your ancestors were in the process of the discovery of the New World. We're older than you as an organized people, but we were living in the Stone Age. We Oneidas existed long before the European community knew about us. Both of our people were far, far behind where we are today.

Yet, since we and white men from Europe met on the Broad acres that would become New York, we have been friendly and cooperative associates. I think this bears repeating. Nothing since 1634 when surgeon, (Dutch) Dr. Van den Bogaert, left Fort Orange and explored our homeland has there been organized, open or covert conflict between our peoples. For over 300 years our association has proven mutually beneficial.

You gave us a more advanced and fruitful way of life, and we gave your infant society help to withstand French invasion south of the St. Lawrence River. Our help gave you the chance to claim a protectorate over Iroquois country before the world at your negotiations in Paris in 1783. In America's struggle for Independence, the Oneidas actively allied with the military force of Congress and helped Washington's generals establish America's claim to sovereignty over 20 million acres of land in present-day New York. Since the Revolution, we Oneidas alone have "released" over 5 million acres of land to New York and its citizens. In other words, we signed away our capital base for the well-being of millions of New Yorkers. Today about one-sixth of the state's economic base rests on former Oneida Lands. By our generosity—naive, perhaps—we contributed greatly to the emergence of New York as the Empire State.

In the process we gained something. We gained the opportunity to be educated, to function effectively in an increasingly progressive world.

Our education has made us realize that we do not want to become stone-age Indians again. Yet our education has brought home to us that our ancestors had values in their way of living that should not be discarded as primitive. We have become cultured people and have learned cultural values. In the process, we now know that all our "releases" of land—our

85

national capital—did not meet the standards of American Equity. Put bluntly, we learned and can prove that we were duped, by practices that might be called illegal, of the means to help us move from a stone-age existence to one blessed with modern technology.

Our education has also shown us that the means for redressing the errors of the past are limited, complicated and arduous. In many ways the whims of state administrators stand between us and the promise of a brighter future.

Our education has given us a vision of what we could achieve if we only had a small portion of our former estate.

Our education tells us that we must work within the framework of our own American Society and in the spirit of cooperation that has always marked the relations between New York and the Oneidas.

From these hopes and values, learned and treasured, we have made two conclusions.

One: We must re-establish the Oneida Reservation as a going concern. It need be only be a modest one of approximately 10,000 acres.

Two: We need a capital fund, perpetually protected against diminishment, held in trust for use by and with the consent of the Oneida Indian Nation, to finance reservation housing, agriculture, and industry; Oneida education for Indian purposes, Iroquois craftsmanship and arts, and the preservation of the enduring vestiges of our ancient culture including practice of its folkways, music, rituals, and arts and language.

These two needs—Reservation and a capital fund—we Oneidas could obtain by righting the wrongs done to us in the 18th and 19th centuries. We do not want to reverse the course of history. Rather we want the State of New York to reappraise its treatment of us by a normal American process. Give us the opportunity to have access to New York State Courts. By obtaining a simple amendment to the constitution, the Oneida Indians and New York State could peacefully, and without rancor, work out their differences—promote both sides—and continue the centuries-old friendship between us.

JACOB THOMPSON—President
Oneida Indian Nation
New York

APPENDIX B

ONEIDA INDIAN NATION PETITION TO THE PRESIDENT OF THE UNITED STATES, 1968

This is a Complaint and Petition for justice submitted to the President of the United States of America pursuant to Articles 2 and 7 of a Treaty of the United States dated November 11, 1794 between the United States and the Iroquois Nation.

This Complaint and Petition is respectfully submitted by the Oneida Nation of Indians.

WHEREAS, the Oneida Nation of Indians, unlike the other Iroquois who sided with Britain, rendered valuable assistance to the United States in the War of Independence from Britain, and

WHEREAS, the United States, in formal treaties in 1784, 1789 and 1794, promised that the Oneida Nation would remain secure in the possession of their lands, and

WHEREAS, the said Treaty of 1794 provided that complaint for injuries done to the Iroquois Nation, including the Oneida Nation, be made to the President of the United States;

NOW, THEREFORE, the Oneida Nation hereby makes Its complaint to the President of the United States as follows:

1. By agreement with New York State, as stated in the Treaty of Ft. Schuyler in 1788, a tract of land comprising about 300,000 acres was set aside as the Reservation of the Oneida Nation in New York State. This was confirmed to the Oneida Nation by the 1794 treaty with the United States.

2. In 1790 the Congress of the United States enacted legislation to protect Indians in respect of their lands. In 1793 the law was re-enacted and has been continued in much the same form to this date as Section 177 of 25 U.S.C.A.

3. From 1795 to 1842 the State of New York, acting in violation of said statute, purchased the entire reservation of the Oneida Nation, excepting about 700 acres, by a series of so-called treaties. Specifically, no Commissioner of the United States, as required by the federal law, was present at the negotiation and signing of the so-called treaties with the State of New York. One exception to this is the purchase of 1798, which was made under U.S. authority.

4. In addition to violating the statute cited above, the State of New York, supposedly acting as fiduciary for the Oneida Nation, purchased their lands for a fraction of their actual value at the time.

5. The Oneida Nation, as soon as some of its members became

89

sufficiently aware of the value placed upon land by the White Man to realize the fraud perpetrated upon them, and up to the present, have asked for redress from the State of New York. They have not received it. In the Summer of 1967 the Oneidas filed a petition for justice with the New York State Constitutional Convention. The Attorney General of New York objected (see memorandum following)* and nothing came of the plea.

6. A case decided by the United States Circuit Court of Appeals, Second Circuit, has renewed the hopes of the Oneida Nation that they can secure redress from the State of New York. *Tuscarora Nation v. N.Y.S. Power Authority, et al.,* 257 F. 2d 885 (1958). That case definitely held that the protective statute referred to in paragraph 2 does now apply and has always applied to Indian Reservations of the State of New York.

7. Be it clearly understood that the Oneida Nation has no purpose or wish to eject from such lands the innocent people who now have record title to them and reside thereon.

8. The Oneida Nation wishes to secure from the State of New York only fair and just compensation for the lands unlawfully taken from them without due process of law.

9. The Oneida Nation of New York wishes to use its share of such compensation to (a) set up a trust fund for the education, health and welfare of future generations of Oneidas, and (b) purchase lands in or near their former Reservation in New York State as Reservation for those members of the Oneida Nation who from time to time may choose to live there.

10. The Oneida Nation of New York proposes to acquire for these purposes only such lands as are freely sold to them by their present owners who take title from so-called patents from the State of New York.

11. A historical and legal statement of the Oneida's case is the Memorandum of Law and Fact, which follows.

12. The Oneida Nation requests the assistance of the President of the United States and his Attorney General and the Department of the Interior in proceeding against the State of New York for redress of the injuries described above. Over the years the Attorney General, in observance of his oath of office and statutory duties, has come to the assistance of Indian Nations in similar circumstances on numerous occasions. He

---

*For clarity, cross references found in the original documents have been omitted if they are not included in this book or have been modified as required.

should now do it for the people who helped the Thirteen Colonies win their independence.

13. This Complaint and Petition is submitted to the President of the United States in reliance upon the sacred word of the United States.

Respectfully submitted,

JACOB THOMPSON, President

Oneida Nation of New York

MEMORANDUM

To: THE CONSTITUTIONAL CONVENTION
COMMITTEE ON INDIAN AFFAIRS

From: LOUIS J. LEFKOWITZ
Attorney general
By: JULIUS L. SACKMAN
Principal Attorney

Re: *Oneida Indian Nation*

The Oneida Indian Nation seeks what, in effect, would be enabling legislation from the Convention authorizing a suit against the State for money damages for approximately five million acres of land. They claim that they were inadequately paid (allegedly $.004 to $.03 per acre). They seek authorization to recover the difference between what they were paid and what similar property was allegedly going for at the same time.

The comparable prices which have been set forth in their memorandum range from 16¢ to 80¢ per acre on "whole-sale" sales and up to $22 per acre on "retail" sales. The differential thus reflected would range approximately from $800,000 to $110,000,000. If interest were to be added at 4% for the 170 years which have elapsed (a total of 680%) the total award would range between the low of $6,240,000 and a high of $858,000,00.

The Oneidas question the validity of the titles derived from them on the ground that the transactions were violative of the Indian Nonintercourse Act (25 U.S. Code, § 177), but they do not challenge the present ownership of the lands. The element of land titles is introduced on the issue of alleged damages (Oneida memorandum, p. 16). But they are in error even on the question of title because the Indian Nonintercourse Act does not apply to the State of New York. This was squarely held by our Court of Appeals as the Oneidas concede in their memorandum (p. 13) in *St. Regis Tribe v. State*, 5 N. Y. 2d 24 (1958) and by the United States District Court for the Northern District of New York in *United States v. Franklin County*, 50 F. Supp. 152 (1943). The decision of the Federal Second Circuit Court of Appeals in the Tuscarora case, 257 F. 2d 885 (1958) to the contrary was firstly, *obiter* in character, and secondly, was rendered moot by subsequent proceedings.

It is pertinent to observe also that the Oneidas presently have an identical claim pending against the United States before the Federal Indian Claims Commission (Oneida memorandum, pp. 5–6).

In any event it should be noted that the Oneidas here seek authorization to sue the State. Such authorization should be sought from the State Legislature which has power to enact such enabling legislation. The Legislature is certainly better equipped than is this Convention to explore the ramifications and implications of the Oneida proposal. Before the State is committed to an obligation of such potentially astronomical a sum there should be ample time for study.

The proposal submitted by the Oneidas should be rejected.

Dated: Albany, New York, August 3, 1967

Julius L. Sackman

Principal Attorney

Department of Law

MEMORANDUM OF LAW AND FACT

Preamble

This memorandum is submitted in behalf of The Oneida Indian Nation. We represent The Oneida Indian Nation (herein sometimes called "Oneidas") under a retainer contract filed with and approved by the United States Department of the Interior. At present, members of the Oneida Indian Nation reside in New York State, in Wisconsin and in Ontario, Canada.

Introduction

The Oneidas appeal to the President of the United States for assistance in asserting against New York State their claim for damages for illegal taking of their former Reservation. After the Revolutionary War, in which the Oneidas fought on the side of the Colonies, the Oneidas owned in good fee title between 4,000,000 and 6,000,000 acres of land in what is now New York State (see map 1). Thereafter this land was acquired from them by the State for completely unfair and inadequate consideration, and in many cases in violation of the Federal Indian Law, Section 177 of 25 U.S.C.A.

A state can be sued only with its own consent and the 11th Amendment to the United States Constitution bars suit against a state in federal courts. Therefore, the Oneidas have never had a forum in which to present their claim against the State. Further, until recently the courts of New York have uniformly held that an Indian Nation had no status to sue in New York courts.

The purpose of this memorandum is to tell you *why* the Oneidas should have their day in court.

Historical Background

History can sometimes best be understood in terms of geography. What happened to the Oneidas is a good example: They were in the way.

The western boundary of the white man's domain was fixed by the Treaty of 1768 at a line roughly north and south from Rome, New York. After the Revolution the move West was irresistible and the fact that the Oneidas had helped New York and the other Colonies during the Revolutionary War did them no good.

In 1783 the New York Legislature empowered commissioners to try to get the Oneidas to leave their lands and move West to land then owned by the Senecas. "The Treaty of Fort Stanwix" by Henry S. Manley, p. 28. Later in 1783 General George Washington visited the Oneidas to investigate their complaints and as a result of his visit, the Continental Congress delegated to its commissioners power to effect a peace treaty with the warring Indians and to reassure the Oneidas and Tuscaroras as to their lands. *Manley,* pp. 44, 46.

In 1795 the Oneidas sold a large part of their Reservation to the State for an annuity of $0.03 per acre forever. This figures out to a price of 50¢ per acre at 6%, or about 43¢ per acre at 7%, the prevailing interest rates. Just two years later the State re-sold the same land to settlers for an average of $3.53 per acre. See Hammond's *"History of Madison County"* p. 699. See *Laws of New York,* 20th Sess. Chap. 80, April 1, 1797. In 1795 Mr. John Lincklaen was selling land just south of the Reservation for $1.50 to $3.00 per acre. *Hammond,* p. 210.

As will be shown below, the 1795 purchase was illegal under federal law. See: Section 4 of the Indian Nonintercourse Act of July 22, 1790 (1 Stat. 138); Section 8 id of March 1, 1793 (1 Stat. 330) and Section 177 of the present *Federal Indian Law* 25 U.S.C.A. The New York Legislature must have been concerned with the federal statute because in 1798 the State treated with a federal commissioner on the further purchase that took place that year. See *Laws of New York,* 22nd Sess. Chap. 87, April 2, 1799.

Over the next 40 years the Oneidas sold the balance of their 300,000 acre Reservation to the State in a series of so-called treaties, all of which were in violation of federal law forbidding such sales without the consent of the United States. Section 177 of 25 U.S.C.A. The last such sale was in 1842. With rare exceptions the Indians signed these treaties only with "X", their mark. (The Oneidas presently have a claim pending against the U. S. and the Indian Claims Commission for allowing this to happen. The United States denies any liability.) A summary of the more important sales follows:

Date of Sale	Annuity Promised	Approx. Per Acre Price
1785	0	$0.04
1788	$ 600	$.0.004
1795	$3269	$0.50
1798	$ 700	—
1802	$ 300	$0.85
1802	$ 300	$0.85
1807	$ 645	$0.75
1809	$ 120	$0.56
1810	?	$0.50
1811	$ 332	$0.50
1811	$ 72	$0.50
1815	$ —	$1.00
1817	$ 121	$2.00
1824	$ 300	$2.60
1826	$ —	$3.00
1827	$ —	$3.50

The entire principal value of all annuities promised to the Oneidas is about $115,000. See "*History of Oneida County*", Everts & Fariss (1878) p. 66. [Even] allowing for down payments, their [consideration was woefully unfair. In the post-1800 sales, while the Oneidas were receiving]* $1.00 to $3.00 per acre, white men were buying and selling for $10.00 per acre and up. Land values can be established from recitals in deeds contemporaneously filed in the Oneida, Chenango and Madison Counties Clerks' offices and from the still extant records of the men who subdivided and made fortunes selling off the former Oneida lands.

To understand this, we must remember that Madison County was fully civilized and a "boom" area in the 1790's and early 1800's. Numerous turnpikes and the Erie Canal were being built right through the center

*For clarity, cross references found in the original documents have been omitted if they are not included in this book or have been modified as required.

of the Reservation. As the current official map and summary history of Madison County indicate "A great influx of settlers to Madison County was promoted by these first highways" and "The County was rapidly settled, growth being stimulated by three main roads which crossed from East to West". By 1810, the County had a population of 25,000; by 1830 it was 39,000; by 1840 it was 40,000 and probably had more working farms and farmers than it has today.

To give some idea of the range of values circa 1785–1800, we submit the following extracts of price information found in official state records:

(a) Massachusetts in 1787 sold to Samuel Brown 230,000 acres, West of the Oneidas' 1788 sale, for $0.125 per acre. Richards "*Historical Atlas of New York State*", p. 65. This was over thirty times per acre more than the Oneidas received for their 1788 sale.

(b) In 1788 Massachusetts sold to Nathaniel Gorham and Oliver Phelps the pre-emption right to purchase 6,000,000 acres of Western New York from the Indians. The consideration was $0.03 per acre. See Richards, p. 65, and Whipple Report, p. 17. Under the Hartford Compact of 1786, the preemption right belonged to Massachusetts and the land itself to New York. The $0.03 per acre was not for the land, but for the right to try to buy it from the Indians—presumably at a fair price in addition.

(c) In 1791 Gorham and Phelps turned back 4,000,000 acres to Massachusetts, which then re-sold the pre-emption right to Robert Morris for $333,000, Richards p. 65. (Per the Whipple Report, p. 18, the price was $225,000.) This comes to $0.08 per acre just for the preemption right.

(d) Over the next few years most of the lands purchased from the Oneidas in 1785 and 1788 were sold off. Richards, p. 65, describes some of the prices:

  —townships sold at auction from 16¢ to 80¢ per acre;
  —Chenango townships, purchased from Oneidas in 1788 for $0.004, sold for 3 shillings three pence (40¢?) per acre in 1794;
  —Macomb's purchase in North Country at 16¢ per acre for 4,000,000 acres in 1791 included former Oneida lands;
  —Scriba's patent in 1791 at 16¢ per acre for land north of Oneida Lake;
  —Holland Land Company purchased 50,000 acres at about $0.62 per acre just South of Reservation in 1792:
  —same company purchased 64,000 additional acres for $0.75 per acre in 1792.

Remember, these lands were purchased from the Oneidas in 1788 for about $0.004 per acre.

If the variations in these wholesale prices make little sense, we must remember that it was New York's policy to get the land settled as quickly as possible. The price it got for the land was not the important thing. In many cases it was sold at auction to the highest bidder.

As between white men, dealing in smaller lots at arm's length, we have a quite different picture. Exhibit "B" is a condensation of early land sales in Chenango County, then just South of the Oneida reservation. This exhibit covers roughly the 1795 period when the Oneidas received 50¢ per acre and includes land just South of the Reservation as of 1795. . . .

Exhibit "B"

FROM EARLY REAL ESTATE RECORDS
CHENANGO COUNTY, NEW YORK

Date	Page	Acres	Price	Price/Acre
1801	1	179	$ 126.00	.71
1800	1	40	$ 200.00	5.00
1798	1	11	$ 34.20	3.00
1798	1	47	$ 225.00	4.90
1799	1	51	$ 375.00	7.40
1798	2	57	$ 400.00	7.00
1800	2	10	$ 100.00	10.00
1795	2	50	£ 50.00	£1.00
1799	2	64	$ 500.00	7.80
1799	2	250	$ 950.00	3.80
1799	2	50	$ 700.00	14.00
1800	2	70	$ 900.00	1.30
1796	2	50	$ 150.00	3.00
1800	2	58	$ 35.00	.60
1799	2	20	$ 100.00	5.00
1801	3	57	$ 25.00	.44
1800	3	40	$ 140.00	3.50
1794	3	250	$ 125.00	2.00
1799	3	20	$ 100.00	5.00
1800	4	4	$ 60.00	15.00
1799	6	20	$ 160.00	8.00
1797	6	50	$ 269.00	5.40
1799	7	20	$ 160.00	8.00
1796	7	323	£ 323.00	£1.00
1797	7	255	£ 267.00	£1.00
1798	7	290		10 shillings
1797	8	100	$ 700.00	7.00
1799	8	313	$1500.00	4.80
1794	8	250	$ 125.00	.50
1799	9	50	$ 227.00	4.50
1798	9	101	$ 267.00	2.60
1800	9	313	$1400.00	4.50
1798	10	79	$ 300.00	3.80
1799	11	150	$ 10.00	.60

Date	Page	Acres	Price	Price/Acre
1799	11	51	$ 375.00	7.40
1800	11	150	$ 75.00	.50
1800	12	150	$ 75.00	.50
1799	12	500	$ 550.00	1.10
1798	12	160	$ 25.00	.50
1801	12	179	$ 126.00	.70
?	13	60	$ 240.00	4.00
?	13	150	$ 318.00	2.10
1800	14	58	$ 35.00	.60
1798*	14	250	$ 858.00	3.40
1801	14	49	$ 71.00	1.40
1798	14	57	$ 400.00	7.00
1801	15	120	$ 340.00	2.80
1801	15	24	$ 209.00	8.80
1799	15	158	$ 160.00	1.00
1796	15	50	$ 200.00	4.00
1797	16	250	$ 500.00	2.00
1800	19	40	$ 140.00	3.50
1793	21	150	£ 116.00	£3.00
1798	21	11	$ 34.00	3.00
1793	21	150	£ 86.00	£1/2
1798	21	150	$ 303.00	2.00
1797	21	250	$ 500.00	2.00
1798	21	250	$1250.00	5.00
1797	21	250	$ 500.00	2.00
1797	21	79	$ 300.00	3.80
1798	21	117	$ 500.00	4.30
1800	22	10	$ 100.00	10.00
1798	22	250	$1250.00	5.00
1798	22	250	$1513.00	6.10
1797**	22	1½	$ 830.00	
1801	23	100	$ 550.00	5.50
1800	23	20	$ 104.00	5.00
1800	23	150	$ 200.00	1.30
1800	24	20	$ 101.00	5.00
1796	24	50	$ 200.00	4.00
	24	60	$ 240.00	4.00
1800	24	4	$ 60.00	15.00
1801	24	100	$ 550.00	5.50

Date	Page	Acres	Price	Price/Acre
1799	25	110	$ 244.00	3.00
1797	25	281	$ 844.00	3.00
1799*	26	158	$ 127.00	5.60
			+ 760.00	Mtg. Due
			$ 887.00	
1800	27	40	$ 900.00	22.00
1801	27	117	$1220.00	10.50
1799*	27	158	$ 160.00	5.80
			+ 760.00	Mtg. Due
			$ 920.00	
1798*	28	250	$ 858.00	3.40
1799	28	50	$ 237.00	4.80
1799*	28	110	$ 244.00	2.20
1801	29	125	$ 390.00	3.10
1799	29	160	$ 250.00	1.50
1801	30	42	$ 213.00	5.00
1797	30	250	$ 250.00	1.00
1799	30	500	$ 550.00	1.10
	30	313	$1400.00	4.50
1797	31	250	$ 250.00	1.00
1798	31	117	$ 500.00	4.30
1800	32	150	$ 133.00	.89
1801	33	50	$ 250.00	5.00
1796	34	50	$ 150.00	3.00
1796	35	323	£1221.00	£3.50
1797	35	4065		5 shillings
1798	35	291		10 shillings
1797	35	281	$ 844.00	3.00
1800	35			5 shillings
1801	36	24	$ 207.00	8.80
1796	36	125	£ 75.00	£ .50
1800	36	70	$ 900.00	12.20

*Former Oneida Reservation

**Town Lot

Note: Because the lists contained both grantors and grantees, there may be considerable duplication in the above transactions. However, they do give a rough idea of what land to the south of the reservation as of 1795–1800 was selling for.

What standards should be applied to measure the difference between what the Oneidas received and should have received are for expert witnesses at a trial of fact. The point is that the Oneidas were defrauded of their land under official state policy. Although the 1785 and 1788 purchases preceded Section 177 of 25 U.S.C.A., this review shows what the policy was. A text on "The Holland Land Company" p. 192, sums this up:

> ". . . Here the usual accounts of the Big Tree Treaty end but unhappily this, like most other treaties with the Indians, has an unsavory side which originally was concealed as far as possible and has rarely been spoken of since. From the time when Indians were recognized as independent nations who possessed rights in the lands they occupied, the Indian status was anomalous. Their ownership was something different from the ownership of Spaniards and Canadians over the border. The morality of the day, not so different after all from that of our own, countenanced universally measures for the purchase of such ownership at prices far below its true value. No one thought of paying the Indian the full worth of his lands. No commissioner, appointed by the President to see justice done at the treaties, felt for a moment that it was his duty to warn the Indians that they were being unfairly treated. He did not indeed believe that they were. Nor did Government at the time. . . ."

Land Titles

This is not the first time the New York Indians have asked for justice. In 1888–89 a special committee of the Legislature, headed by Assemblyman Whipple of Salamanca, made a complete investigation of the "Indian Problem". See Assembly Document #51, February 1, 1889, commonly known as the "Whipple Report". This document sets forth the history of the Oneidas' land cessions in detail, including all their treaties with the United States and New York.

In 1919 the Legislature again created a special committee to investigate the New York Indians' status. The Chairman of the Committee, Assemblyman Edward A. Everett, published a report that the Iroquois Indians were still the fee owners of most of New York State. The other members of the Committee refused to sign this report, one saying it was not their job to "dig up irrelevant matters from the past". Whatever the basis for Mr. Everett's conclusions, it appears that there may be a question of title to lands derived from the Oneidas sold without federal consent after enactment of Section 177 of 25 U.S.C. in 1790. For legal authority on the title issue, we can look to the four-square holding of the Second Circuit Court of Appeals in the Tuscarora case, 257 F. 2d 885 (1958). The main issue there was whether Section 177 applied to condemnation of Indian Reservations by the State of New York. The State and its agencies claimed that it could acquire title from Indians without the presence of a U.S. Commissioner and without consent of the United States. The brief of Louis J. Lefkowitz, Attorney General, states at page 34:

> "The Indian Intercourse Act of 1802 (2 Stat. 103) provides that title to Indian lands must be extinguished by a treaty made in the presence of a United States Commissioner. The provisions of that act, however, are not applicable to the thirteen original states which, it will be remembered, derived their title to Indian lands directly from the British Crown and not from the Federal Government.—(Citations)—"*Actually, a very large number of agreements were made with the New York Indians extinguishing their titles without the presence of a United States Commissioner . . .*" (Emphasis added.)

The brief of Thomas F. Moore, Jr., attorney for the New York Power Authority, makes this same point at pages 12–23. It states in part:

> "Except for the Period from 1790 to 1793, New York made a practice of purchasing Indian rights of aboriginal occupany without the intervention of the Federal Government." p. 12.***

> "While as our memorandum below shows, at pages 27, 49, 52, New York purchased some Indian land rights at Federal treaties subsequent to 1793, in most instances when it purchased such rights it did so without Federal intervention. A vast part of the territory within the State was purchased by the State without such intervention. *The present day title to this area depends upon the validity of these purchases.* Invariably when such purchases were challenged the courts have sustained them." (Emphasis added.)

The cases cited by Mr. Moore for the above are interesting. *Seneca Nation v. Christie,* 126 N.Y. 122, 162 U.D. 283, was decided on the narrow issue of the statute of limitations. *Deere v. State Power Authority,* 32 F. 2d 550 (1927), was decided on the issue that an action of ejectment under a Federal treaty does not present a federal question. *U.S. v. Franklin Co.,* 50 F. Supp. 152 (1943), and *St. Regis v. State,* 5 N.Y. 2d 24 (1958), do squarely hold that Section 177 does not apply to New York State. The *St. Regis* case was decided by the New York Court of Appeals in June 1958 and the Tuscarora case by the Second Circuit in July 1958. This presents a square conflict between state and federal courts, which even now the New York Courts may be resolving in favor of federal constitutional pre-eminence. See *Pierce v. The State Tax Commission of the State of New York* discussed below.

An article, *"Drums Along the Power Ways"*, Albany Law Review, 1958, says:

> "The decision of the federal court—(Tuscarora case)—impugns the validity of past and contemporary takings of Indian lands and throws many Indian alienated titles in the State of New York into chaos and confusion."

The memorandum referred to in the Power Authority's brief (quoted above) states that:

> "Since 1793, the Federal statute—(Section 177)—has not been considered a prohibition applicable to purchases of Indian lands in New York State. At least thirty-nine agreements or 'treaties' have been entered into since then by which Indian land rights were acquired without the presence or supervision of a United States Commissioner. Titles to hundreds of thousands of acres in New York State stem from such agreements or 'treaties'." p. 27.

* * *

> "No participation by the United States was invited or given during the years 1793–1845 when the State of New York made 24 other treaties with various bands of Oneidas, 6 with the St. Regis, 5 with the Onondagas, 3 with the Cayugas, and at least one with the Senecas. Titles to very large and important parts of the State are held under these treaties and they always have been and still are regarded as valid." p. 52.

A fairly complete history of these "treaties" and the federal-state relation is set out in the affidavit of Henry S. Manley which appears in the record of the Tuscarora case. This affidavit, which was submitted in behalf of the Power Authority, states in a footnote on page 7:

> "Titles to large areas of the State would be invalidated, as well as important rights upon the existing reservations (such as railroad line and utility lines and highways across the reservation now involved) if the plaintiffs' contentions were upheld."

As we know, the "plaintiffs' contentions", the Indians' contentions, were upheld by the Second Circuit on this point. The final holding of the U.S. Supreme Court clearly reinforces the Second Circuit's decision on the applicability of Section 177 to New York State. See footnote #18 of opinion at 80 S. Ct. 556, which states that the U.S.

> "promised to hold the Oneidas and Tuscaroras secure in the lands on which they lived—which were the lands in Central New York about 200 miles east of the lands in question."

It distinguished the Tuscarora lands near Niagara Falls on the ground that title there derived from the Holland Land Company by purchase and that the particular land was not the same as referred to in the treaties with the U.S. The lands involved in this petition are the very same lands which they owned when the U.S. treaties were made and which they had owned, occupied and protected as their ancestral hunting grounds long before Columbus was born. They are the very same lands referred to in the Supreme Court's footnote cited above.

The implications of the Tuscarora decision are staggering. The State in its legal papers admitted that title to large areas of the State were at stake—and then lost. An article in the Buffalo Law Review, Fall 1958, assesses the effect of the Tuscarora decision of the Second Circuit:

> "The Tuscarora decision of the Court of Appeals came, after all, in a case which the State deliberately chose to make the most elaborate presentation of its position and to argue on the broadest possible grounds. All the greater the significance then — and all the more penetrating the likely impact—of the repudiation of New York's contentions." p. 21.

The Oneida Indian Nation wants it very clearly understood that it does not want to challenge the ownership of any persons holding record title to their lands. The element of land titles is introduced at this time only on the issue of damages. A court might find that there was a cloud on titles derived from New York State patents which should be extinguished for some recompense to the Oneidas in addition to the difference in value between what they received from New York and what they ceded to New York. The people who now occupy the former Reservation should be left peacefully there, but the Oneida Nation should have justice too.

Legal Status of Oneidas

The Oneidas are a nation within a nation. It seems strange in this day that there exist in New York State several independent nations, among them the Oneida Indian Nation. Yet this is so. Several U.S. treaties recognize and deal with the "Oneida Nation" and these are in effect today with the full force of law. See Treaties of 1784, 1789 and 1794. They are the law of the land. At least twenty-four "treaties" with New York also recognize and deal with the Oneida Indian Nation, the first in 1785 and the last in 1846.

A generation ago, the federal courts reaffirmed the status of the Oneidas in *U.S. v. Boylan,* 256 F. 468 (2d Cir. 265 F. 165). Last Spring, right on schedule, the Oneidas received their quota of unbleached muslin cloth as promised under the federal treaty of 1794. In appropriating money for this purpose, Congress has continually reaffirmed the treaty obligations of the United States. A very recent decision of the Appellate Division, Fourth Department, New York Supreme Court, affirms the vitality of the Six Nations Treaty:

". . . The power of Congress to deal with them—(the New York Indians)—regardless of New York's actions or desires is unquestioned."

*   *   *

"Legislative power over Indian affairs is vested in Congress. 'The Congress shall have power . . . to regulate Commerce with foreign Nations . . . and with the Indian Tribes.' (U.S. Const. art I, O8, cl.3. See, e.g., Hallowell v. United States, 221 U.S. 317; Worcester v. Georgia, 31 U.S. (6 Pet.) 515; United States v. Kagama, 118 U.S. 375; United States v. Thomas, 151 U.S. 577.) There is no doubt that legislation implementing this Constitutional mandate ousts state law on the same subject and to the extent that a state enactment otherwise valid interferes with or impedes the operation of a federally-created scheme to fulfill the obligation toward the Indians, the state law must fall. (McCulloch v. Maryland, supra; Board of County Commr's. v. United States, 308 U.S. 343.) Thus if any interference with the federal program for the Indians can be shown to result from the taxes sought to be imposed, the taxes must be struck down and the judgment below affirmed."

The above quoted language is from *Pierce vs. The State Tax Commission of the State of New York,* decided January 11, 1968, by the Appellate Division, Fourth Department. This case holds that the State cannot tax sales of articles made and sold on an Indian Reservation.

The Purchase of 1795

This memorandum has sought to picture a broad sweep of history from the time of the American Revolution, when the Oneidas helped feed Washington's Army at Valley Forge and stood in battle at the side of Colonial troops at the battles of Oriskany and Fort Plain, to the mid-1840's when the last pitiful remnants of the Oneida Reservation were bartered away to their former allies.

Perhaps this is too much to present in one draft. To put things in a sharper focus this section deals with a limited phase of the history of the Oneidas. This is unlike the usual "Indian case" where experts and historians theorize on what land hundreds of miles West of the Frontier was worth. In much of the period described herein, the Oneidas' Reservation was hundreds of miles East of the Frontier, in settled, civilized and organized country. Land values here are not a matter of speculation. They are established by recorded deeds of nearby parcels, state laws and other contemporary records including the books of account of the very men who sub-divided and sold off the Oneidas' Reservation. (This writer has studied the books of John Lincklaen, agent for the Holland Land Company, at his home in Cazenovia, New York. The books and journals of Peter Smith, who bought and sold land over the entire area, are in the Library of Syracuse University.)

Let's take a look at the "treaty" of 1795 between the Oneidas and New York State in which they sold to the State a huge slice of the Reservation confirmed and guaranteed to the Oneidas by federal treaties and federal law. The consideration for the 1795 sale was expressed in terms of a perpetual annuity in dollars for measured land plus an annuity of three dollars per year for every hundred acres on certain unmeasured land. This amounts to a principal price of $0.50 per acre for very valuable and desirable land. No U.S. Commissioner was present and the United States has never ratified this sale. Every Indian who signed the treaty used an "X".

In the period 1792–1795 the Holland Land Company, through its agent, John Lincklaen of Cazenovia, was selling nearby land (not part of the Reservation) at from $1.50 to $4.00 per acre unimproved. From 1795 to the early 1800's nearby land was sold to settlers at $4.00, $5.00, and $6.00 per acre. According to Lincklaen's records, land involved in the 1795 purchase, the New Peterbourgh Tract, was sold off at from $6.00 to $10.00 per acre from 1800 to 1805.

Despite some tapering off of the land boom after 1795 the land purchased by the State for $.50 per acre in 1795 was sold off in 1797 to white settlers and developers, including the aforementioned Peter Smith, for $3.53½ per acre. This represented a profit to the State of $3.03½ per acre in just two years. Also the Oneidas did not receive cash, they received only a perpetual annuity of $0.03 per acre (6%).

As of 1795 the Indian Non-Intercourse Act of March 1, 1793 (1 Stat. 330), substantially the same as the present section 177, was in effect. New York cannot argue now that this statute was not applicable to New York because the State Legislature in 1796 and 1798 recognized the power of the U.S. Commissioner for Indian Affairs in New York. See *Laws of New York*, Nineteenth Session, Chap. 39 (1796) and Twenty-Second Session, Chap. 87 (1798). The minutes of the New York Land Office, p. 99, Vol. 3, recite that the U.S. Commissioner, Joseph Hopkinson, was present at the Oneidas' 1798 cession to the State. One wonders why the State, in 1795 and after the 1798 purchase, disregarded federal law which its own legislature recognized as applicable.

The 1795 purchase was only one of a series of similar transactions in which the Oneidas lost their entire 300,000 acre Reservation.

The United States Can Help

The Oneida Nation asks the United States to intercede with New York State for a fair monetary settlement of their claim. If intercession fails, the United States should bring an action in the Supreme Court against New York State. This was done in *United States v. State of Minnesota*, 270 U.S. 181 46 S. Ct. 298 (1926), in a suit to secure redress for the Chippewa Indians as wards of the United States. The Court then held that as to the lands wrongfully taken:

". . . the United States is entitled to a decree cancelling the patents for such as have not been sold by the state and charging her—(the State of Minnesota)—with the value of such as she has sold." If Section 177 of 25 U.S.C.A. applies to New York State, and recent court decisions uniformly hold that it does, then Section 194 also applies:

"In all trials about the right of property in which an Indian may be a party on one side, and a white person on the other, the burden of proof shall rest upon the white person, whenever the Indian shall make out a presumption of title in himself from the fact of previous possession or ownership." § 194, 25 U.S.C.A. . . .

This section is evidence of the policy of the government to give Indians the benefit of the doubt on questions of fact or construction of treaties or statutes relating to their welfare. *Anno. to Section 194 in official report referring to 34 Op. Atty. Gen.* 439 (1925).

It may be asserted by the State that too much time has passed for the Oneidas now to press their claim. The other side of this coin is that 173 years is a long time to wait for justice. No statute of limitation or equitable laches bars the claim. *U.S. v. State of Minnesota,* supra; *U.S. v. 7405.3 Acres of Land,* 97 F. 2d 417 (CCA 4, 1938); *U.S. v. Forness,* 125 F. 2d 928 (CCA 2, 1942).

Even if the suit were by the Indians and not the United States, no state statute of limitations would be allowed to frustrate federal law and federal constitutional policy. *Schrimpscher v. Stockton,* 183 U.S. 290, 22 S. Ct. 107 (1902). In fact, until very recently an Indian nation or tribe had no capacity to sue as such in the State Courts of New York. See, "*New York Jurisprudence*", § 17; *Pharaoh v. Benson,* 164 A.D. 51(1914), affd.

222 N.Y. 665 *St. Regis Tribe v. State of New York,* 4 Misc. 2d 110 (1956), reversed on other grounds 5 A.D. 2d 117.

For these 170 years the New York Indians have been precluded from recovering their lands by a maze of legal technicalities, *Pharaoh v. Benson,* supra; *Seneca Indians v. Christie,* 126 N.Y. 122 (1891), and *Deere v. St. Lawrence Pow. Co., et al.,* 32 F. 2d 550 (CCA 2, 1929). The help of the United States can free the Oneidas from the legal bondage imposed on them by the Courts of New York.

The United States Should Help the Oneidas

The Congress of the United States was empowered to regulate commerce with the Indian Tribes under Article IX of the Articles of Confederation and under Article 1, Section 8, of the United States Constitution. Under this power, treaties were made with the Oneidas, which read in part as follows:

Treaty with Six Nations—Ft. Stanwix 1784

"Article 2. The Oneida and Tuscarora Nations shall be secured in the possession of lands on which they are settled."

Treaty with Six Nations—Ft. Harmar 1789

"Article 3. The Oneida and Tuscarora Nations are also again secured and confirmed in the possession of their respective lands."

Treaty with Six Nations—Canandaigua 1794

"Article 2. The United States acknowledge the lands reserved to the Oneida, Onondaga and Cayuga Nations, in their respective treaties with the State of New York, and called their reservations to be their property; and the United States will never claim the same, nor disturb them . . . in the free use and enjoyment thereof; but the said reservation shall remain theirs until they choose to sell the same to the people of the United States, who have the right to purchase."

*   *   *

"Article 7. Lest the firm peace and friendship now established should be interrupted by the misconduct of individuals, the United States and

Six Nations agree that for injuries done by individuals on either side no private revenge or retaliation shall take place, but instead complaint shall be made by the party injured to the other: by the Six Nations or any of them to the President of the United States . . . and such prudent measures shall then be pursued as shall be necessary to preserve our peace and friendship unbroken . . ."

Treaty with Oneida, Tuscarora and Stockbridge Indians — Oneida 1794

"Whereas, In the late war between Great Britain and the United States of America, a body of the Oneida and Tuscarora and Stockbridge Indians adhered faith fully to the United States and assisted them with their warriors, . . . and as the United States in the time of their distress, acknowledged their obligations to these faithful friends, and promised to reward them . . ." (Here followed promises to erect a sawmill and other improvements on the Reservation and to compensate the Oneidas for damages suffered in the War.)

To implement their treaty obligations to the Oneidas and other Indians, the United States enacted in 1790 what is now Section 177 of the Federal Indian Law, 25 U.S.C.A. The meaning of the protection promised in these treaties was explained by President George Washington to a delegation of Senecas on December 29, 1790. Interpreting the 1784 treaty he said:

"Here, then, is the security for the remainder of your lands. No state, nor person, can purchase your lands, unless at some public treaty, held under the authority of the United States. The General Government will never consent to your being defrauded, but it will protect you in all your just rights.

"Hear well and let it be heard by every person in your nation, that the President of the United States declares, that the General Government considers itself bound to protect you in all the lands secured to you by the treaty of Fort Stanwix, the 22d day of October, 1784, excepting such parts as you may since have fairly sold, to persons properly authorized to purchase of You."

Thus, the United States by formal treaties, the supreme law of the land, and George Washington, our first President, have given their sacred word and promise: "The General Government will never consent to your being defrauded, but it will protect you in all your just rights."

The Oneida Indians now ask the United States to keep its promise.

Summary

The Oneida Nation was in the way of America's expansion to the West. Unfortunately their Reservation was square across the gateway. They were moved out by official act and policy of New York State. In truth, their property was condemned for public purpose, but without fair and adequate consideration. This is demonstrable from the very records of New York State. The property was also taken in contravention of specific federal law which is even now in effect.

The Oneidas have been denied property without due process of law and the State has never granted them a forum where they could seek redress. What they want now is their day in court.

The United States in formal treaty has promised to help their former allies in time of need. "Great nations, like great men, should keep their word." The Oneidas ask that the United States keep its word to them given by George Washington and in three formal treaties.

Respectfully,
BOND, SCHOENECK & KING

By: George C. Shattuck

ASSISTANT SECRETARY OF THE INTERIOR
HARRY R. ANDERSON TO JACOB THOMPSON
JULY 1, 1968

Dear Mr. Thompson:

Pursuant to the petition dated May 19, and discussions at our May 15 meeting, we have further considered the Oneida Nation's request that the United States prosecute a claim against the State of New York for the allegedly wrongful taking of Oneida lands during the period from 1788 to 1842, and concur in the Commissioner of Indian Affairs' conclusion, as stated in his letter of March 15, that it would be inappropriate for the Government to act upon the Oneidas' request at this time.

Careful examination of this matter indicates that the proposed suit would present serious problems. To begin with, it is not clear that the United States is even capable of maintaining such an action. The United States may prosecute a claim on behalf of an Indian tribe only if it has a pecuniary interest in the remedy sought or is under an obligation to sustain the action in behalf of the tribe. *United States v. San Jacinto Tin Company*, 125 U.S. 273 (1888); *United States v. Winans*, 198 U.S. 371 (1905); *Heckman v. United States*, 224 U.S. 412 (1912). Since the Government would have no pecuniary interest in the recovery sought from New York, it would have to demonstrate that it was somehow obligated to being the proposed suit for the Oneidas.

It is extremely doubtful that such an obligation could be found in the Treaty of Canandaigua of November 11, 1894 (7 Stat. 44), as you maintain, since the Court of Claims has specifically held that there was "nothing in the text of the treaty or the treaty negotiations implying or acknowledging that the United States could thereafter guard the Six Nations in their transactions with the states or private individuals." *Six Nations v. United States*, 173 Ct. Cl. 899, 905 (1965). This does not imply that any of the provisions of the treaty are deemed ineffective or abrogated, as you suggest; it merely means that the responsibility assumed by the United States under the treaty does not extend to matters arising as a result of dealings with third parties.

The only other potential source of federal obligation or standing to maintain the proposed suit is the Trade and Intercourse Act of July 22, 1790 (1 Stat. 137), presently embodied in 25 U.S.C. §177, which forbade any sale or conveyance of Indian lands without the consent of the United States. In *Seneca Nation of Indians v. United States*, 173 Ct. Cl. 917 (1965), the court found that Act obligated the Federal Government to protect and guard

115

the Indians of New York against unfair treatment in land transactions with private individuals. The opinion went on to note, however, that there are several decisions which suggest that the Trade and Intercourse Act is inapplicable to purchases or condemnations by the State of New York itself, *United States v. Franklin County,* 50 F. Supp. 152, 155–56 (N.D.N.Y., 1943); *United States v. Cattaraugus County,* 71 F. Supp. 413 (W.D.N.Y. 1947); *St. Regis Tribe of Mohawk Indians v. United States,* 5 N.Y.2d 24, 39–40, 152 NE2d 411, 419 (1958), *cert. denied,* 359 U.S. 910 (1959). Accordingly, the *Seneca* holding was specifically limited to transactions involving private individuals, as opposed to states.

The question of the applicability of the Trade and Intercourse Act to the dealings of the State of New York with its Indians, left unanswered in the *Seneca* decision, has been presented to the Indian Claims Commission in the claim the Oneidas now have pending, Docket No. 301. It is the position of the United States in that case that the Act is not so applicable. Until it is abandoned by the Government or rejected by the Indian Claims Commission or the Court of Claims on appeal, that position precludes reliance upon the Act as a basis for federal action against New York. Our review of the matter has not persuaded us that the Government's position is incorrect. Under these circumstances, we are in agreement with the Department of Justice that there is no present legal justification for altering the United States' position and undertaking an action against the state on the very theory which the Government is currently opposing before the Indian Claims Commission.

We note that this obstacle to a federal action against New York will disappear if the United States if found liable to the Oneidas in Docket 301. In that event, the possibility of a subsequent federal suit against New York could be reconsidered.

Sincerely yours,
(Sgd.) HARRY R. ANDERSON
Assistant Secretary of the Interior

APPENDIX D

ONEIDA SUPREME COURT BRIEF, 1973

IN THE

Supreme Court of the United States

October Term, 1972

No. 72-851

THE ONEIDA INDIAN NATION OF NEW YORK STATE, also known
as the ONEIDA NATION OF NEW YORK, also known as the
ONEIDA INDIANS OF NEW YORK, and THE ONEIDA INDIAN
NATION OF WISCONSIN, also known as the ONEIDA TRIBE OF
INDIANS OF WISCONSIN, INC.,

Petitioners,

v.

THE COUNTY OF ONEIDA, NEW YORK, and THE COUNTY OF
MADISON, NEW YORK,

Respondents.

BRIEF FOR THE PETITIONERS

OPINION BELOW

The opinion of the Court of Appeals appears in the petition,
Appendix pp. 14-29, and is reported at 464 F. 2d 916.

JURISDICTION

The judgment of the Court of Appeals was entered on July 12,
1972, and motion for rehearing was denied on September 11,
1972. The petition was filed on December 9, 1972 and was
granted on June 4, 1973. The jurisdiction of this Court rests on
28 USC 1254(1).

QUESTIONS PRESENTED

1. Whether the federal court has jurisdiction of this suit as arising under the Constitution, laws, or treaties of the United States pursuant to 28 U.S.C. 1331, headed "Federal question; amount in controversy; costs".

2. Whether the federal court has jurisdiction of this claim of the Oneida Indians as arising under the Constitution, laws, or treaties of the United States pursuant to 28 U.S.C. 1362, headed "Indian tribes".

3. In a broader sense, the question presented by this case is whether an Indian tribe can protect its tribal lands where: (a) the federal authorities refuse to help and (b) the Indian tribe is denied access to state courts.

STATUTES INVOLVED

Federal

25 USC 175

§ 175. United States attorneys to represent Indians

> In all States and Territories where there are reservations or allotted Indians the United States attorney shall represent them in all suits at law and in equity. Mar. 3, 1893, c.209, § 1,27 Stat.631; June 25, 1948, c.646, § 1,62 Stat.909.

25 USC 177

§ 177. Purchases or grants of lands from Indians

> No purchase, grant, lease, or other conveyance of lands, or of any title or claim thereto, from any Indian nation or tribe of Indians, shall be of any validity in law or equity, unless the same be made by treaty or convention entered into pursuant to the Constitution. Every person who, not being employed under the authority of the United States, attempts to negotiate such treaty or convention, directly or indirectly, or to treat with any such nation or tribe of Indians for the title or purchase of any lands by them held or claimed, is liable to a penalty of $1,000. The agent of any State who may be present at any treaty held with Indians under the authority of

the United States, in the presence and with the approbation of the commissioner of the United States appointed to hold the same, may however, propose to, and adjust with, the Indians the compensation to be made for their claim to lands within such State, which shall be extinguished by treaty. R.S. §2116.

25 USC 233

§233. Jurisdiction of New York State courts in civil actions

The courts of the State of New York under the laws of such State shall have jurisdiction in civil actions and proceedings between Indians or between one or more Indians and any other person or persons to the same extent as the courts of the State shall have jurisdiction in other civil actions and proceedings, as now or hereafter defined by the laws of such State: ... Provided further, That nothing herein contained shall be construed as subjecting the lands within any Indian reservation in the State of New York to taxation for State or local purposes, nor as subjecting any such lands, or any Federal or State annuity in favor of Indians or Indian tribes, to execution on any judgment rendered in the State courts, except in the enforcement of a judgment in a suit by one tribal member against another in the matter of the use or possession of land: And provided further, That nothing herein contained shall be construed as authorizing the alienation from any Indian nation, tribe, or band of Indians of any lands within any Indian reservation in the State of New York: Provided further, *That nothing herein contained shall be construed as conferring jurisdiction on the courts of the State of New York or making applicable the laws of the State of New York in civil actions involving Indian lands or claims with respect thereto which relate to transactions or events transpiring prior to September 13, 1952.* Sept. 13, 1950, c.845, § 1,64 Stat. 845. [Emphasis added.]

28 USC 1331

§1331. Federal question; amount in controversy; costs

(a) The district courts shall have original jurisdiction of all civil actions wherein the matter in controversy exceeds the sum or value of $10,000, exclusive of interest and costs, and arises under the Constitution, laws, or treaties of the United States.

28 USC 1362

§ 1362. Indian tribes

The district courts shall have original jurisdiction of all civil actions, brought by any Indian tribe or band with a governing body duly recognized by the Secretary of the Interior, wherein the matter in controversy arises under the Constitution, laws, or treaties of the United States. Added Pub.L. 89-635, § 1, Oct. 10, 1966, 80 Stat. 880.

EXCERPTS FROM FEDERAL TREATIES INVOLVED

Treaty with Six Nations — Ft. Stanwix 1784

"Article 2. The Oneida and Tuscarora Nations shall be secured and confirmed in the possession of lands on which they are settled."

Treaty with Six Nations — Ft. Harmar 1789

"Article 3. The Oneida and Tuscarora Nations are also again secured and confirmed in the possession of their respective lands."

Treaty with Six Nations — Canandaigua 1794

"Article 2. The United States acknowledge the lands reserved to the Oneida, Onondaga and Cayuga Nations, in their respective treaties with the State of New York, and called their reservations to be their property; and the United States will never claim the same, nor disturb them . . . in the free use and enjoyment thereof; but the said reservation shall remain theirs until they choose to sell the same to the people of the United States, who have the right to purchase."

"Article 7. Lest the firm peace and friendship now established should be interrupted by the misconduct of individuals, the United States and Six Nations agree that for injuries done by individuals on either side no private revenge or retaliation shall take place, but instead complaint shall be made by the party injured to the other: by the Six Nations or any of them to the President of the United States . . . and such prudent measures shall then be pursued as shall be necessary to preserve our peace and friendship unbroken . . ."

Treaty with Oneida, Tuscarora and Stockbridge Indians —
Oneida 1794

"Whereas, In the late war between Great Britain and the United States of America, a body of the Oneida and Tuscarora and Stockbridge Indians adhered faithfully to the United States and assisted them with their warriors, . . . and as the United States in the time of their distress, acknowledged their obligations to these faithful friends, and promised to reward them . . ." (Here followed promises to erect a sawmill and other improvements on the Reservation and to compensate the Oneidas for damages suffered in the War.)

STATEMENT OF FEDERAL POLICY
BY PRESIDENT GEORGE WASHINGTON
TO NEW YORK INDIANS 1790

"I the President of the United States, by my own mouth, and by a written speech signed with my own hand, and sealed with the seal of the United States, speak to the Seneca nation, and that they would keep this speech in remembrance of the friendship of the United States.

* * * * *

"I am not uninformed, that the Six Nations have been led into some difficulties, with respect to the sale of their lands, since the peace. But I must inform you that these evils arose before the present Government of the United States was established, when the Separate States, and individuals under their authority, undertook to treat with the Indian tribes respecting the sale of their lands. But the case is now entirely altered; the General Government, only, has the power to treat with the Indian nations, and any treaty formed, and held without its authority, will not be binding.

"Here, then, is the security for the remainder of your lands. No State, nor person, can purchase your lands, unless at some public treaty, held under the authority of the United States. The General Government will never consent to your being defrauded, but it will protect you in all your just rights.

"Hear well, and let it be heard by every person in your nation, that the President of the United States declares, that the *General Government considers itself bound to protect you* in all the lands secured to you by the treaty of fort Stanwix, the 22d of October, 1784, excepting such parts as you may since have fairly sold, to persons properly authorized to purchase of you. You complain that John Livingston and Oliver Phelps, assisted by Mr. Street, of Niagara, have obtained your lands, and that they have not complied with their agreement. It appears, upon inquiry of the Governor of New York, that John Livingston was not legally authorized to treat with you, and that every thing that he did with you has been declared null and void, so that you may rest easy on that account. But it does not appear, from any proofs yet in possession of Government, that Oliver Phelps has defrauded you.

"If, however, you have any just cause of complaint against him, and can make satisfactory proof thereof, the federal courts will be open to you for redress, as to all other persons. But your great object seems to be, the security of your remaining lands; and I have, therefore, upon this point, meant to be sufficiently strong and clear, that, in future, you cannot be defrauded of your lands; that you possess the right to sell, and the right of refusing to sell, your lands; that, therefore, the sale of your lands, in future, will depend entirely upon yourselves. But that, when you find it for your interest to sell any part of your lands, the United States must be present, by their agent, and will be your security that you shall not be defrauded in the bargain you may make.

* * * * *

"That besides the before mentioned security for your land, you will perceive, by the law of Congress for regulating trade and intercourse with the Indian tribes, the fatherly care the United States intend to take of the Indians. For the particular meaning of this law, I refer you to the explanation given thereof by Colonel Timothy Pickering, at Tioga, which, with the law, are herewith delivered to you." 1/ (Emphasis added)

1/ American State Papers (Indian Affairs, Vol. 1, 1832), p. 142. From a statement made by President George Washington to a delegation of New York Indians in 1790. Colonel Pickering's explanation at Tioga, to which the President referred, mentioned previous frauds practiced by "some white men", and then said: "Now, Brothers, to prevent these great evils in future, the Congress declare That no sale of lands made by any Indians, *to any person or persons, or even to any state,* shall be valid (or of force) unless the same be

[footnote continued]

STATEMENT OF FACTS

The Oneida Indian Nation of New York and The Oneida Indian Nation of Wisconsin brought this suit against the Counties of Oneida and Madison, located in the State of New York.

Plaintiffs contend that the respondents occupy lands which the State of New York obtained in 1795 in violation of the Indian Non-Intercourse Act, 1 Stat. 137 (1790), later Rev. Stat. §2116, and now 25 U.S.C. §177. The 1790 Act provided, *inter alia:*

> No purchase, grant, lease or other conveyance of lands, or of any title or claim thereto, from any Indian nation or tribe of Indians, shall be of any validity in law or equity, unless the same be made by treaty or convention entered into pursuant to the Constitution.

Prior to the contested cession in 1795, the Plaintiffs had a Reservation in Upstate New York. In 1795, representatives of the State of New York negotiated a "treaty" with the Plaintiffs whereby the Plaintiffs ceded a portion of their land, for what the complaint alleges was unfair and inadequate consideration. This 1795 "treaty" was obtained without federal consent and was never ratified in any way by the United States, and, consequently, was in violation of the above cited Indian Non-Intercourse Act and the treaties invoked in the complaint. 2/

1/ [continued]

made at some public treaty held under the authority of the United States. For at such public treaty *wise and good men* will be appointed by the President to attend, *to prevent all deception and fraud.* These Wise & Good men will examine every deed before it is signed and sealed, *and see that every lease or purchase of the Indians be openly and fairly made"* (emphasis added). See Op. of Court of Claims in *Seneca Nation of Indians* v. *United States,* Ind. Cl. Com. Docket #342-A, 368-A (Ct. Cl., Dec. 17, 1965), from which Pickering quote is taken.

2/ Pursuant to their treaties, the Oneida Indians have petitioned for relief herein to both the President of the U.S. (1968) and the Governor of NY (1967); both petitions were denied.

Plaintiffs in this suit claim damages for the respondents' occupancy of the Plaintiffs' land for the period January 1, 1968 to December 31, 1969. The fair rental value of such premises for this period amount to at least $10,000 exclusive of interest and costs.

In the United States District Court for the Northern District of New York, petitioners asserted jurisdiction under 28 U.S.C. §1331 and 28 U.S.C. §1362 and other sections of 28 U.S.C.

The District Court dismissed the complaint for lack of jurisdiction and held that the case should properly be tried in New York State Courts. In affirming, the Court of Appeals reasoned that the Plaintiffs' complaint was an action "basically in ejectment" and therefore a well-pleaded complaint need not contain allegations of the Oneidas' source of asserted title to the contested property. Consequently, held the Court, the action did not "arise under" the Constitution, laws, or treaties of the United States (28 U.S.C. §1331), even though the Plaintiffs' assertion of title in their complaint is founded on federal statutes and treaties. The Court of Appeals concluded that the "arising under" language of §1362 should be interpreted similarly to the "arising under" language of §1331, and hence under §1362 there was likewise no federal question.

Judge Lumbard dissented, suggesting that the "arising under" language of §1362, passed into law in 1966, should not necessarily be interpreted as the same language in §1331. Judge Lumbard also noted that since the case would turn exclusively on interpretation of federal law and federal treaties, this case "should be considered to arise under the laws, as well as the treaties of the United States."

SUMMARY OF ARGUMENT

Jurisdiction is claimed under two statutes, 28 U.S.C. 1331 and 28 U.S.C. 1362.

28 U.S.C. 1331

With respect to Section 1331, the case arises under the treaties and laws of the United States in the classic sense. The Second Circuit in our case and in *Deere v. St Lawrence River Power Co.*, 32 F2d 550 (2d Cir. 1929), did not recognize the distinction between *Taylor v. Anderson*, 234 U.S. 74 (1914), and cases arising in New York; namely, that the courts of New York may not hear this case, whereas the state court in *Taylor* did have jurisdiction. In another Second Circuit case, *Tuscarora Nations of Indians v. New York Power Authority*, 257 F.2d 885 (2d Cir. 1958), *vacated as moot sub nom. McMorran v. Tuscarora Nation of Indians*, 362 U.S. 608 (1960), *modifying* 164 F. Supp. 107 (W.D.N.Y. 1958), the lack of a state court forum was a factor in the court's assuming jurisdiction.

In Indian land cases, "possession"or the presumed lack of it should not be controlling where U.S. laws and treaties guarantee such possession to the Indians. Prior decisions of the Second and Ninth Circuits assuming jurisdiction in land cases are analyzed to demonstrate that possession has not uniformly been used as the sole criterion of whether a case "arises under" the treaties and laws of the United States.

In the view of the majority of the Second Circuit, the treaties' guaranty of possession would be self-cancelling: If the Oneidas do not have the possession which treaties guarantee, they may not have a federal forum in which to assert their rights to the guaranted possession. This is not a tenable use of the "arising under" test.

28 U.S.C. 1362

Jurisdiction is also claimed under the broader scope of Section 1362. See dissent of Judge Lumbard in the Court below. Legislative history shows clearly that 28 U.S.C. 1362 was enacted to cover cases, like the Oneidas' case, where the United States Attorney General refuses to act under 25 U.S.C. 175.

Congress intended 1362 to be a remedial "Indian" statute, rather than just a limited exception of the $10,000 jurisdictional amount rule. It used "arising under the Constitution, laws or treaties of the United States" in the constitutional grant sense, rather than with the more restrictive meaning that has developed for 28 U.S.C. 1331. The examples given to Congress by Senator Burdick, who introduced the bill, and in the Committee Reports have no relation to the "arising under" rule as interpreted by the Second Circuit in our case and in the *Deere* case, 32 F.2d 550 (2d Cir. 1929). The Ninth Circuit in May 1973 decided the same issue contra to the Second Circuit and in favor of jurisdiction under 28 U.S.C. 1362. See Exhibit B of this brief.

This case has a broad policy impact on American Indians, who are precluded by federal law from commencing land cases in courts of many states. 25 U.S.C. 233, 28 U.S.C. 1360. As recognized by the drafters of 28 U.S.C. 1362, there are many instances where the United States Attorney may not or will not act to protect Indian lands. If the decision below stands, an Indian tribe in such case, once ousted from possession, will have no legal forum to assert its rights.

OUTLINE OF ARGUMENT

ARGUMENT

I.

THE OVERRIDING LEGAL PREMISE FOR JURISDICTION IS THAT THE UNITED STATES GOVERNMENT, NO LESS THAN ANY INDIVIDUAL CITIZEN, MUST OBEY ITS OWN TREATIES, LAWS, AND PROMISES.

The cases under 28 U.S.C. 1331 and the legislative history of 1362 should be considered with the above premise in mind. The dignity of the treaties herein involved is exemplified in the opinion of this Court in *Federal Power Comm'n.* v. *Tuscarora Indian Nation,* 362 U.S. 99, 121-25 (1960) expecially footnote 18 at 121-22.

In the *Tuscarora* case, the Supreme Court held that the taking of land for a reservoir:

> "...did not breach the faith of the United States, or any treaty or other contractual agreement...in respect to these lands for the *conclusive reason that there is none."* *Id.* at 124 (emphasis added).

In other words, no treaty or agreement concerning the lands near Niagara Falls taken from the Tuscaroras was before the Court. Footnote 18, *Id.* at 121-22 held that the treaty invoked by the Tuscaroras referred only to "...lands in central New York about 200 miles east of the lands in question..." These lands "200 miles east" are the very Reservation lands involved in the Oneidas' case.

In the Oneidas' case, now before this Court, there are *three treaties* promising the Oneidas "possession" of their Reservation.

Therefore, the failure of the United States to take action with respect to the Oneidas' Reservation would constitute a breach of treaties and laws of the United States.

II.

THE ONEIDA INDIANS DO NOT HERE SEEK DRASTIC REMEDIES, SUCH AS EJECTMENT, BUT ONLY AN EQUITABLE RECOGNITION OF THE CURRENT VALUE OF THEIR LOST RESERVATION.

The complaint asks, in effect, for an equitable accounting for the value of the Oneidas' interest in their Reservation.   This action is not one in ejectment, as the Second Circuit concluded. The relief demanded in the complaint was modeled on the remedy ordered by the Second Circuit Court of Appeals in *United States* v. *Forness*, 125 F.2d 928 (2d Cir.), *cert. denied*, 316 U.S. 694 (1942). (The City of Salamanca, N.Y. was ordered to pay a modest ground rent to the Senecas.)

III.

THE ONEIDA INDIANS DO NOT HAVE ACCESS TO THE COURTS OF NEW YORK STATE.

A. NEW YORK LAW HAS BARRED INDIAN TRIBES FROM STATE COURTS.

Even in the days when New York courts did not recognize federal supremacy in Indian land matters, the courts of New York barred Indian claims from being heard therein. This is a basic element of the fairness of the Oneida Indians' cause.

It is the law in New York that an Indian Tribe is not a person or entity capable of initiating a lawsuit. This is demonstrated by the fact that under Section 8 of the New York Indian Law, the responsibility of protecting tribal lands rested with the County Judge and not with the tribe as plaintiff. 3/

3/ See discussion of Section 11-A of the New York Indian Law below.

A tribe cannot sue or be sued in New York except where authority has been conferred by statute. Likewise, a suit cannot be brought by an individual in the name of the tribe in the absence of statutory authority, or by a portion of the tribe separated therefrom.

In *Strong* v. *Waterman,* 11 Paige 607 (1845), the chancellor of the State of New York was asked to review an injunction granted to the Indians of the Seneca Nation against trespasses on their lands. The court found no common law or statutory basis for jurisdiction but permitted the injunction to stand since the Indians had rights but no remedies.

However, the Court of Appeals of New York has specifically overruled this decision, thus denying Indians access to New York courts in land cases. In *Johnson* v. *Long Island Railroad Co.,* 162 N.Y. 462, 56 N.E. 992 (1900), the court discussed *Strong* v. *Waterman* and overruled it,holding that neither an Indian tribe, an individual Indian or a group of Indians with similar causes of action have access to the courts of New York without specific legislation:

> "As already intimated, we do not regard *Strong* v. *Waterman* (supra) as authorizing this action.
>
> A decision holding that this action could be maintained either by the tribe, or an individual member thereof, on behalf of himself and all others who should come in and contribute, would be contrary to the policy and practice which have been long established in our treatment of the Indian tribes. They are regarded as the wards of the state, and generally speaking, possessed of only such rights to appear and litigate in courts of justice as are conferred upon them by statute.
>
> It is conceded by the complaint in this action 'that the tribe have no legal capacity to sue therefor and have no corporate name by which they can institute such a suit.'
>
> The theory of an action by one for the benefit of all is, that where a large number of persons, not incorporated, are vested with a cause of action, it may be enforced in that manner, but when it is admitted, as in this case, that the tribe has no cause of action, it follows, logically, that no one member of the tribe could sue for the benefit of all, as the cause of action does not exist.

We are of opinion, however, that the Montauk Tribe of Indians are not without legal redress in the premises, as by an application to the legislature an enabling act can be obtained allowing action to be brought on behalf of the tribe, in the name of its chief or head, or in the name of such member or members thereof as may be selected." *Id.* at 466-67.

The Court's reasoning seems circular but the legal effect continued: Indian land actions like the Montauks' were barred from New York State Courts, until state enabling legislation could be passed.

As it happened, the Montauks *did* obtain an enabling act in 1906 and the case again went to the Court of Appeals, *Pharoah* v. *Benson,* 164 App. Div. 51, 149 N.Y.S. 438, *aff'd.,* 222 N.Y. 665, 118 N.E. 1079 (1918), which confirmed the *Johnson* rule:

"In the absence of express statutory authority therefore, no action will lie in the courts of this state in the name of any tribe of Indians, nor in the name of any Indian a member of such tribe suing in behalf of himself and all others similarly situated." *Id.* at 52.

The New York Court then utilized a second line of defense and held that the Montauk Indians were not an Indian tribe under the enabling statute, and therefore had no right to sue.

A more recent declaration of this rule is found in *Andrews* v. *State,* 192 Misc. 429, 79 N.Y.S. 2d 479 (Ct. Cl. 1948), *aff'd.,* 276 App. Div. 814, 93 N.Y.S. 2d 705 (1949):

"The general rule seems to be that a tribe cannot sue or be sued in this state, except where authority has been conferred by statute...Likewise, a suit cannot be brought by an individual in the name of the tribe in the absence of statutory authority...or by a portion of the tribe separated therefrom." *Id.* at 485.

In the case of *St. Regis Tribe* v. *State,* 4 Misc. 2d 110, 158 N.Y.S. 2d 540 (Ct. Cl. 1956), *rev'd on other grounds,* 5 App. Div. 2d 117, 168 N.Y.S. 2d 894 (1957), *aff'd.,* 5 N.Y. 2d 152 N.E. 2d 411, 177 N.Y.S. 2d 289 (1958), *cert. denied,* 359 U.S. 910 (1959), the State in a Court of Claims action contended that the

Tribe lacked legal status to sue. In his affidavit in support of the State's motion to dismiss, Assistant Attorney General, Donald C. Glenn, deposed and said:

"3. Relating to capacity to sue:

Assuming, but not conceding, that the American St. Regis Tribe of Indians had any independent interest in Barnhart's Island, which was appropriated by the State of New York, such interest belonged to the Tribe collectively. *In the absence of specific statutory authority, an Indian Tribe does not have capacity to sue since it is not a recognized legal entity.* Similarly, an action involving tribal property cannot be maintained by the Chiefs or members of the Tribe, suing in their individual capacity and also for the benefit of all other tribal members, because the interest is tribal, not individual. *Only the Legislature may permit bringing of a suit pertaining to a tribal interest in real property;* but neither the general provisions of the Indian Law, nor Article eight thereof which specifically deals with the St. Regis Tribe, authorize claimants to prosecute the instant claim.

Since there is no enabling act which would allow this suit, claimants lack legal capacity to sue and the claim must be dismissed." (Emphasis added.)

[From *Record on Appeal to N.Y. Court of Appeals, St. Regis Tribe, etc.,* v. *State of New York,* at 31-32.]

The St. Regis Indians did not dispute this point as a general rule, but claimed specific statutory permission. The Court of Claims held that such specific permission *did* exist in the *St. Regis* case:

"The — [State's] — motion must be and hereby is denied on this particular ground. We limit our decision specifically to the cited and quoted statutes as they authorize or may authorize the exercise of the right of eminent domain." *St. Regis Tribe* v. *State,* 4 Misc. 2d 110, 117, 158 N.Y.S. 2d 540, 549 (Ct. Cl. 1956).

In effect, the *St. Regis* case confirmed the long-standing rule that an Indian Tribe, as such, cannot sue in New York courts.

The New York legislature in 1958 added the following to the Indian Law:

§ 11-a. Recovering possession of reservation land.

"In addition to any other remedy provided by this chapter or by any other law, the council, chiefs, trustees or headmen constituting the governing body of any nation, tribe or band of Indians may in the name and on behalf of such nation, tribe or band, maintain any action or proceeding to recover the possession lands of such nation, tribe or band unlawfully occupied by others and for damages resulting from such occupation. Added L. 1958, c. 400, eff. April 7, 1958." N.Y. Indian Law § 11A (McKinney Supp. 1972).

This statute and 25 USC §33 (discussed below) must be construed together. The result must be that Indian land cases which "relate to transactions or events transpiring prior to September 13, 1952" are foreclosed from the jurisdiction of New York Courts since that jurisdiction was not granted to New York State by Congress.

B.   FEDERAL LAW HAS BARRED INDIAN LAND CLAIMS FROM NEW YORK STATE COURTS.

Since the challenged transaction occurred in 1795, the New York State courts are barred from entertaining claims of the Oneida tribes by the Fifth proviso to 25 U.S.C. 233:

"*Provided further,* That nothing herein contained shall be construed as conferring jurisdiction on the courts of the State of New York or making applicable the laws of the State of New York in civil actions involving Indian lands or claims with respect thereto which relate to transactions or events transpiring prior to September 13, 1953."

Despite the clear statutory bar to the jurisdiction of the New York State courts over the land claims of the Oneida tribes, the United States has argued in Footnote 3 of its amicus curiae memorandum that New York courts may have jurisdiction here apart from 25 U.S.C. Section 233.

The United States has ignored this Court's decisions, discussed in detail in *Williams* v. *Lee,* 258 U.S. 217 (1959) and the legislative history of 25 U.S.C. §233. *Williams* v. *Lee,* supra, affirmed the long-standing principle of *Worcester* v. *Georgia,* 31 U.S. (6 Pet.) 515 (1932) that state courts are without jurisdiction over Indian affairs. While recognizing that there have been some judicial modifications to the rule of *Worcester v. Georgia,* this Court stated at page 221 of its *Williams* opinion:

> "Significantly, when Congress has wished the states to exercise this power [civil and criminal jurisdiction] it has expressly granted them the jurisdiction which *Worcester v. Georgia* had denied."

Therefore, the New York courts have no jurisdiction apart from the section 233 unless specifically granted by Congress. Research has not disclosed any Congressional or judicial grant of jurisdiction to the New York courts over Indian land claims arising out or pre-1953 events. The issue is not an open question for the state courts.

The fifth proviso in Sec. 233, as quoted above was not in the bill (S. 192) as originally introduced in Congress. It was added at the request of certain New York Indians. See Congressional Record—House for July 27, 1950, page 11400. The explanation given by Congressman Morris therein shows clearly that Congress assumed that Indian land claims arising before September 13, 1952 could be heard in federal courts. See following excerpt:

> "These amendments will preserve those -(treaty)- rights. Then in addition thereto they will preserve their right to go into the United States courts in regard to claims that they might have growing out of any transactions in regard to land dealings and so forth, with the State of New York. In other words, Mr. Speaker, I believe that these particular amendments are such that there can be no real objection now."

The Congressional Record—House for August 14, 1950, at page 12664, contains further explanation:

> "In addition thereto, of course, they may go into the Federal courts and adjudicate any differences they have had between themselves and the great State of New York relative to their lands or claims in regard thereto, and I am sure that the State of New York should have and no doubt will have, no objection to such provision."

Rep. Morris also stated

> "This just [the Fifth proviso] assures the Indians of an absolutely fair and impartial determination of any claims they might have had growing out of any relationship they have had with the great state of New York in regard to their lands."

In expressly denying jurisdiction to the New York State courts over Indian land claims arising out of pre-1953 events, Representative Morris and Congress seemed to have the instant situation in mind. Although New York State is not a party defendant, it is indirectly involved in this litigation. To avoid any conflict, apparent or real, Congress deprived the courts of New York of jurisdiction in civil actions involving Indian lands or claims relating to events occurring before 1953. 4/

IV.

BECAUSE OF THE THREE TREATIES INVOKED THEREIN, THE COMPLAINT STATES A CAUSE OF ACTION ARISING UNDER THE LAWS OF THE UNITED STATES WITHIN THE MEANING OF 28 U.S.C. 1331.

A. PREAMBLE

This section of the Oneidas' brief will analyze the law under 28 U.S.C. 1331 as applied to the particular facts before the Court. Initially, the analysis shows that the three treaties, in and of themselves, bring this case under 1331. Next, the concept of "possession", which the majority opinion below thought crucial, is examined in the light of prior decisions of the Second and Ninth Circuits. Finally, the point is made that this is not an action in ejectment, but rather a plea for equity and justice in form which will leave undisturbed the occupancy of the persons presently residing on the Oneidas' Reservation.

4/ The Court of Appeals, 464 F. 2d 916 (1972) in Footnote 9 of its opinion assumed that the New York courts would not have jurisdiction over the claim of the Oneida tribes. See also "Federal Indian Law" 363-64.

B. THIS CASE "ARISES UNDER" THE THREE TREATIES INVOKED IN THE COMPLAINT

To the majority of the Court below, the fact that the Oneida Indians are not in possession of their Reservation is fatal to federal jurisdiction. It distinguished the *Tuscarora*, 257 F.2d 885 (2d Cir. 1958), case on the basis that there the Indians were in possession of their land and stated that, because the Oneidas were not in possession:

> "...on the rather technical view taken by the Supreme Court, their action does not 'arise' thereunder." (Meaning under the laws, etc. of the United States.) Petition, p. 21.

We believe the Second Circuit's distinction on the basis of possession to be untenable because the very treaties under which the Oneidas are suing and invoke in their complaint promise them "possession" of the land in question:

> "The Oneida and Tuscarora Nations shall be secured in the *possession* of lands on which they are settled." (Emphasis added; Treaty of 1784.)

> "The Oneida and Tuscarora Nations are also *again secured and confirmed* in the *possession* of their respective lands." (Emphasis added; Treaty of 1789)

> "...the said reservation *shall remain theirs* until they choose to sell the same to the people of the United States...". (Emphasis added; Treaty of 1794)

> "No purchase, grant, lease, or other conveyance of lands...*shall be of any validity in law or equity...*" (Emphasis added; 25 U.S.C. 177)

> "...The General Government will never consent to your being defrauded, but it will protect you in your just rights..." (Promise of George Washington)

> "...the burden of proof shall rest upon the white person, whenever the Indian shall make out a presumption of title in himself *from the fact of previous possession* or ownership." (Emphasis added; 25 U.S.C. 194)

Since all of the foregoing were quoted and invoked in the Oneidas' complaint, the cause of action is not one of ejectment but rather a special one created by the treaties and laws and promises of the United States.

Whatever policies existed, or may exist, requiring the "ejectment" rule are not applicable to the factual situation presented in this case. The United States has refused to honor its statutory duty, to represent the interest of the Oneidas and the Oneidas have been and are now barred from state courts. 5/

Under these facts in a suit under a federal treaty guaranteeing "possession", the fact of non-possession should not bar the recipient of the guaranty from federal court.

C. THE USE OF POSSESSION VS. NON-POSSESSION AS THE SOLE CRITERION OF FEDERAL JURISDICTION IS NOT IN ACCORD WITH OTHER DECISIONS OF THE SECOND AND NINTH CIRCUIT COURTS OF APPEAL.

In two prior cases, Circuit Courts of Appeal have held that Indian tribes *not in possession* of the disputed land could protect their rights in federal court. The first such case was *Tuscarora Nation of Indians* v. *New York Power Authority,* 257 F. 2d 885 (2 Cir. 1958). As shown in the opinion of the District Court, which raised the jurisdictional issue and then assumed jurisdiction, the Superintendent of Public Works of New York State was authorized to "obtain possession according to the procedure provided by Section thirty of the highway law..." *Tuscarora Nation of Indians* v. *New York Power Authority,* 164 F. Supp. 107, 109 (W.D.N.Y. 1958). In April 15, 1958, the Power Authority did take over the right to possession of the land in question by filing a condemnation map under Section 30 of the State Highway Law. See Opinion of Second Circuit 257 F. 2d 887, 888. As alleged in paragraph 9 of the Tuscarora

5/ 25 U.S.C. 195. The Oneidas have requested the help of the U.S. Attorney in the basic issue, and also on appeal to the Second Circuit on the sole issue of jurisdiction. In each case the help was denied because of an alleged conflict of interest in a case the Oneidas have before the Indian Claims Commission relating to the same "treaties" with New York State.

complaint, dated April 18, 1958, the power authority asserted its right to possession under Section 30 and attempted to enter the Tuscaroras' property. 6/

The other relevant "possession" case is *Skokomish Indian Tribe* v. *France*, 269 F.2d 555 (9th Cir. 1959). In that case the Indians claimed certain tidelands located adjacent to their acknowledged reservation. In 1889 the State of Washington asserted ownership of the tidelands, adversely to the Indians, and granted and leased them to the non-Indian predecessors of the defendants in the action. The Indians *were not in possession* of the lands claimed at the time of commencement of the action.

The defendants there raised the same jurisdictional issues as did the defendants in our case. The Ninth Circuit held that there was jurisdiction under 28 U.S.C.A. 1331, because interpretation of the treaty was the crux of the case. It did not find controlling the fact that the Indians were not in possession. (Ultimately the Indians lost because the Court, having taken jurisdiction, held that the legal description of the reservation did not cover the disputed tidelands.)

The main factual difference between the *Skokomish*, *Tuscarora*, and *Oneida* cases is the fraction of the original land currently possessed as compared to the fraction possessed by the defendant. The difference is one of degree, not of kind.

D. TAYLOR V. ANDERSON, 234 U.S. 74, DISTINGUISHED

Both the majority opinion below and counsel for defendants have cited the decision in *Taylor* v. *Anderson*, 234 U.S. 74 (1914), as controlling here. The Second Circuit also relied on *Taylor* in its decision in *Deere* v. *St. Lawrence River Power Co.*, 32 F.2d

---

6/ According to Edmund Wilson's "Apologies To The Iroquois", the state's engineers and work crews had already moved onto the land and several Indians were arrested for trying to oust them and to prevent further entry.

550 (2d Cir. 1929). The *Taylor* case is unlike the Oneidas' case in that the plaintiffs in *Taylor* had an available remedy in the courts of the State of Oklahoma. The Oklahoma District Court, *Taylor* v. *Anderson*, 197 F.Supp. 383, 388 (E.D. Okla. 1911) pointed out:

> "[3] Should the plaintiffs hereafter commence this action in the proper state court, and the defendants there set up in their answer the defense which the plaintiffs anticipate, then a federal question will be presented which the state court in the first instance has jurisdiction to determine. If the decision of the trial court on this federal question be adverse to the plaintiffs, they may appeal to the Supreme Court of the state. If the decision of that court on that question be again adverse the plaintiffs, they may appeal to the Supreme Court of the United States and thus finally have the question decided by a federal court."

and the Supreme Court referred to this alternative in saying:

> "Whether or not in other respects the plaintiffs overlooked an authorized mode of securing relief to which they may be entitled need not now be considered." 34 S. Ct. 725.

In *Taylor* the plaintiffs were individuals bringing an avowed ejectment action to regain possession of land allotted to an Indian predecessor in title, and the federal district court assumed that the plaintiffs as individual Indians could sue in the courts of the State of Oklahoma (as distinguished from New York where they may not).

SUMMARY: 28 U.S.C. 1131

Under the facts here, the District Court does have jurisdiction under 28 U.S.C. 1331.

The Second Circuit's use of the "arising under" test as applied to ejectment cases would be appropriate in the great majority of real property cases. As pointed out in *Shulthis* v. *McDougal*, 225 U.S. 561, 569 (1912), much of the land in the United States has its source in a federal grant and federal courts might have been engulfed in land litigation if every ejectment or other land case had original jurisdiction in federal court. A more appropriate procedure in most cases, as the District Court pointed out in

Taylor v. *Anderson,* is to initiate the suit in state court and then pursue a federal appeal if federal law not applied by state court. This procedure is not, however, available to the Oneidas.

The Oneida Indians' case, as shown by the complaint as amended, is vitally different from *Taylor* and the many "arising under" cases cited by the Second Circuit and by opposing counsel:

First, the Oneidas are now and always have been forbidden by federal law to bring their case in the courts of New York State. The alternate procedure available to the plaintiffs in *Taylor* v. *Anderson* is not and never has been available to the Oneidas.

Second, until 1958 an Indian tribe was not considered a person competent to bring an action in New York State courts; thus these courts have always been closed to the Oneidas under *state* law as well as federal. By the time Section 11-A of the New York Indian Law had been passed, Congress had enacted 25 U.S.C. 233 which specifically reserved to federal courts actions accruing before September 13, 1952.

Third, the United States has guaranteed to the *Oneidas* the "possession" of their Reservation. Following proper petition by the Oneidas, both the Executive and Legislative branches of the United States Government have failed to keep the word of the United States because of an alleged "conflict of interest". Thus the courts of the United States are the only avenue by which the Oneidas can pursue justice and have their day in court.

Fourth, this is *not* an ejectment action, nor one whose essential allegation is a right to possession. It is an appeal to the equitable jurisdiction of federal courts based on a very singular factual and legal situation.

Fifth, based on the decisions in the *Tuscarora* and *Skokomish* cases, "possession" in the sense of complete dominion and control is not the key to federal court. In neither of these cases did the Indians have, under state law, a right of possession of the property involved.

V.

APART FROM THE SPECIAL FACTS WHICH BRING THIS CASE UNDER 25 U.S.C. 1331, THE BROADER JURISDICTIONAL CONCEPT OF 25 U.S.C. 1362 ALSO APPLIES.

A. THE WORDS "ARISES UNDER THE CONSTITUTION, LAWS, OR TREATIES OF THE UNITED STATES" AS USED IN 28 U.S.C. 1362 NEED NOT HAVE THE SAME RESTRICTIVE MEANING AS UNDER 28 U.S.C. 1331.

When Congress enacted 28 U.S.C. §1362, extending the jurisdiction of the federal district courts to entertain suits brought by federally-recognized Indian tribes on questions arising under the Constitution, laws or treaties of the United States, Congress intended to include in this jurisdictional grant a suit brought by a recognized Tribe involving land of which the Tribe had been dispossessed in violation of federal laws and treaties.

The Court below assumed, without analysis, that Congress, when it enacted 28 U.S.C. §1362 in 1966, intended that the conditioning phrase "where in the matter in controversy arises under the Constitution, laws, or treaties of the United States" (28 U.S.C. §1362) would be subject to the "well pleaded complaint rule", a judicially ingrained interpretation of the similar phrase contained in 28 U.S.C. §1331. Plaintiffs assert that this assumption is belied by the legislative history of 28 U.S.C. §1362. Before addressing the legislative history of 28 U.S.C. §1362, this brief will focus on two preliminary points.

First, although the "arising under" phrases of 28 U.S.C. §§1331 and 1362 closely parallel the provision in Article III, Section 2 of the Constitution delimiting the permissible ambit of federal court jurisdiction, this Court has recognized that the congressional grant of federal court jurisdiction contained in 28 U.S.C. §1331 is less generous than the jurisdiction authorized by the Constitution and that the "well pleaded complaint rule" is not an interpretation of the constitutional language but rather an interpretation of 28 U.S.C. §1331. *Shoshone Mining Co.* v. *Rutler*, 170 U.S. 505 (1900); *Romero* v. *International Terminal Operating Co.*, 358 U.S. 354 (1959); see *Osborn* v. *Bank of United States*, 9 Wheat. 738 (1824); *Louisville & Nashville Ry. Co.* v. *Mottley*, 211 U.S. 149 (1908). Consequently, the decision below was not constitutionally compelled, and the Constitution would permit this Court's reversal. See *Osborn* v. *Bank of United States*, 9 Wheat. 738 (1824); *Textile Workers Union* v. *Lincoln Mills*, 353 U.S. 448 (1957).

Second, this Court has recently cautioned that "[w]ords generally have different shades of meaning, and are to be construed if reasonably possible to effectuate the intent of the lawmakers; and this meaning in particular instances is to be arrived at not only by a consideration of the words themselves, but by considering, as well, the context, the purposes of the law, and the circumstances under which the words were employed." *District of Columbia* v. *Carter*, 93 S.Ct. 602, 604 (1973), citing *Puerto Rico* v. *The Shell Co.* (*P.R.*), *Ltd.*, 302 U.S. 253, 258 (1937); see *Helvering* v. *Stockholms Enskilda Bank*, 293 U.S. 84, 86, 87-88 (1934); *Atlantic Cleaners & Dyers* v. *United States*, 286 U.S. 427, 433 (1932).

In *District of Columbia* v. *Carter*, this Court was reviewing a decision of the United States Court of Appeals for the District of Columbia that the District of Columbia was a "State or Territory" for the purpose of 42 U.S.C. §1983. The Court of Appeals' decision was founded on a Supreme Court holding that "the District of Columbia is included within the phrase 'every State and Territory' as employed in 42 U.S.C. §1982.... *Hurd* v. *Hodge*, 334 U.S. 24, 31, 92 L. Ed. 1187, 68 S. Ct. 847 (1948)." *District of Columbia* v. *Carter, supra*, at 604. In reversing the decision below, this Court stated:

At first glance, it might seem logical simply to assume, as did the Court of Appeals, that identical words used in two related statutes were intended to have the same effect. Nevertheless, "[w]here the subject matter to which the words refer is not the same in the several places where they are used, or the conditions are different, or the scope of the legislative power exercised in one case is broader than that exercised in another, the meaning well may vary to meet the purposes of the law..." *Atlantic Cleaners & Dyers* v. *United States, supra,* 286 U.S., at 433, 52 S.Ct., at 609. *District of Columbia* v. *Carter, supra,* at 604.

The relevance of the above language from *District of Columbia* v. *Carter* to the instant case is readily apparent. The Court below in this case automatically assumed that the "arising under" language of 28 U.S.C. §1361 should be interpreted in exactly the same fashion as the "arising under" language of 28 U.S.C. §1331, and in so doing, the Court below clearly violated this Court's standards as enunciated in *District of Columbia* v. *Carter.* Furthermore, as we will demonstrate below, "the logic underlying the Court of Appeals' assumption breaks down completely where, as here, 'there is such variation in the connection in which the words are used as reasonably to warrant the conclusion that they were employed...with different intent.' [*Atlantic Cleaners & Dyers* v. *United States, supra,* 286 U.S. at 433; 52 S.Ct., at 609.]" *District of Columbia* v. *Carter, supra,* at 604.

B. 28 U.S.C. §1362 WAS INTENDED TO BE A REMEDIAL "INDIAN" STATUTE, EXTENDING FEDERAL JURISDICTION TO LAND CASES LIKE THE INSTANT ONE.

The legislative history of 28 U.S.C. §1362 is replete with references indicating that Congress, by enacting 28 U.S.C. §1362 in 1966, understood that federal courts would have jurisdiction of suits presenting for judicial action the issues raised by the instant suit.

In recommending the enactment of what is now 28 U.S.C. §1362, the Judiciary Committee of the House of Representatives noted that:

> "In its report to the Senate Committee, the Department of the Interior specifically pointed out that the issues involved in cases involving tribal lands that either are held in trust or were so held by the United States or are held by the tribe subject to restriction against alienation imposed by the United States are Federal issues. The Department therefore observed that particularly as to this class of cases, it is appropriate that the actions be brought in a U.S. district court." H.R.Rep. No. 2040, 89th Cong., 2d Sess. 3146 (1966).

The Oneida complaint presents exactly the fact pattern which the above language demonstrates was intended by Congress to fall within the ambit of 28 U.S.C. §1362. The Oneidas are suing for lands taken from them allegedly in violation of the Indian Non-Intercourse Act (now 25 U.S.C. §177), by which Congress imposed a restriction against alienation of Indian land throughout the country. Petitioners assert that if the decision of the Court below is affirmed by this Court, the congressional will as expressed in the above quotation will be violated since this case and, indeed, any other case brought by an Indian tribe for lands of which the tribe was dispossessed in violation of the restriction against alienation imposed by the Indian Non-Intercourse Act will not be heard by federal courts.

Furthermore, this same Committee was cognizant that federal courts have jurisdiction over suits brought by the United States as trustee for Indians or Indian tribes (28 U.S.C. §1345), and that, for a variety of reasons, the United States frequently declines to litigate some Indian actions. The Committee stated as a justification for the passage of 28 U.S.C. §1362 that:

> "The enactment of this bill would provide for U.S. district court jurisdiction in those cases where the U.S. attorney declines to bring an action and the tribe elects to bring the action. As is observed in the Department of the Interior report, the tribes would then have access to the Federal courts through their own attorneys. It can therefore be seen that the bill provides the means whereby the tribes are

assured of the same judicial determination whether the action is brought in their behalf by the Government or by their own attorneys. There is a large body of Federal law which states the relationship, obligations and duties which exists between the United States and the Indian tribes. The Federal forum is therefore appropriate for litigation involving such issues." H.R. Rep. No. 2040, 89th Cong., 2d Sess. 3147 (1966).

This legislative history is again specifically relevant to the instant case. The United States could have instituted this action (see *United States* v. *Boylan*, 265 F. 165 [2d Cir. 1920]; 25 U.S.C. §175), and, in fact, the Oneidas have requested the assistance of the United States. The request was denied because of an alleged conflict of interest, engendered by the Oneidas' suit against the United States in the Indian Claims Commission. If the Oneida Tribes and other Indian tribes are to be afforded the same right to a federal court forum as would the United States suing on their behalf in a trustee capacity, which was certainly the Congress' intent in enacting 28 U.S.C. §1362, this Court must reverse the decision below.

Other instances of Legislative Intent on §1362 are as follows:

(1) The memorandum of the Solicitor General of the United States on certiorari describes the issue under 25 U.S.C. 1362 as turning on whether 1362 should be construed as a statute involving Indian claims or more narrowly as a statute involving the $10,000 limit on federal jurisdiction. This is an accurate description of the 1362 issue, and we submit that the legislative history of 1362 discloses that it is to be interpreted as an Indian statute rather than a jurisdictional statute. In addition to the legislative history, it should be pointed out that the official heading of the bill as submitted to Congress reads as follows:

"AN ACT

To amend the Judicial Code to permit Indian tribes to maintain civil actions in Federal district courts without regard to the $10,000 limitation, *and for other purposes.*" [Emphasis added.]

Thus removal of the $10,000 jurisdictional limit was not the sole purpose for if it were, the act would not specify "for other purposes". Further, 1362 was included in the chapter analysis of Chapter 85 of Title 28 with the heading "1362 Indian tribes". This it was officially characterized as an *Indian statute* as distinguished from a jurisdictional limit change.

(2)   It should be noted further that the legislation did not take the form of an exception to 1331, eliminating the $10,000 requirement as to Indians. It was introduced and passed as a separate statute, which as Judge Lumbard of the Second Circuit pointed out can be considered as an entirely new section with meaning independent of 1331. *Romero* v. *Intl. Terminal Operating Co.,* 358 U.S. 354, 379-380 (1959); *Gully* v. *First National Bank* 299 U.S. 109, 113 (1936); "The Broken Compass", 115 Penn. Law Rev. 890, 891 (1969).

An examination of the legislative history of 1362 confirms the view of the Acting Solicitor of the Department of Interior as set forth in his letter to the United States Solicitor General, dated March 21, 1973, which states in part:

> "We think the legislative history of §1362 clearly shows that it is a statute intended to enable Federally recognized Indian tribes to litigate in the Federal courts all questions pertaining to their rights arising from lands claimed by them. ..." p. 11. 7/

(3)   House Report #2040, September 12, 1966, U.S. Code Congr. & Adm. News 1966, pp. 3145-3149, states in its introduction that the purpose of the bill is "to permit Indian tribes to maintain civil actions in federal courts without regard to the $10,000 limitation and *for other purposes. ...*" *Id.* p. 3145. [Emphasis added.]

7/   Exhibit A of this brief is a reprint of such letter as set forth in the Memorandum of the Solicitor General of the United States to the Supreme Court.

(4)   The same House report cites a case similar to the Oneidas', where the U.S. Attorney declines to bring an action: "As is observed in the Department of Interior Report, the tribes would then have access to the federal courts through their own attorneys." *Id*. p. 3147. This example is *not* given in the context of the $10,000 limitation but is, rather, listed as "another factor which is relevant in this situation and serves to emphasize the justification for enactment of this bill." *Id*. p. 3147. The next paragraph of the House Report clearly differentiates the cases where the U.S. Attorney refuses to bring the suit from cases where the $10,000 limitation is applicable.

(5)   The House Report contains a letter from Harry R. Anderson, Assistant Secretary of Interior, which refers to lands which are *or were held* by the United States in trust or by a tribe subject to restrictions on alienation, thus indicating that the Indians need not be in possession to sue in Federal Court. *Id*. p. 3148.

(6)   The House Report also contains a letter from Ramsey Clark, Deputy Attorney General, setting forth the views of the Department of Justice. He states that "*one of the purposes of this bill...*" is to remove the problem of the $10,000 limitation. *Id*. p. 3149.

(7)   The Senate Report adds certain clarification to the House Report. *S. Rep. No. 1507*, August 24, 1966, states in part:

> "...In many instances claims arise under special treaties between the United States and the tribes, but because of the limitation the matter cannot be litigated in Federal courts. As an example, several parcels of land may be claimed by the tribes, each of the parcels being valued at under $10,000 even though the aggregate constitutes more than $10,000. However, these claims may not be added together for the purpose of meeting the jurisdictional amount, and the tribes are denied a Federal forum.

> "There is great hesitancy on the part of tribes to use State courts.   This reluctance is founded partially on the traditional fear that tribes have had of the States in which their reservations are situated.   Additionally, the Federal

courts have more expertise in deciding questions involving treaties with the Federal Government, as well as interpreting the relevant body of Federal law that has developed over the years.

"Currently, the right of the Attorney General of the United States to bring civil actions on behalf of tribes without regard to jurisdictional amount, a power conferred on him by special statutes, is insufficient in those cases wherein the interest of the Federal Government as guardian of the Indian tribes and as Federal sovereign conflict, in which case the Attorney General will decline to bring the action.

"The proposed legislation will remedy these defects by making it possible for the Indian tribes to seek redress using their own resources and attorneys."

Note that the above language refers to several parcels which "may be *claimed* by the tribes". [Emphasis added.] The floor report on this bill, as reported in Congressional Record-Senate, August 26, 1966, p. 19, 885, contains essentially the same language as quoted above in explanation of the purpose of the bill.

(8) With his Memorandum to the Supreme Court on this case, dated May 1973, the United States Solicitor General lodged with the Court a copy of the Congressional hearings on 28 U.S.C. 1362, held July 15, 1966. At these hearings, Senator Quentin N. Burdick, who sponsored the bill gave several examples of its intended application, which are quoted in part below:

"For example, an Indian tribe claims title to a tract of land on the reservation by reason of a treaty or act of Congress. But the value of the land is less than $10,000.

"And I might say, Mr. Chairman, that the fraction there is one of the problems we have in Indian tribes, where there is a multiplicity of ownership in small pieces and small fractions.

"So there may be eight or ten of such parcels, each claimed by different owners. Added together the value of the parcels would exceed $10,000. But the separate value of each parcel cannot be added up to make the $10,000. As a result, a tribe cannot maintain suit in Federal court to establish its right to substantial land areas even though the matter arises under laws or treaties of the United States."
at 4.

*   *   *

"There are cases where a conflict arises on the question of
whether land, or minerals, is public land or minerals of the
United States or the trust property of a tribe. The Secretary
of the Interior has the responsibility for both kinds of land,
on request of a public land applicant, unbeknown to the
tribe or even the Bureau of Indian Affairs, the Secretary of
the Interior issues a patent to the land. The tribe is
prohibited from maintaining suit in Federal court to cancel
the patent. Only the United States can do that. But the
Attorney General will not bring suit unless asked and the
Secretary of the Interior, who issued the patent, could not be
expected to ask for cancellation because to do so would in
effect admit error on his part originally. The tribe may bring
suit against the patentee and ask the court to declare the
tribe the owner on the ground that the tribe's title depends
on Federal laws or treaties. But here again, unless the land
has a value in excess of $10,000 the Federal district court has
no jurisdiction." at 4, 5.

Both the examples given by Senator Burdick are instances
where the Indians would not be in possession of the land
involved. The second example very specifically refers to the case
where the United States has patented alleged Indian land to a
third party, who would presumably then be in possession of it.
This is very similar to the Oneidas' case except that it was the
State of New York and not the United States which patented the
Reservation to the predecessors of the defendants herein. 8/

(9) The Congressional hearings referred to above also contain
a statement by Attorney Marvin J. Sonosky, at 12-15, to the
Congressional Committee in part as follows:

"I might add one other point, and I should have put it in
my memorandum, that as a general proposition state courts
have no jurisdiction over civil matters affecting restricted
property, or tribal relations of Indians, unless Congress has
specifically conferred such jurisdiction. In many instances,
particularly in Oklahoma, Congress has conferred such

8/ A reading of the legislative history of 25 U.S.C. 233 and 28
U.S.C. 1362 clearly shows that Congress, in enacting these
sections, had no idea that "arising under" would be given the
very restricted meaning adopted by the majority of the
Second Circuit.

jurisdiction. Now, this statement can be found in Federal Indian Law at page 363, with supporting citations. Federal Indian Law is a government publication, a Government Printing Office publication, sponsored by the Department of the Interior. It is hard to generalize in these things. But as a general rule this is true. And we feel that Indians, through S. 1336, would be put in at least as good a position as so many of the non-Indians who are permitted to test their rights under Federal laws, treaties and constitutions without regard to the jurisdiction of the court.

Senator Tydings. Thank you very much, Mr. Sonosky. I think you have answered our questions, and any that are left in mind.

I will recommend to the Subcommittee prompt favorable report on this legislation to the full committee." at 14-15.

This statement bears out, not only the general remedial intent of 1362, but also the fact that in the State of Oklahoma where *Taylor* v. *Anderson* originated, the state courts have jurisdiction over Indian land cases. Compare 25 U.S.C. 233 and 28 U.S.C. 1360.

The Oneidas' view of 1362 and its impact upon federal jurisdiction was adopted by Judge Lumbard of the Second Circuit in his dissenting opinion and also has been adopted by the Ninth Circuit Court of Appeals in the case of *Fort Mojave Tribe* v. *Lafollette*, No. 71-1967 (9th Cir., May 16, 1973). The opinion in this case is reproduced as Exhibit B to this brief and was called to the attention of the Supreme Court by the Solicitor General of the United States in a supplemental memorandum to the Supreme Court.

A further case upholding the Oneidas' view of the effect of 1362 is the case of *Salt River Pima-Maricopa Indian Community* v. *Arizona Sand and Rock Co.*, No. Civ. 72-376-Phx. (D. Ariz., Dec. 11, 1972), an unreported decision filed in December 1972 after the Oneidas' petition for certiorari was filed. A copy of this decision is reproduced as Exhibit C to this brief.

Two law review articles recently published have also analyzed this case from the viewpoint of 28 U.S.C. 1362. In "*Federal*

Question Jurisdiction in Cases Involving Indian Land", by Gail Alpern, 39 Brooklyn Law Review 880 (1973), the author states:

"Section 1362 of Title 28 of the United States Code (hereinafter referred to as Section 1362) was also enacted to define the unique status of the Indians within the scheme of federal jurisdiction. The legislative history of this statute reveals that it was enacted to do more than merely abrogate the need for civil actions of this kind to meet the required jurisdictional amount. It also provides 'the means whereby the tribes are assured of the same judicial determination whether the action is brought in their behalf by the Government or by their own attorneys'."

In *"Toward a New System for the Resolution of Indian Resource Claims"*, 47 N.Y.U. Law Rev. 1107 (1972), the author analyzed 28 U.S.C. 1362 and concludes as follows:

"Based on this analysis, it is submitted that to determine the scope and purpose of section 1362, one must consider its historical background and the problems its passage sought to remedy. The legislative history of section 1362 indicates that its primary purpose was to remove the amount in controversy requirement in suits brought by Indian tribes; however, the history does not limit the purpose of the act to this alone. In fact, examples of the applicability of the bill given by the Committee reports indicate that Congress expected that certain actions which would be denied jurisdiction under the well-pleaded complaint rule, such as those in ejectment, should be heard in federal courts. Thus, the legislative history may be the basis for giving a broader meaning to the 'arising under' clause of section 1362 than is presently given to the 'arising under' clause of section 1331. Moreover, it is a general rule of construction that statutes applying to Indians, and remedial statutes generally, are to be construed liberally. Therefore, when one considers that the section manifests Congress' concern for its [Indian wards, the argument to read the section 1362]* grant of jurisdiction liberally, as was done in the Salt River decision, is compelling."

SUMMARY: 28 U.S.C. 1362

Under the legislative history noted above, and following the two Ninth Circuit cases included as Exhibits B and C, it is our conclusion that 28 U.S.C. 1362 was intended to be enacted as a jurisdictional relief statute for Indians and should not be given the strict "arising under" interpretation heretofore used under 28 U.S.C. 1331.

*Copy omitted from the original.

CONCLUSION

This suit is brought under three federal treaties which guarantee to the plaintiffs, the Oneida Indians, the *possession* of the specific land in question. According to the Court below, the lack of such possession precludes federal court jurisdiction; if this be so, then the lack of that which is guaranteed by the treaties also precludes the treaties' implementation.

As the legal principles are applied to our facts by the Court below, the three treaties and 28 U.S.C. 1331 and 1362 cancel each other out. That condition which brings the treaties into play also renders them unenforceable; this is not the intent of the treaties or the laws.

Under the very singular facts before this Court, 25 U.S.C. 1331 and 1362 should be applied in favor of federal court jurisdiction.

Respectfully submitted,

George C. Shattuck
Attorney for Petitioners
c/o Bond, Schoeneck & King
One Lincoln Center
Syracuse, New York   13202

July 18, 1973.

ONEIDA INDIAN NATION v.
ONEIDA & MADISON COUNTIES,
UNITED STATES SUPREME COURT DECISION,
JANUARY 21, 1974

414 U.S. 661, 39 L.Ed.2d 73

The ONEIDA INDIAN NATION OF
NEW YORK STATE et al.,
Petitioners,

v.

The COUNTY OF ONEIDA,
NEW YORK, et al.

No. 72–851.

Argued Nov. 6 and 7, 1973.

Decided Jan. 21, 1974.

Indian nations brought action seeking to recover from counties in New
York state the fair rental values of certain lands ceded in 1795 by Indians to
the state, on theory that the cession was
invalid under treaties and laws of the
United States. The United States District Court for the Northern District of
New York dismissed the action, and
plaintiffs appealed. The United States
Court of Appeals for the Second Circuit
affirmed, 464 F.2d 916, and certiorari
was granted. The Supreme Court, Mr.
Justice White, held that, assuming that
the case was essentially a possessory action, the threshold allegation required of
such a well-pleaded complaint, i.e., the
right to possession, asserted a current
right to possession conferred by federal
law, wholly independent of state law,
and not asserted solely in anticipation of
a defense; that assertion of federal
right to possession was not wholly insubstantial, implausible, foreclosed by
prior decisions of the Court, or otherwise devoid of merit; that, accordingly,
the complaint asserted a controversy
arising under the Constitution, laws or
treaties of the United States within
meaning of federal question jurisdiction-

al statutes; that the "well-pleaded complaint" rule is not changed; and that upholding federal jurisdiction was not inconsistent with statute granting, with certain exceptions, civil jurisdiction over Indians to the state.

Reversed and remanded.

Mr. Justice Rehnquist, with whom Mr. Justice Powell joined, filed a concurring opinion.

1. Courts ⚖299.3(2)

Assuming that action brought by Indians against counties seeking fair rental value of certain lands ceded to State in 1795, on ground that the Indians' right to possession of such lands had been confirmed by treaties with the United States and that the cession was without the consent of the United States as required by the Nonintercourse Act, was essentially a possessory action, the threshold allegation required of such a well-pleaded complaint, i.e., the right to possession, asserted a current right to possession conferred by federal law wholly independent of state law, and not asserted solely in anticipation of a defense, and thus complaint asserted a controversy "arising under" the Constitution, laws or treaties of the United States within federal question jurisdictional statutes. 28 U.S.C.A. §§ 1331(a), 1362; Treaty with the Six Nations, 7 Stat. 15, 33, 44; Act of July 22, 1790, 1 Stat. 137; 25 U.S.C.A. § 177.

> See publication Words and Phrases for other judicial constructions and definitions.

2. Courts ⚖281

Assertion by Indian nations that they had a federal right to possession to certain lands governed wholly by federal law, by reason of treaties confirming their right to possession of such land and on theory that 1795 cession of such lands to the state of New York was without consent of the United States and thus in violation of the Nonintercourse Act, was not so insubstantial, implausible, foreclosed by prior decisions of the Supreme Court, or otherwise completely devoid of merit as not to involve a federal controversy within the jurisdiction of the district court, whatever might be ultimate resolution of the federal issues on the merits. 28 U.S.C.A. §§ 1331, 1362; Treaty with the Six Nations, 7 Stat. 15, 33, 44; Act of July 22, 1790, 1 Stat. 137.

3. Indians ⚖10

Once the United States was organized and the Constitution adopted, tribal rights to Indian lands became the exclusive province of federal law and Indian title, though recognized to be only a right of occupancy, is extinguishable only by the United States, and such rule applies in all the states, including the original 13. Act of July 22, 1790, 1 Stat. 137; Act of March 1, 1793, 1 Stat. 329; Act of May 19, 1796, 1 Stat. 469; Act of March 3, 1799, 1 Stat. 743; Act of March 30, 1802, 2 Stat. 139; Act of June 30, 1834, 4 Stat. 729; 25 U.S.C.A. § 177.

4. Courts ⚖299.4

Rule that possessory action is not one "arising under" the Constitution, laws, or treaties of the United States within federal question jurisdictional statutes if federal issue is not one of the essential elements of a "well-pleaded complaint," without anticipation of any defense, is not disturbed. 28 U.S.C.A. §§ 1331, 1362.

5. Courts ⚖299.3(2)

Once a patent issues, the incidents of ownership of land are, for the most part, matters of local property law to be vindicated in local courts, and in such situations it is normally insufficient for "arising under" jurisdiction merely to allege that ownership or possession is claimed under a United States patent. 28 U.S.C.A. §§ 1331, 1362.

6. Courts ⚖299.3(2)

Complaint by Indian nations seeking to recover from certain counties in New York State the fair rental value of lands ceded by the Indians to the state in 1795, on theory that the Indians' right to possession of such lands had been confirmed by United States treaties and that the 1795 cession was without the consent of the United States and hence ineffective to terminate such right of possession, under the Nonintercourse Act, met requirement for federal question jurisdiction that it reveal a dispute or controversy respecting the validity, construction, or effect of a federal law, on the determination of which the result depends. Act of July 22, 1790, 1 Stat. 137; 28 U.S.C.A. §§ 1331, 1362.

7. Courts ☞284(3), 298
Indians ☞27(2)

Conclusion that case wherein Indian nations sought to recover fair rental value of certain lands on theory that 1795 cession of such lands to the state of New York was ineffective under federal treaties and applicable federal statutes was one arising under the laws of the United States, and thus within the jurisdiction of federal district court, was not inconsistent with, but on the contrary was in furtherance of the intent of Congress as expressed in, statutes granting civil jurisdiction over Indians to the state of New York, with specified exceptions. Act of July 22, 1790, 1 Stat. 137; 25 U.S.C.A. §§ 232, 233; 28 U.S.C.A. §§ 1331, 1362.

Syllabus *

Petitioners brought this action for the fair rental value for a specified period of certain land in New York that the Oneidas had ceded to the State in 1795, alleging, *inter alia*, that the Oneidas had owned and occupied the land from time immemorial to the time of the American Revolution; that in the 1780's and 1790's various treaties with the United States had confirmed their right to possession of the land until purchased by the United States; that in 1790 the treaties had been implemented by the Nonintercourse Act forbidding the conveyance of Indian lands without the United States' consent; and that the 1795 cession was without such consent

and hence ineffective to terminate the Oneidas' right to possession under the treaties and applicable federal statutes. The District Court, ruling that the action arose under state law, dismissed the complaint for failure to raise a question arising under the laws of the United States within the meaning of either 28 U.S.C. § 1331 or 28 U.S.C. § 1362. The Court of Appeals, relying on the "well-pleaded complaint rule" of Taylor v. Anderson, 234 U.S. 74, 34 S.Ct. 724, 58 L. Ed. 1218, affirmed and held that although the decision would ultimately depend on whether the 1795 cession complied with the Nonintercourse Act, and what the consequences would be if it did not, this alone did not establish "arising under" jurisdiction because the federal issue was not one of the necessary elements of the complaint, which essentially sought relief based on the right to possession of real property. *Held*: The complaint states a controversy arising under the Constitution, laws, or treaties of the United States sufficient to invoke the jurisdiction of the District Court under 28 U.S.C. §§ 1331 and 1362. Pp. 777–785.

(a) Petitioners asserted a current right to possession conferred by federal law, wholly independent of state law, the threshold allegation required of such a well-pleaded complaint—the right to possession—being plainly enough alleged to be based on federal law so that the federal law issue did not arise solely in anticipation of a defense. Pp. 776–777, 782.

(b) Petitioners' claim of a federal |662 right to possession governed wholly by federal law is not so insubstantial or devoid of merit as to preclude a federal controversy within the District Court's jurisdiction, regardless of how the federal issue is ultimately resolved. Pp. 776–777.

(c) Indian title is a matter of federal law and can be extinguished only with federal consent. Pp. 778–781.

* The syllabus constitutes no part of the opinion of the Court but has been prepared by the Reporter of Decisions for the convenience of the reader. See United States v. Detroit Timber & Lumber Co., 200 U.S. 321, 337, 26 S.Ct. 282, 287, 50 L.Ed. 499.

(d) This is not a case where the underlying right or obligation arises only under state law and federal law is merely alleged as a barrier to its effectuation. Gully v. First National Bank, 299 U.S. 109, 57 S.Ct. 96, 81 L.Ed. 70, distinguished. Pp. 781–782.

(e) In sustaining the District Court's jurisdiction, the well-pleaded complaint rule of Taylor v. Anderson, *supra*, is not disturbed, since here the right to possession itself is claimed to arise under federal law in the first instance, and allegedly aboriginal title of an Indian tribe guaranteed by treaty and protected by statute has never been extinguished. Pp. 781–782.

(f) The complaint satisfies the requirement that it reveal a dispute or controversy respecting the validity, construction, or effect of a federal law, upon the determination of which the result depends. Pp. 782–783.

(g) The conclusion that this case arises under the laws of the United States comports with the language and legislative history of 25 U.S.C. § 233 granting to New York civil jurisdiction over disputes between Indians or between Indians and others. Pp. 783–785.

2 Cir., 464 F.2d 916, reversed and remanded.

———◆———

George C. Shattuck, Syracuse, N. Y., for petitioners.

William L. Burke for respondent.

1. Section 1331(a) provides:
  "The district courts shall have original jurisdiction of all civil actions wherein the matter in controversy exceeds the sum or value of $10,000, exclusive of interest and costs, and arises under the Constitution, laws, or treaties of the United States."
  Under § 1362:
  "The district courts shall have original jurisdiction of all civil actions, brought by any Indian tribe or band with a governing body duly recognized by the Secretary of the Interior, wherein the matter in controversy arises under the Constitution, laws, or treaties of the United States."

Jeremiah Jochnowitz, Albany, N. Y. for the State of New York, as amicus curiae, by special leave of Court.

⌊Mr. Justice WHITE delivered the ⌊663 opinion of the Court.

Both § 1331 and § 1362 of Title 28 of the United States Code confer jurisdiction on the district courts to hear cases "aris[ing] under the Constitution, laws, or treaties of the United States." [1] Section 1331 requires that the amount in controversy exceed $10,000. Under § 1362, Indian tribes may bring such suits without regard to the amount in controversy. The question now before us is whether the District Court had jurisdiction over this case under either of these sections.

I

The complaint was filed in the United States District Court for the Northern District of New York by the Oneida Indian Nation of New York State and the Oneida Indian Nation of Wisconsin against the Counties of Oneida and Madison in the State of New York.[2] The⌊complaint alleged that from time ⌊664 immemorial down to the time of the American Revolution the Oneidas had owned and occupied some six million acres of land in the State of New York. The complaint also alleged that in the 1780's and 1790's various treaties had been entered into between the Oneidas and the United States confirming the Indians' right to possession of their lands until purchased by the United States[3] and that in 1790 the treaties

2. Initially, only diversity jurisdiction under 28 U.S.C. § 1332 was alleged in the complaint. The necessary jurisdictional amount was averred. Federal-question jurisdiction was asserted by an amendment to the complaint. Jurisdiction under § 1332 was rejected by the District Court and the Court of Appeals and is not at issue here.

3. Three treaties with the Six Indian Nations of the Iroquois Confederacy in New York were alleged: the Treaty of Fort Stanwix of 1784, which provides in part that "[t]he Oneida and Tuscarora nations shall be secured in the possession of the lands on which they are settled"; the Treaty of Fort

had been implemented by federal statute the Nonintercourse Act, 1 Stat. 137, forbidding the conveyance of Indian lands without the consent of the United States. It was then alleged that in 1788 the Oneidas had ceded five million acres to the State of New York, 300,000 acres being withheld as a reservation, and that in 1795 a portion of these reserved lands was also ceded to the State. Assertedly, the 1795 cession was without the consent of the United States and hence ineffective to terminate the Indians' right to possession under the federal treaties and the applicable federal statutes. Also alleging that the 1795 cession was for an unconscionable and inadequate price and that portions of the premises were now in possession of and being used by the defendant counties, the complaint prayed for damages representing the fair rental value of the land for the period January 1, 1968, through December 31, 1969.

The District Court ruled that the cause of action, regardless of the label given it, was created under state law and required only allegations of the plaintiffs' possessory rights and the defendants' interference therewith. The possible necessity of interpreting a federal statute or treaties to resolve a potential defense was deemed insufficient to sustain federal-question jurisdiction. The complaint was accordingly dismissed for want of subject matter jurisdiction for failure of the complaint to raise a question arising under the laws of the United States within the meaning of either § 1331 or § 1362.

The Court of Appeals affirmed, with one judge dissenting, ruling that the jurisdictional claim "shatters on the rock of the 'well-pleaded complaint' rule for determining federal question jurisdiction." 464 F.2d 916, 918 (CA2 1972). Although "[d]ecision would ultimately turn on whether the deed of 1795 complied with what is now 25 U.S.C. § 177 and what the consequences would be if it did not," id., at 919, this alone did not establish "arising under" jurisdiction because the federal issue was not one of the necessary elements of the complaint, which was read as essentially seeking relief based on the right to possession of real property. The Court of Appeals thought Taylor v. Anderson, 234 U.S. 74, 34 S.Ct. 724, 58 L.Ed. 1218 (1914), directly in point. There, a complaint in ejectment did not state a claim arising under the laws of the United States even though it alleged that the defendants were claiming under a deed that was void under acts of Congress restraining the alienation of lands allotted to Choctaw and Chickasaw Indians. The Court applied the principle that whether a case arises under federal law for purposes of the jurisdictional statute "must be determined from what necessarily appears in the plaintiff's statement of his own claim in the bill or declaration, unaided by anything alleged in anticipation of avoidance of defenses which it is thought the defendant may interpose." Id., at 75–76, 34 S.Ct. at 724. Because the only essential allegations were plaintiffs' rights to possession, defendants' wrongful holding and the damage claim, the complaint did not properly assert a federal issue, however likely it might be that it would be relevant to or determinative of a defense. In the present case, noting that the District Judge was correct in holding that under New York law these allegations would suffice to state a cause of action in ejectment, the Court of Appeals considered Taylor to be dispositive.

Harmar of 1789 where the Oneida and the Tuscarora nations were "again secured and confirmed in the possession of their respective lands"; and the Treaty of Canandaigua of 1794, Art. II of which provides: "The United States acknowledge the lands reserved to the Oneida, Onondaga and Cayuga Nations, in their respective treaties with the state of New-York, and called their reserva-

tions, to be their property; and the United States will never claim the same, nor disturb them . . . in the free use and enjoyment thereof: but the said reservations shall remain theirs, until they choose to sell the same to the people of the United States, who have the right to purchase." The treaties referred to are found at 7 Stat. 15, 7 Stat. 33, and 7 Stat. 44, respectively.

Both the District Court and the Court of Appeals were in error, and we reverse the judgment of the Court of Appeals.

II

[1, 2] Accepting the premise of the Court of Appeals that the case was essentially a possessory action, we are of the view that the complaint asserted a current right to possession conferred by federal law, wholly independent of state law. The threshold allegation required of such a well-pleaded complaint—the right to possession—was plainly enough alleged to be based on federal law. The federal law issue, therefore, did not arise solely in anticipation of a defense. Moreover, we think that the basis for petitioners' assertion that they had a federal right to possession governed wholly by federal law cannot be said to be so insubstantial, implausible, foreclosed by prior decisions of this Court, or otherwise completely devoid of merit as not to involve a federal controversy within the jurisdiction of the District Court, whatever may be the ultimate resolution of the federal issues on the merits. See, *e.g.*, The Fair v. Kohler Die & Specialty Co., 228 U.S. 22, 25, 33 S.Ct. 410, 411, 27 L.Ed. 716 (1913); Montana Catholic Missions v. Missoula County, 200 U.S. 118, 130, 26 S.Ct. 197, 201, 50 L.Ed. 398 (1906); Levering & Garrigues Co. v. Morrin, 289 U.S. 103, 105–106, 53 S.Ct. 549, 550, 77 L.Ed. 1062 (1933); Montana-Dakota Utilities Co. v. Northwestern Public Service Co., 341 U.S. 246, 249, 71 S.Ct. 692, 694, 95 L.Ed. 912 (1951). Given the nature and source of the possessory rights of Indian tribes to their aboriginal lands, particularly when confirmed by treaty, it is plain that the complaint asserted a con-

troversy arising under the Constitution, laws, or treaties of the United States within the meaning of both § 1331 and § 1362.

[3] It very early became accepted doctrine in this Court that although fee title to the lands occupied by Indians when the colonists arrived became vested in the sovereign—first the discovering European nation and later the original States and the United States—a right of occupancy in the Indian tribes was nevertheless recognized. That right, sometimes called Indian title and good against all but the sovereign, could be terminated only by sovereign act. Once the United States was organized and the Constitution adopted, these tribal rights to Indian lands became the exclusive province of the federal law. Indian title, recognized to be only a right of occupancy, was extinguishable only by the United States. The Federal Government took early steps to deal with the Indians through treaty, the principal purpose often being to recognize and guarantee the rights of Indians to specified areas of land. This the United States did with respect to the various New York Indian tribes, including the Oneidas. The United States also asserted the primacy of federal law in the first Nonintercourse Act passed in 1790, 1 Stat. 137, 138, which provided that "no sale of lands made by any Indians . . . within the United States, shall be valid to any person . . . or to any state . . . unless the same shall be made and duly executed at some public treaty, held under the authority of the United States."[4]   This has remained the policy of the United States to this day. See 25 U.S.C. § 177.

---

4. Section 4 of the Act provided that "no sale of lands made by any Indians, or any nation or tribe of Indians within the United States, shall be valid to any person or persons, or to any state, whether having the right of pre-emption to such lands or not, unless the same shall be made and duly executed at some public treaty, held under the authority of the United States." The second Nonintercourse Act passed in 1793 made it a misdemeanor to negotiate for Indian lands with-

out federal authority, but it was made lawful for state agents who were present at any treaty held with the Indians under the authority of the United States, in the presence and with the approbation of the United States Commissioner, "to propose to, and adjust with the Indians, the compensation to be made for their claims to lands within such state, which shall be extinguished by the treaty." 1 Stat. 329, 330–331 § 8. This statutory policy, without major change, was carried for-

In United States v. Santa Fe Pacific R. Co., 314 U.S. 339, 345, 62 S.Ct. 248, 251, 86 L.Ed. 1116 (1941), a unanimous Court succinctly summarized the essence of past cases in relevant respects:

"'Unquestionably it has been the policy of the federal government from the beginning to respect the Indian right of occupancy, which could only be interfered with or determined by the United States.' Cramer v. United States, 261 U.S. 219, 227, 43 S.Ct. 342, [344,] 67 L.Ed. 622. This policy was first recognized in Johnson v. M'Intosh, 8 Wheat. 543, 5 L.Ed. 681, and has been repeatedly reaffirmed. Worcester v. Georgia, 6 Pet. 515, 8 L.Ed. 483; Mitchel v. United States, 9 Pet. 711, 9 L.Ed. 283; Chouteau v. Molony, 16 How. 203, 14 L.Ed. 905; Holden v. Joy, 17 Wall. 211, 21 L.Ed. 523; Buttz v. Northern Pacific Railroad [119 U.S. 55, 7 S.Ct. 100, 30 L.Ed. 330]; United States v. Shoshone Tribe, 304 U.S. 111, 58 S.Ct. 794, 82 L.Ed. 1213. As stated in Mitchel v. United States, *supra,* 9 Pet. 746, 9 L. Ed. 283, Indian 'right of occupancy is considered as sacred as the fee simple of the whites.'"

⌊669

The *Santa Fe* case also reaffirmed prior decisions to the effect that a tribal right of occupancy, to be protected, need not be "based upon a treaty, statute, or other formal government action." *Id.,* at

347, 62 S.Ct., at 252. Tribal rights were nevertheless entitled to the protection of federal law, and with respect to Indian title based on aboriginal possession, the "power of Congress . . . is supreme." *Ibid.*

As indicated in *Santa Fe,* the fundamental propositions which it restated were firmly rooted in earlier cases. In Johnson v. M'Intosh, 8 Wheat. 543, 5 L. Ed 681 (1823), the Court refused to recognize land titles originating in grants by Indians to private parties in 1773 and 1775; those grants were contrary to the accepted principle that Indian title could be extinguished only by or with the consent of the general government. The land in question, when ceded to the United States by the State of Virginia, was "occupied by numerous and warlike tribes of Indians; but the exclusive right of the United States to extinguish their title, and to grant the soil, has never, we believe, been doubted." *Id.,* at 586, 5 L.Ed. 681. See also *id.,* at 591–597, 603, 5 L.Ed. 681. The possessory and treaty rights of Indian tribes to their lands have been the recurring theme of many other cases.[5]

⌊The rudimentary propositions that Indian title is a matter of federal law and can be extinguished only with federal consent apply in all of the States, including the original 13. It is true that the United States never held fee title to the Indian lands in the original States

⌊670

---

ward in § 12 of the 1796 Act, 1 Stat. 469, 472; § 12 of the 1799 Act, 1 Stat. 743, 746; § 12 of the 1802 Act, 2 Stat. 139, 143; § 12 of the Act of 1834, 4 Stat. 729, 730–731; and in Rev.Stat. § 2116, now 25 U.S.C. § 177.

5. Representative of almost countless cases are Cherokee Nation v. Georgia, 5 Pet. 1, 8 L.Ed. 25 (1831); United States v. Rogers, 4 How. 567, 11 L.Ed. 1105 (1846); The Kansas Indians, 5 Wall. 737, 18 L.Ed. 667 (1866); The New York Indians, 5 Wall. 761, 18 L.Ed. 708 (1867); Holden v. Joy, 17 Wall. 211, 21 L.Ed. 523 (1872); Beecher v. Wetherby, 95 U.S. 517, 24 L.Ed. 440 (1877); United States v. Kagama, 118 U.S. 375, 6 S. Ct. 1109, 30 L.Ed. 228 (1886); Spalding v. Chandler, 160 U.S. 394, 16 S.Ct. 360, 40 L.

Ed. 469 (1896); United States v. Sandoval, 231 U.S. 28, 34 S.Ct. 1, 58 L.Ed. 107 (1913); Nadeau v. Union Pacific R. Co., 253 U.S. 442, 40 S.Ct. 570, 64 L.Ed. 1002 (1920); Minnesota v. United States, 305 U. S. 382, 59 S.Ct. 292, 83 L.Ed. 235 (1939); United States v. Alcea Band of Tillamooks, 329 U.S. 40, 67 S.Ct. 167, 91 L.Ed. 29 (1946); Tee-Hit-Ton Indians v. United States, 348 U.S. 272, 75 S.Ct. 313, 99 L.Ed. 314 (1955).

U. S. Dept. of Interior, Federal Indian Law 32–43, 583–645, 675–687 (1958) (hereinafter Federal Indian Law), sets out some of the fundamentals of the law dealing with Indian possessory rights to real property stemming from aboriginal title, treaty, and statute.

as it did to almost all the rest of the continental United States and that fee title to Indian lands in these States, or the pre-emptive right to purchase from the Indians, was in the State, Fletcher v. Peck, 6 Cranch 87, 3 L.Ed. 162 (1810).[6] But this reality did not alter the doctrine that federal law, treaties, and statutes protected Indian occupancy and that its termination was exclusively the province of federal law.

For example, in Worcester v. Georgia, 6 Pet. 515, 8 L.Ed. 483 (1832), the State of Georgia sought to prosecute a white man for residing in Indian country contrary to the laws of the State. This Court held the prosecution a nullity, the Chief Justice referring to the treaties with the Cherokees and to the

"universal conviction that the Indian nations possessed a full right to the lands they occupied, until that right should be extinguished by the United States, with their consent: that their territory was separated from that of any state within whose chartered limits they might reside, by a boundary ⌊671 ⌊line, established by treaties: that, within their boundary, they possessed rights with which no state could interfere: and that the whole power of regulating the intercourse with them, was vested in the United States." *Id.*, at 560, 8 L.Ed. 483.

The Cherokee Nation was said to be occupying its own territory "in which the laws of Georgia can have no force . . . ." The Georgia law was declared unconstitutional because it interfered with the relations "between the United States and the Cherokee nation, the regulation of which, according to the settled principles of our constitution, are committed exclusively to the government of the union." *Id.*, at 561, 8 L.Ed. 483.

There are cases of similar import with respect to the New York Indians. These cases lend substance to petitioners' assertion that the possessory right claimed is a *federal* right to the lands at issue in this case. Fellows v. Blacksmith, 19 How. 366, 372, 15 L.Ed. 684 (1857), which concerned the Seneca Indians, held that the "forcible removal [of Indians] must be made, if made at all, under the direction of the United States [and] that this interpretation is in accordance with the usages and practice of the Government in providing for the removal of Indian tribes from their ancient possessions." In The New York Indians, 5 Wall. 761, 18 L.Ed. 708 (1867), the State sought to tax the reservation lands of the Senecas. The Court held the tax void. The Court referred to the Indian right of occupancy as creating "an indefeasible title to the reservations that may extend from generation to generation, and will cease only by the dissolution of the tribe, or their consent to sell to the party possessed of the right of pre-emption," *id.*, at 771, 18 L.Ed. 708, and noted that New York "possessed no power to deal with Indian rights or title," *id.*, at 769, 18 L.Ed. 708. Of major importance, however, was the treaty of 1794 in which the United States acknowledged⌊certain territory to be the ⌊672 property of the Seneca Nation and promised that "it shall remain theirs until they choose to sell the same to the people of the United States . . . ." *Id.*, at 766–767, 18 L.Ed. 708. The rights of the Indians to occupy those lands "do not depend on . . . any . . . statutes of the State, but upon treaties, which are the supreme law of the land; it is to these treaties we must look to ascertain the nature of these rights, and the extent of

6. See also Cherokee Nation v. Georgia, *supra*, 5 Pet., at 38, 8 L.Ed. 25; Clark v. Smith, 13 Pet. 195, 10 L.Ed. 123 (1839); Lattimer's Lessee v. Poteet, 14 Pet. 4, 10 L. Ed. 328 (1840); Seneca Nation v. Christy, 162 U.S. 283, 16 S.Ct. 828, 40 L.Ed. 970 (1896). "Outside of the territory of the original colonies, the ultimate fee is located in the United States and may be granted to individuals subject to the Indian right of occupancy." Federal Indian Law 599; Missouri v. Iowa, 7 How. 660, 12 L.Ed. 861 (1849).

them." *Id.*, at 768, 18 L.Ed. 708.[7] The State's attempt to tax reservation lands was invalidated as an interference with Indian possessory rights guaranteed by the Federal Government.

Much later, in United States v. Forness, 125 F.2d 928 (CA2), cert. denied, sub. nom. City of Salamanca v. United States, 316 U.S. 694, 62 S.Ct. 1293, 86 L.Ed. 1764 (1942),[8] the Government sued to set aside certain leases granted by the Seneca tribe on certain reservation lands. It was argued in opposition that the suit was merely an action for ejectment which under state law could be defeated by a tender; but the Court of Appeals for the Second Circuit held that the Indian rights were federal and that "state

|673

|674

---

7. In an earlier case, New York ex rel. Cutler v. Dibble, 21 How. 366, 16 L.Ed. 149 (1859), the Court had upheld New York statutes which protected the Indians from intrusion by others on their tribal lands, and had asserted that "[n]otwithstanding the peculiar relation which these Indian nations hold to the Government of the United States, the State of New York had the power of a sovereign over their persons and property, so far as it was necessary to preserve the peace of the Commonwealth, and protect these feeble and helpless bands from imposition and intrusion." *Id.*, at 370, 16 L.Ed. 149. It is apparent that by the later decision in *The New York Indians, supra,* the Court did not consider the potential implications of the dictum expressed in *Dibble* applicable in situations where the State's power was exercised other than for the protection of the Indians on their tribal lands. In any event, whatever *Dibble* may have held with respect to state power to protect Indian possession, it does not question the Indians' right to possession under *federal* law.

8. The question of the application of federal law to Indian tribal property in New York was litigated in the state courts in the intervening years as well. In 1870, an unreported decision of the New York Supreme Court held that tribal leases of Seneca reservation lands, ratified by the New York Legislature, were invalid in the absence of approval from the United States. See United States v. Forness, *supra*, at 930–931; H.R.Rep.Misc. Doc.No.75, 43d Cong., 2d Sess. (1875); Brief for the Warden and the State of New York 26–27, New York ex rel. Ray v. Martin, No. 158, O.T.1945, 326 U.S. 496, 66 S.Ct. 307, 90 L.Ed. 261 (1946). In the mid-1890's, in Buffalo, R. & P. R. Co. v. Lavery, 75 Hun. 396, 27 N.Y.S. 443 (5th Dept., App.Div.1894), affirmed on opinion below, 149 N.Y. 576, 43 N.E. 986 (1896), a private non-Indian lessee of Indian land under a lease first granted by the Senecas in 1866, which was concededly not legally effective until an 1875 Act of Congress validated such leases, was nonetheless held to have priority over a railroad claiming under an 1872 lease from the Senecas and a state statute purportedly validating the lease as one to a railroad which had

been ratified by a state court, because the state statute which would have given the railroad a superior right to possession was incapable of confirming possessory rights to Indian tribal lands without federal authority. The New York courts held that it was "not within the legislative power of the State to enable the Indian nation to make, or others to take from the Indians, grants or leases of lands within their reservations. In that matter the Federal government, having the power under the Constitution to do so, has assumed to control it by . . . act of Congress [referring to the Indian Nonintercourse Act]. . . . As respects their lands, subject only to the pre-emptive title, the Indians are treated as the wards of the United States, and it is only pursuant to the Federal authority that their lands can be granted or demised by or acquired by conveyance or leased from them." 75 Hun., at 399–400, 27 N.Y.S., at 445.

Still later, in People ex rel. Cusick v. Daly, 212 N.Y. 183, 105 N.E. 1048 (1914), the New York Court of Appeals held that without the consent of Congress New York could not prosecute Indian crimes on reservations. Relying on the classic federal cases, the court held that federal power was pre-eminent and that the Federal Government had made treaties with the Indians which confirmed their territorial possession, although the Federal Government never owned the fee of the land within the State's confines. *Id.*, at 192, 105 N.E. 1048. Within the reservation federal power, when exercised, foreclosed the exercise of power by the State. "It is said that there is a difference between the Indians whose reservations are the direct gift of the federal government and those whose reservations have been derived from the state or from other sources. We find no such distinction in the statute, and we can think of none that logically differentiates one from the other. Even if we assume that, in the absence of federal legislation, the state has the most ample power to legislate for the Indians within its borders, there seems to be no escape from the conclusion that when Congress does act the power of the state must yield to the paramount authority of the federal government." *Id.*, at 196–197, 105 N.E., at 1052.

law cannot be invoked to limit the rights in lands granted by the United States to the Indians, because, as the court below recognized, state law does not apply to the Indians except so far as the United States has given its consent." *Id.,* at 932. There being no federal statute making the statutory or decisional law of the State of New York applicable to the reservations, the controlling law remained federal law; and, absent federal statutory guidance, the governing rule of decision would be fashioned by the federal court in the mode of the common law.[9]

|675

|III

Enough has been said, we think, to indicate that the complaint in this case asserts a present right to possession under federal law. The claim may fail at a

later stage for a variety of reasons; but for jurisdictional purposes, this is not a case where the underlying right or obligation arises only under state law and federal law is merely alleged as a barrier to its effectuation, as was the case in Gully v. First National Bank, 299 U. S. 109, 57 S.Ct. 96, 81 L.Ed. 70 (1936). There, the suit was on a contract having its genesis in state law, and the tax that |676 the defendant had promised to pay was imposed by a state statute. The possibility that a federal statute might bar its collection was insufficient to make the case one arising under the laws of the United States.

[4, 5] Nor in sustaining the jurisdiction of the District Court do we disturb the well-pleaded complaint rule of Taylor v. Anderson, *supra,* and like cases.[10]

9. Still later, federal authority over Indian lands was again challenged. In Tuscarora Nation of Indians v. Power Authority, 257 F.2d 885 (1958), the Court of Appeals for the Second Circuit rejected New York's claim that the Nonintercourse Act did not apply to the State of New York and that, as one of the original 13 States, it never surrendered to the United States its power to condemn Indian lands. The Court of Appeals also held that the Act of Sept. 13, 1950, 64 Stat. 845, 25 U.S.C. § 233, whereby the United States ceded civil jurisdiction over Indian reservations to the State of New York, expressly and effectively excepted from its coverage the alienation of reservation lands, a matter over which the United States had reaffirmed its paramount authority. Nonetheless, the Court of Appeals held that the Niagara River Power Project Act, 71 Stat. 401 (1957), 16 U.S.C. §§ 836, 836a, by which Congress directed the Federal Power Commission to issue a license to the New York Power Authority for the construction and operation of a power project to utilize water made available to the United States by a 1950 treaty with Canada, constituted federal authorization for the Power Authority to exercise the right of eminent domain, but only in accordance with § 21 of the Federal Power Act, 41 Stat. 1074, 16 U.S.C. § 814, which permits the acquisition of sites for the purpose of developing waterways by the exercise of the right of eminent domain in the federal district court in which the land is located or in the state courts. Because the Power Authority had proceeded to appropriate a portion of the Tuscaroras' reservation lands by filing a map and other documents pursuant to procedures established by the State's Highway Law and Public

Authorities Law, those proceedings were vacated and annulled. Subsequently, the Power Authority abandoned efforts to obtain possession of the land by appropriation pursuant to those statutes and instead proceeded by condemnation proceedings in the District Court for the Western District of New York. The Tuscaroras petitioned for review of the Court of Appeals decision, but the Court denied certiorari. 358 U.S. 841, 79 S.Ct. 66, 3 L.Ed.2d 76 (1958). The Superintendent of Public Works of the State of New York simultaneously appealed from it under 28 U.S.C. § 1254(2), and the Court, on the Tuscaroras' subsequent suggestion of mootness, which the Power Authority supported and the Superintendent continued to oppose, and which was based on the Power Authority's abandonment of its appropriation proceedings in favor of the condemnation suit, vacated the Court of Appeals' judgment and remanded to the District Court with directions to dismiss the complaint as moot. 362 U.S. 608, 80 S.Ct. 960, 4 L.Ed.2d 1009 (1960). See Records and Briefs in No. 384, O.T.1958; Records and Briefs in No. 4, O.T. 1959.

10. See, *e. g.,* Gold-Washing & Water Co. v. Keyes, 96 U.S. 199, 24 L.Ed. 656 (1878); Florida C. & P. R. Co. v. Bell, 176 U.S. 321, 20 S.Ct. 399, 44 L.Ed. 486 (1900); Filhiol v. Maurice, 185 U.S. 108, 22 S.Ct. 560, 46 L.Ed. 827 (1902); Filhiol v. Torney, 194 U.S. 356, 24 S.Ct. 698, 48 L.Ed. 1014 (1904); Joy v. City of St. Louis, 201 U.S. 332, 26 S.Ct. 478, 50 L.Ed. 776 (1906); White v. Sparkill Realty Corp., 280 U.S. 500, 50 S.Ct. 186, 74 L.Ed. 578 (1930).

Here, the right to possession itself is claimed to arise under federal law in the first instance. Allegedly, aboriginal title of an Indian tribe guaranteed by treaty and protected by statute has never been extinguished. In *Taylor*, the plaintiffs were individual Indians, not an Indian tribe; and the suit concerned lands allocated to individual Indians, not tribal rights to lands. See 32 Stat. 641. Individual patents had been issued with only the right to alienation being restricted for a period of time. Cf. Minnesota v. United States, 305 U.S. 382, 386 n. 1, 59 S.Ct. 292, 294, 83 L.Ed. 235 (1939); McKay v. Kalyton, 204 U.S. 458, 27 S.Ct. 346, 51 L.Ed. 566 (1907). Insofar as the underlying right to possession is concerned, *Taylor* is more like those cases indicating that "a controversy in respect of lands has never been regarded as presenting a Federal question merely because one of the parties to it has derived his title under an act of Congress." Shulthis v. McDougal, 225 U.S. 561, 570, 32 S.Ct. 704, 707, 56 L.Ed. 1205 (1912).[11] Once patent issues, the incidents of ownership are, for the most part, matters of local property law to be vindicated in local courts, and in such situations it is normally insufficient for "arising under" jurisdiction merely to |677 allege that ownership or possession is claimed under a United States patent. Joy v. City of St. Louis, 201 U.S. 332, 342–343, 26 S.Ct. 478, 481, 50 L.Ed. 776 (1906). As the Court stated in Packer v. Bird, 137 U.S. 661, 669, 11 S.Ct. 210, 212, 34 L.Ed. 819 (1891):

"The courts of the United States will construe the grants of the general government without reference to the rules of construction adopted by the states for their grants; but whatever incidents or rights attach to the ownership of property conveyed by the government will be determined by the states, subject to the condition that their rules do not impair the efficacy of the grants or the use and enjoyment of the property by the grantee."

In the present case, however, the assertion of a federal controversy does not rest solely on the claim of a right to possession derived from a federal grant of title whose scope will be governed by state law. Rather, it rests on the not insubstantial claim that federal law now protects, and has continuously protected from the time of the formation of the United States, possessory rights to tribal lands, wholly apart from the application of state law principles which normally and separately protect a valid right of possession.

[6] For the same reasons, we think the complaint before us satisfies the additional requirement formulated in some cases that the complaint reveal a "dispute or controversy respecting the validity, construction, or effect of such a law, upon the determination of which the result depends." Shulthis v. McDougal, *supra*, 225 U.S. at 569, 32 S.Ct. at 706; Gold-Washing & Water Co. v. Keyes, 96 U.S. 199, 203, 24 L.Ed. 656 (1878).[12] Here, the Oneidas assert a present right to possession based in part on their aboriginal right of occupancy which was not terminable except by act of the United States. Their claim is also asserted to arise from treaties guaranteeing their possessory right until terminated by the United States, and "it is to these treaties [that] we must look to ascertain the nature of these [Indian] rights, and the extent of them." The New York Indians, 5 Wall., at 768, 18 L.Ed. 708. Finally, the complaint asserts a claim under the Nonintercourse Acts which put in statutory form what was or came to be the accepted rule—that the extinguishment of Indian title required the consent of the United States. To us, it is sufficiently clear that the controversy stated in the com- |678

---

11. Florida C. & P. R. Co. v. Bell, *supra*, 176 U.S., at 328–329, 20 S.Ct., at 402; Joy v. City of St. Louis, *supra*, 201 U.S., at 341–342, 26 S.Ct., at 480.

12. Tennessee v. Union & Planters' Bank, 152 U.S. 454, 460, 14 S.Ct. 654, 656, 38 L.Ed. 511 (1894); Joy v. City of St. Louis, *supra*, 201 U.S., at 340, 26 S.Ct., at 480.

plaint arises under the federal law within the meaning of the jurisdictional statutes and our decided cases.

IV

This is not to ignore the obvious fact that New York had legitimate and far-reaching connections with its Indian tribes antedating the Constitution and that the State has continued to play a substantial role with respect to the Indians in that State.[13] There has been recurring tension between federal and state law; state authorities have not easily accepted the notion that federal law and federal courts must be deemed the controlling considerations in dealing with the Indians. Fellows v. Blacksmith, The New York Indians, United States v. Forness, and the *Tuscarora* litigation are sufficient evidence that the reach and exclusivity of federal law with respect to reservation lands and reserva-

tion Indians did not go unchallenged; and it may be that they are to some extent challenged here. But this only underlines the legal reality that the controversy alleged in the complaint may well depend on what the reach and impact of the federal law will prove to be in this case. |679

[7] We are also aware that New York and federal authorities eventually reached partial agreement in 1948 when criminal jurisdiction over New York Indian reservations was ceded to the State. 62 Stat. 1224, 25 U.S.C. § 232. In addition, in 1950 civil disputes between Indians or between Indians and others were placed within the jurisdiction of the state courts "to the same extent as the courts of the State shall have jurisdiction in other civil actions and proceedings, as now or hereafter defined by the laws of such State." 64 Stat. 845, 25 U.S.C. § 233.[14] The latter statute,

13. For brief accounts of the New York experience with its Indians, see Federal Indian Law, 965–979; Gunther, Governmental Power and New York Indian Lands—A Reassessment of a Persistent Problem of Federal-State Relations, 8 Buffalo L.Rev. 1 (1958); Brief for the Warden and the State of New York, New York ex rel. Ray v. Martin, No. 158, O.T.1945, 326 U.S. 496, 66 S.Ct. 307, 90 L.Ed. 261 (1946).

14. Section 233 provides:
"Jurisdiction of New York State courts in civil actions.
"The courts of the State of New York under the laws of such State shall have jurisdiction in civil actions and proceedings between Indians or between one or more Indians and any other person or persons to the same extent as the courts of the State shall have jurisdiction in other civil actions and proceedings, as now or hereafter defined by the laws of such State: *Provided*, That the governing body of any recognized tribe of Indians in the State of New York shall have the right to declare, by appropriate enactment prior to September 13, 1952, those tribal laws and customs which they desire to preserve, which, on certification to the Secretary of the Interior by the governing body of such tribe shall be published in the Federal Register and thereafter shall govern in all civil cases involving reservation Indians when the subject matter of such tribal laws and customs is involved or at issue, but nothing herein contained shall be construed

to prevent such courts from recognizing and giving effect to any tribal law or custom which may be proven to the satisfaction of such courts: *Provided further*, That nothing in this section shall be construed to require any such tribe or the members thereof to obtain fish and game licenses from the State of New York for the exercise of any hunting and fishing rights provided for such Indians under any agreement, treaty, or custom: *Provided further*, That nothing herein contained shall be construed as subjecting the lands within any Indian reservation in the State of New York to taxation for State or local purposes, nor as subjecting any such lands, or any Federal or State annuity in favor of Indians or Indian tribes, to execution on any judgment rendered in the State courts, except in the enforcement of a judgment in a suit by one tribal member against another in the matter of the use or possession of land: *And provided further*, That nothing herein contained shall be construed as authorizing the alienation from any Indian nation, tribe, or band of Indians of any lands within any Indian reservation in the State of New York: *Provided further*, That nothing herein contained shall be construed as conferring jurisdiction on the courts of the State of New York or making applicable the laws of the State of New York in civil actions involving Indian lands or claims with respect thereto which relate to transactions or events transpiring prior to September 13, 1952."

⌐680 however, provided for the preservation of tribal laws and customs and saved Indian reservation lands from taxation and, with certain exceptions, from execution to satisfy state court judgments. Furthermore, it provided that nothing in the statute "shall be construed as authorizing the alienation from any Indian nation, tribe, or band of Indians of any lands within any Indian reservation in the State of New York" or as "conferring jurisdiction on the courts of the State of New York or making applicable the laws of the State of New York in civil actions involving Indian lands or claims with respect thereto which relate to transactions or events transpiring prior to September 13, 1952." The Senate report on the bill disclaimed any intention of "impairing any of their property or rights under existing treaties with the United States." S.Rep.No.1836, 81st Cong., 2d Sess., 2 (1950). Under the penultimate proviso the matter of alienating tribal reservation lands would appear to have been left precisely where it was prior to the Act.[15] Moreover, the ⌐681 final proviso of the statute negativing the application of state law with respect to transactions prior to the adoption of the Act was added by amendment on the floor of the Senate, and its purpose was explained by the gentleman who offered it to be as follows:

"Mr. Chairman, I do not think there will be any objection from any source with regard to this particular amendment. This just assures the Indians of an absolutely fair and impartial determination of any claims they might have had growing out of any relationship they have had with the great State of New York in regard to their lands.

"I think there will be no objection to that; they certainly ought to have a right to have those claims properly adjudicated. . . .

⌐ "In addition thereto, of course, they ⌐682 may go into the Federal courts and adjudicate any differences they have had between themselves and the great State of New York relative to their lands, or claims in regard thereto, and I am sure that the State of New York should have and no doubt will have, no objection to such provision." 96 Cong.Rec. 12460 (1950) (remarks of Congressman Morris).

Our conclusion that this case arises under the laws of the United States is, therefore, wholly consistent with and in furtherance of the intent of Congress as expressed by its grant of civil jurisdiction to the State of New York with the indicated exceptions.[16]

15. "The text and history of the new legislation are replete with indications that congressional consent is necessary to validate the exercise of state power over tribal Indians and, most significantly, that New York cannot unilaterally deprive Indians of their tribal lands or authorize such deprivations. The civil jurisdiction law, to make assurance doubly sure, contains a proviso that explicitly exempts reservations from state and local taxation and that negatives any authorization of 'the alienation from any Indian nation, tribe, or band of Indians of any land within any Indian reservation in the State of New York.' The Senate Committee's report on that law emphasizes that 'State law does not apply to Indians except so far as the United States has given its consent' and points out that the law provides that 'no lands within any reservation be alienated.' During the congressional hearings, most Indian leaders continued to oppose the bills, partly because of fear of state attempts to deprive them of their reservations, despite the New York Joint Committee's repeated assurances. Accordingly, New York's representatives once more disavowed any intention to break up the reservations and, more clearly than some state officials in the history of the controversy, disclaimed any state power to do so. Moreover, both federal and state officials agreed that the bills would retain ultimate federal power over the Indians and that federal guardianship, particularly with respect to property rights, would continue." Gunther, supra, n. 13, 8 Buffalo L.Rev., at 16. (Footnotes omitted.)

16. Because of our determination that the complaint states a controversy arising under the laws of the United States sufficient to invoke the jurisdiction of the District Court under §§ 1331 and 1362, in accordance with prior decisions of this Court, we have no occasion to address and do not reach the con-

The judgment of the Court of Appeals is reversed and the case is remanded for further proceedings consistent with this opinion.

It is so ordered.

Reversed and remanded.

Mr. Justice REHNQUIST, with whom Mr. Justice POWELL joins, concurring.

The majority opinion persuasively demonstrates that the plaintiffs' right to possession in this case was and is rooted firmly in federal law. Thus, I agree that this is not a case which depends for its federal character solely on possible federal defenses or on expected responses to possible defenses. I also agree that the majority decision is consistent with our decision in Gully v. First National Bank, 299 U.S. 109, 57 S.Ct. 96, 81 L.Ed. 70 (1936). However, I think it worthwhile to add a brief concurrence to emphasize that the majority opinion does not disturb the long line of this Court's cases narrowly applying the principles of 28 U.S.C. § 1331 and the well-pleaded complaint rule to possessory land actions brought in federal court.

As the majority seems willing to accept, the complaint in this action is basically one in ejectment. Plaintiffs are out of possession; the defendants are in possession, allegedly wrongfully; and the plaintiffs claim damages because of the allegedly wrongful possession. These allegations appear to meet the pleading requirements for an ejectment action as stated in Taylor v. Anderson, 234 U.S. 74, 34 S.Ct. 724, 58 L.Ed. 1218 (1914). Thus the complaint must be judged according to the rules applicable to such cases.

The federal courts have traditionally been inhospitable forums for plaintiffs asserting federal-question jurisdiction of possessory land claims. The narrow view of the scope of federal-question ju-

risdiction taken by the federal courts in such cases probably reflects a recognition that federal issues were seldom apt to be dispositive of the lawsuit. Commonly, the grant of a land patent to a private party carries with it no guarantee of continuing federal interest and certainly carries with it no indefinitely redeemable passport into federal court. On the contrary, as the majority points out, the land thus conveyed was generally subject to state law thereafter.

Thus, this Court's decisions have established a strict rule that mere allegation of a federal source of title does not convert an ordinary ejectment action into a federal case. As the Court noted in Shoshone Mining Co. v. Rutter, 177 U.S. 505, 507, 20 S.Ct. 726, 44 L.Ed. 864 (1900), "a suit to enforce a right which takes its origin in the laws of the United States is not necessarily one arising under the Constitution or laws of the United States, within the meaning of the jurisdiction clauses, for if it did every action to establish title to real estate (at least in the newer States) would be such a one, as all titles in those States come from the United States or by virtue of its laws." This rule was even applied to cases in which land grants to Indians, subject to limited restrictions on alienation, were involved. See Taylor, supra.

The majority today finds this strict rule inapplicable to this case, and for good reason. In contrast to the typical instance in which the Federal Government conveys land to a private entity, the Government, by transferring land rights to Indian tribes, has not placed the land beyond federal supervision. Rather the Federal Government has shown a continuing solicitude for the rights of the Indians in their land. The Nonintercourse Act of 1790 manifests this concern in statutory form. Thus, the Indians' right to possession in this

tention pressed by petitioners that the Congress, in enacting § 1362 in 1966, 80 Stat. 880, intended to expand the scope of "arising under" jurisdiction in the District Courts, beyond what judicial interpretations

of that language have allowed under § 1331, for that category of suits brought by Indian tribes, in addition to eliminating the amount in controversy requirement when Indian tribes sue.

case is based not solely on the *original* grant of rights in the land but also upon the Federal Government's subsequent guarantee. Their claim is clearly distinguishable from the claims of land grantees for whom the Federal Government has taken no such responsibility.

The opinion for the Court today should give no comfort to persons with garden-variety ejectment claims who, for one reason or another, are covetously eyeing the door to the federal courthouse. The general standards for determining federal jurisdiction, and in particular the standards for evaluating compliance with the well-pleaded complaint rule, will retain their traditional vigor tomorrow as today.

APPENDIX F

JUDGE PORT'S 1977 DECISION

The ONEIDA INDIAN NATION OF NEW YORK STATE, also known as the Oneida Nation of New York, also known as the Oneida Indians of New York, and the Oneida Indian Nation of Wisconsin, also known as the Oneida Tribe of Indians of Wisconsin, Inc., and the Oneida of the Thames Band Council, Plaintiffs,

v.

The COUNTY OF ONEIDA, New York, and the County of Madison, New York, Defendants.

No. 70–CV–35.

United States District Court,
N. D. New York.

July 12, 1977.

Indians brought action against two counties in New York to recover damages for allegedly illegal use of aboriginal land which had been purchased from the Oneida Indians in 1795 by the State of New York in a transaction which allegedly violated the Indian Nonintercourse Act. The District Court, Port, Senior District Judge, held that: (1) good faith in acquiring property will not render good a title which otherwise is not valid for failure to comply with the Nonintercourse Act; (2) purchase in question was in violation of the Nonintercourse Act; (3) Indians had not abandoned the land; (4) the action was timely; (5) neither state statute of limitations nor state doctrines of laches and adverse possession could serve to render valid a transaction which was otherwise invalid under the Nonintercourse Act; (6) complaint was not required to conform to requirements of state law causes of action, and (7) neither the United States nor the State of New York was an indispensable party.

Order accordingly.

1. Indians ⟷15(1)

Good faith in acquisition of property will not render good a title which is otherwise not valid for failure to comply with the Indian Nonintercourse Act. 25 U.S. C.A. § 177.

2. United States ⟷105

Where case brought in district court challenged validity of 1795 purchase of land from Oneida Indians by the State of New York and sought money damages from two New York counties who currently owned the land and allegedly lacked valid title to the land and where suit in the Indian Claims Commission charged the United States with breach of its fiduciary duty to protect the Oneidas in land dealings with the State of New York, pendency of proceedings before the Indian Claims Commission did not preclude the district court action. 25 U.S.C.A. § 177.

3. United States ⟷105

Indian Claims Commission is to consider only claims against the United States; there was no intention to supplant Indian claims against other parties, governmental or private, through creation of the Commission.

4. Indians ⟷27(6)

In order to establish prima facie case under the Nonintercourse Act, plaintiff must show that it is or represents an Indian tribe within the meaning of the Act, that the parcels of land at issue are covered by the Act as tribal land, that the United States has never consented to the alienation of the tribal land, and that the trust relationship between the United States and the tribe, which was established by coverage of the Act, has never been terminated or abandoned. 25 U.S.C.A. § 177.

5. Indians ⟷2

Oneida Indian Nation of New York, which is a tribe presently recognized by the Bureau of Indian Affairs, whose members still receive annuities under 1794 Treaty with the Six Nations, and who, along with the Oneida Indian Nation of Wisconsin and the Oneida of the Thames Band Council, represent direct descendants of the Oneida Indian Nation which inhabited the area in question before and after the passage of the first Nonintercourse Act is a "tribe" within meaning of the Act. 25 U.S.C.A. § 177; Treaty with the Six Nations, 7 Stat. 44.

6. Indians ⊂⇒ 10

Land which was part of an area reserved for the Oneida Indians in earlier treaty with the State of New York, which was occupied by the Oneidas at the time of the enactment of the first Nonintercourse Act, and which was part of the Oneidas' aboriginal land was covered by the Nonintercourse Act. 25 U.S.C.A. § 177.

7. Indians ⊂⇒ 15(2)

Evidence that no United States commissioner was present in Albany when the State of New York consummated cession of certain Indian lands, that the federal agent for the Six Nations had earlier traveled to Oneida to dissuade the Indians from dealing with New York, and that there was no subsequent treaty or Act of Congress ratifying the transaction demonstrated that the United States did not consent to 1795 purchase of land from the Oneidas by the State of New York. 25 U.S.C.A. § 177.

8. Indians ⊂⇒ 3

Termination of congressional responsibility under the Indian Nonintercourse Act must be explicit. 25 U.S.C.A. § 177.

9. Indians ⊂⇒ 15(2)

Federal policy of removal of Oneida Indians from New York did not affect ratification of purchase of Oneida land by the State of New York as required by the Nonintercourse Act. 25 U.S.C.A. § 177.

10. Indians ⊂⇒ 15(2)

Treaty of Buffalo Creek which ceded Indian rights in land only in Wisconsin and which made no reference to Oneida land in New York or any mention of 1795 agreement between the tribe and New York State did not constitute approval of the United States for 1795 purchase of land from the Oneidas by the State of New

York. 25 U.S.C.A. § 177; Treaty of Buffalo Creek, Art. I, 7 Stat. 550.

11. Indians ⊂⇒ 15(2)

Opinion of the Court of Claims which merely decided which Indians would participate in award of damages for disposition of reservation land in Kansas did not establish either federal ratification of 1795 purchase of land from Oneida Indians by the State of New York or abandonment of the New York land by the Oneidas. 25 U.S.C.A. § 177.

12. Indians ⊂⇒ 15(2)

Evidence that Oneidas are a federally recognized Indian nation and that members of the tribe continue to receive annuities under 1794 Treaty with the Six Nations demonstrated that United States had never terminated or abandoned its trust relationship with the United States so that purchase of Oneida land by the State of New York was required to receive federal approval. 25 U.S.C.A. § 177; Treaty with the Six Nations, 7 Stat. 44.

13. Indians ⊂⇒ 3

Nonintercourse Act does not exempt from its coverage states having a right of preemption. 25 U.S.C.A. § 177.

14. Indians ⊂⇒ 15(1)

Purchase by the State of New York of land from the Oneida Indians in 1795 was in violation of the Nonintercourse Act and thus void. 25 U.S.C.A. § 177.

15. Indians ⊂⇒ 15(1)

Oneida Indians who had never abandoned their claim to their aboriginal homeland and who never acquiesced in the loss of their land but rather continued to protest its diminishment had not abandoned land which was purchased from them by the State of New York in 1795 in violation of the Nonintercourse Act. 25 U.S.C.A. § 177.

16. Indians ⊂⇒ 27(4)

Action brought by Oneida Indians to recover damages for allegedly illegal use and occupancy of a part of their aboriginal land by two counties and which was commenced within the time permitted by statute governing actions brought by the United States for or on behalf of Indian tribes was not time barred even though the land was purchased from the Indians, allegedly in violation of the Nonintercourse Act, by the State of New York in 1795. 25 U.S.C.A. § 177; 28 U.S.C.A. § 2415.

17. Indians ⊕27(4)

Statute of limitations governing actions brought by the United States for or on behalf of Indian tribes applies to a case brought by Indian tribes in their own behalf to recover damages for allegedly illegal use of aboriginal land. 28 U.S.C.A. § 2415.

18. Indians ⊕27(4)

State statutes of limitations and state laws of adverse possessions and laches do not bar suit brought by the United States on behalf of an Indian nation; where the United States holds title to land in trust for Indians, adverse possession cannot run against the land.

19. Indians ⊕15(1)

Where individual Indians sue to rescind transfers of restricted Indian land, state defenses cannot render the transactions effective.

20. Indians ⊕15(1)

If transfer of Indian land is void under a federal law, such as the Nonintercourse Act, it cannot later be made valid by operation of state law. 25 U.S.C.A. § 177.

21. Indians ⊕15(1), 27(4)

New York statute of limitations, doctrine of laches, doctrine of adverse possession, or doctrine of bona fide purchaser, could not validate 1795 purchase of land from the Oneida Indians by the State of New York in violation of the Nonintercourse Act. 25 U.S.C.A. § 177.

22. Federal Civil Procedure ⊕219

United States was not an indispensable party to action brought by Oneida Indians against two counties of New York to recover damages for allegedly illegal use of aboriginal land which had been purchased by the State of New York from the Oneidas in 1795 in violation of the Nonintercourse Act.

25 U.S.C.A. § 177; Fed.Rules Civ.Proc. rule 19, 28 U.S.C.A.

23. Federal Civil Procedure ⊕219

State of New York was not an indispensable party in action brought against two New York counties by Oneida Indians to recover damages for allegedly illegal use by the counties of Indian aboriginal land which had been purchased from the Oneidas in 1795 by the State of New York in a transaction which was in violation of the Nonintercourse Act. 25 U.S.C.A. § 177; Fed.Rules Civ.Proc. rule 19, 28 U.S.C.A.; County Law N.Y. § 215.

24. Counties ⊕103

Land which is held by county in New York is not held merely by the county as an agent for the State. County Law N.Y. § 215.

25. Federal Civil Procedure ⊕673

Under the Federal Rules of Civil Procedure, question is not how plaintiff has characterized the form of its action but rather whether plaintiff is entitled to relief. Fed. Rules Civ.Proc. rule 54(c), 28 U.S.C.A.

26. Indians ⊕27(6)

Complaint and proof in action brought by Oneida Indians to recover damages for allegedly illegal use of aboriginal land which had been purchased by the State of New York in 1795 in a transaction which violated the Nonintercourse Act were not required to meet requirements of state law forms of action. 25 U.S.C.A. § 177.

―――――――――

Bond, Schoeneck & King, Syracuse, N.Y., for plaintiffs; George C. Shattuck, Syracuse, N.Y., of counsel.

Donald E. Keinz, Utica, N.Y., for defendant County of Oneida; James P. O'Rourke, Boonville, N.Y., of counsel.

William L. Burke, Hamilton, N.Y., for defendant County of Madison.

MEMORANDUM–DECISION
AND ORDER

PORT, Senior District Judge.

This case tests the consequences of the failure of the State of New York to comply with the provisions of the Indian Nonintercourse Act, enacted by the first Congress in 1790 and reenacted in substance by subsequent Congresses to the present date. 25 U.S.C. § 177. Familiarity with the prior opinions in the case is assumed.[1]

In 1795, the State of New York acquired from the Oneida Indians, by an instrument variously denominated as a deed or treaty, 100,000 acres in Central New York. The counties of Oneida and Madison have acquired and now occupy undesignated but small portions of that acreage. The claim made in this case is limited to damages for the use and occupancy during the years 1968 and 1969 of those "parts of said premises [currently occupied by defendants] for buildings, roads, and other public improvements."[2]

The issues can be summed up as follows: (1) Have the plaintiffs established that the transfer of land by the 1795 treaty to the State of New York was in violation of the Nonintercourse Act? (2) Have any of the defenses asserted by the defendants been established? (3) Are the defendants liable to the plaintiffs for damages resulting from defendants' use and occupancy of part of the subject land during 1968 and 1969? The answer to the first question is yes; to the second, no; and to the third, yes.

[1] Although the present owners of the 100,000 acres may have acted in good faith when acquiring their property, such good faith will not render good a title otherwise not valid for failure to comply with the Nonintercourse Act.

Although it may appear harsh to condemn an apparently good-faith use as a trespass after 90 years of acquiescence by the owners, we conclude that an even older policy of Indian law compels this result.

United States v. Southern Pacific Transportation Co., 543 F.2d 676, 699 (9th Cir. 1976). Furthermore, it is incumbent upon "[g]reat nations, like great men, [to] keep their word." *Federal Power Commission v. Tuscarora Indian Nation,* 362 U.S. 99, 142, 80 S.Ct. 543, 567, 4 L.Ed.2d 584 (1960) (Black, J., dissenting).

The posture in which this case has been presented is reminiscent of *United States v. Forness,* 125 F.2d 928 (2d Cir.), *cert. denied,* 316 U.S. 694, 62 S.Ct. 1293, 86 L.Ed. 1764 (1942), in which the Second Circuit said:

Although there is directly before us only one lease, on which the annual rent is but $4, the question is of greater importance because the Nation, by resolution, has cancelled hundreds of similar leases.

Id. at 930. Likewise, the impact of the Oneidas' claim will reach far beyond the boundaries of the present suit. In my initial decision dismissing the claim for lack of jurisdiction, I pointed out that, "it obvious that there are, of necessity, numerous other parties occupying the balance of the 100,000 acre parcel under title derived from New York State, against whom . . . claims could be made." *Oneida Indian Nation v. County of Oneida,* 70–CV–35, slip op. at 9 n. 3 (N.D.N.Y., November 9, 1971).

Nor is the problem limited to this case,[3] this particular land transaction, the Oneida Indian Nation, or even this area. Other Indian tribes have similar claims[4] in several

---

1. *Oneida Indian Nation v. County of Oneida,* 70–CV–35 (N.D.N.Y. November 9, 1971), *aff'd,* 464 F.2d 916 (2d Cir. 1972), *rev'd,* 414 U.S. 661, 94 S.Ct. 772, 39 L.Ed.2d 73 (1974).

2. Plaintiffs' amended complaint ¶ 22.

3. The Oneida Nations presently have two other actions pending in this district. *Oneida Indian Nation v. County of Oneida,* 74–CV–187 (N.D.N.Y.) (action for damages challenging some 25 treaties with New York State); *Oneida Indian*

Nation v. Williams, 74–CV–167 (N.D.N.Y.) (action for ejectment against 23 landowners).

4. These Indian claims have not all been pursued through the orderly mechanism of litigation. *See New York v. White,* 528 F.2d 336 (2d Cir. 1975). *White* arose out of the seizure of land in the Adirondacks by members of the Mohawk and other Indian tribes.

other states. Litigation brought by the tribes themselves,[5] or by the federal government in their behalf,[6] is already pending. Further suits brought by the United States are imminent. The Department of Justice has alerted the United States Marshal for this district that, unless Congress extends the statute of limitations for such suits beyond July 18, 1977,[7] an action on behalf of the Cayuga and St. Regis Mohawk tribes will be commenced immediately. The Marshal was given this advance notice because it is anticipated that the suit will involve some 10,000 defendants. The potential for disruption in the real estate market is obvious and is already being felt. News reports indicate that title companies have refused to insure titles in areas where Indian land claims exist, even if law suits have not yet been commenced.

5. *Mashpee Tribe v. New Seabury Corp.*, 427 F.Supp. 899 (D.Mass.1977); *Schaghticoke Tribe of Indians v. Kent School Corp.*, 423 F.Supp. 780 (D.Conn.1976); *Narragansett Tribe of Indians v. Southern Rhode Island Land Development Corp.*, 418 F.Supp. 798 (D.R.I.1976).

6. *See Joint Tribal Council of the Passamaquoddy Tribe v. Morton*, 388 F.Supp. 649 (D.Me.), aff'd, 528 F.2d 370 (1st Cir. 1975) (*Passamaquoddy*).

7. *See* 28 U.S.C. § 2415.

8. *See* Tr. 198–99; Exhs. 46–48, 51. The parties have advised the court that the United States plans to institute a suit on behalf of the Oneidas to prosecute the tribe's land claims. *Compare, Passamaquoddy, supra* note 6.

9. The progress of the Oneidas' action in the Indian Claims Commission can be ascertained by reference to the opinions of the Commission. *See* 26 Ind.Cl.Comm. 138 (Aug. 18, 1971); 37 Ind.Cl.Comm. 522 (Mar. 19, 1976), and the intervening opinion of the Court of Claims, *United States v. Oneida Nation of New York*, 477 F.2d 939, 201 Ct.Cl. 546 (1973). In their answer, defendants raised as an affirmative defense the pendency of proceedings before the Indian Claims Commission. They allege that, "[t]his issue is presently before the . . . Commission." Defendants' answers ¶ 11. The simple rejoinder to this defense is that the same issue is not before this court and the Commission. The case at bar challenges the validity of the 1795 purchase of Oneida land; it seeks money damages from the defendants, present landowners who allegedly lack

[2, 3] The greater part of the disruption and individual hardships caused by litigation such as this could be avoided by seeking solutions through other available vehicles. This in no way is intended to be critical of the plaintiffs' conduct. The trial of this case demonstrated that they have patiently for many years sought a remedy by other means—but to no avail. The aid of the United States as guardian has been sought for the purpose of instituting claims against the State of New York, to challenge not only the 1795 sale but other treaties with the state.[8] The remedy afforded by Congress against the United States for alleged breach of trust has been and is presently being pursued before the Indian Claims Commission.[9] Finally, it is within the power of Congress to dispose of the matter under the constitutional delegation of power.[10]

valid title to the land. The suit in the Indian Claims Commission charges the United States with breach of its fiduciary duty to protect the Oneidas in land dealings with the State of New York. *United States v. Oneida Nation of New York*, 477 F.2d 939, 201 Ct.Cl. 546 (1973). Although these are separate claims, recovery against the United States might well render any other suit academic.

A more important question, whether the Indian Claims Commission was created to provide an exclusive remedy for redress of wrongs to the Indian nations, was not raised by defendants but deserves comment. The Indian Claims Commission was created in 1946 "to right a continuing wrong to our Indian citizens", H.R.Rep.No.1466, 79th Cong., 2d Sess. (1945); 1946 U.S.C.C.S. 1347, by creating a forum for Indian claims against the United States. The legislative history makes clear that the Commission was to consider only claims against the United States; no intent to supplant Indian claims against other parties, governmental or private, is evidenced. In discussing the nature of the claims to be considered by the Indian Claims Commission, the House Report mentions solely claims against the federal government. *See Id.* Section 1; 1946 U.S.C.C.S. 1350–51.

10. *See* U.S.Const. art. I, § 8; *Federal Power Commission v. Tuscarora Indian Nation*, 362 U.S. 99, 80 S.Ct. 543, 4 L.Ed.2d 584 (1960); *United States v. Santa Fe Pacific Railroad Co.*, 314 U.S. 339, 62 S.Ct. 248, 86 L.Ed. 260 (1941); *cf. Rosebud Sioux Tribe v. Kneip*, 430 U.S. 584, 97 S.Ct. 1361, 51 L.Ed.2d 660 (1977).

The aptness of what was recently said by Chief Judge Kaufman is striking. "As in so many cases in which a political solution is preferable, the parties find themselves in a court of law." *British Airways Board v. Port Authority of New York and New Jersey,* 558 F.2d 75 at 78 (2d Cir. 1977).

I. NATURE OF THE PROCEEDING

The Oneida Indian Nations are suing for damages arising from the allegedly illegal use and occupancy of a part of their aboriginal land. In 1795, the State of New York purchased a large tract of the aboriginal land of the Oneida Nation. Plaintiffs claims that this purchase violated United States treaties and the Indian Nonintercourse Act, 25 U.S.C. § 177. Therefore, plaintiffs contend that the purchase was void and of no effect.

Part of the 1795 purchase is now occupied by the defendant counties. Plaintiffs measure their damages by the fair rental value of such land for the years 1968 and 1969, the period covered by the complaint.

II. BACKGROUND

The action was commenced in 1970. Following a motion for summary judgment by the defendants, this court dismissed the action for lack of federal jurisdiction. It was decided that diversity of citizenship was absent, 28 U.S.C. § 1332, and that federal question jurisdiction was lacking because the case did not "[arise] under the Constitution, laws, or treaties of the United States." 28 U.S.C. § 1331(a). This court held that the federal question failed to appear on the face of the complaint; it only appeared in anticipation of various defenses. The Court of Appeals affirmed, holding that the jurisdictional claim "shatters on the rock of the 'well-pleaded complaint' rule." *Oneida Indian Nation v. County of Oneida,* 464 F.2d 916, 918 (2d Cir. 1972). However, the Supreme Court reversed, stating that plaintiffs'

assertion of a federal controversy . . . rests on the not insubstantial claim that

federal law now protects, and has continuously protected from the time of the formation of the United States, possessory right to tribal lands, wholly apart from the application of state law principles which normally and separately protect a valid right of possession.

Oneida Indian Nation v. County of Oneida, 414 U.S. 661, 677, 94 S.Ct. 772, 782, 39 L.Ed.2d 73 (1974). Because the "Oneidas assert a present right to possession based in part on their aboriginal right of occupancy", *Id.,* the complaint on its face raises a federal question.

After remand, plaintiffs moved for summary judgment, but the motion was denied summarily. I held that summary judgment was inappropriate in such a complex and far-reaching case; a full exploration of all the facts was in order. However, trial of the issues was trifurcated. The parties agreed to try the issue of liability first, reserving the question of damages and that of liability of the State of New York to the defendant counties for later disposition.[11] Subsequently, the plaintiffs developed their proof, largely through documentary exhibits, in a three day trial. The defendants, relying only on the plaintiffs' proof and the law, submitted no evidence.

III. FACTS

The Parties

Originally, there were two plaintiffs, the Oneida Indian Nation of New York and the Oneida Indian Nation of Wisconsin. During the trial, plaintiffs moved to amend their complaint to join the Oneida of the Thames Band Council, a band of Oneidas from Ontario, Canada, as party plaintiffs. The motion was granted.

The three plaintiffs are the direct descendants of the Oneida Indian Nation which inhabited Central New York prior to the Revolutionary War. According to expert testimony, this conclusion is supported by extensive research into the kinship and genealogies of the Oneida Nation. (Tr. 63–66, 163–65). Furthermore, the United

---

11. Transcript (Tr.) 8–9.

States is presently paying annuities, which are owed to the Oneida Nation under the Treaty with the Six Nations, executed on November 11, 1794, to the Oneidas in New York and Wisconsin. The Wisconsin Oneidas receive their payments in cash, and the New York Oneidas in cloth. (Tr. 25–26). Also, the Bureau of Indian Affairs recognizes both the Wisconsin and New York Oneidas as the successors in interest to the Oneida Nation of 1794. (Tr. 26, Exh. 49).

This finding is not disturbed by defendants' allegations that the present leadership of the Oneida Nation of New York is in dispute. Regardless of which individuals hold office within the tribe, the tribe is recognized as the direct descendant of the Oneida Nation which inhabited New York 200 years ago. Nothing else is required.

The defendants are the Counties of Oneida and Madison. The parties agree that the defendants now occupy and claim to be the record owners of part of the aboriginal Oneida land, more specifically, part of that area of Oneida land purchased by New York State in 1795.

Historical Background

The Oneidas' aboriginal land ran from the Pennsylvania border north to the St. Lawrence River, from the shores of Lake Ontario to the western foothills of the Adirondack Mountains. (Tr. 69). This region can be described as a band, about fifty miles wide, running north-south through eastern central New York. According to the records of the earliest white missionaries who came to upstate New York, the Oneidas were occupying this land during the early 17th Century. (Tr. 69, 137). They continued to occupy this land until shortly after the birth of the United States.

During the Revolutionary War, the Oneidas fought alongside the Colonists against the British. (Tr. 73). Aside from their service as scouts and their active participation in various battles in upstate New York, the Oneidas performed another valuable function for the Colonies—they prevented the Six Nations or Iroquois from taking a unified stand as allies of the British. (Tr. 73). The Iroquois were the most influential and powerful tribe in the Northeast and had traditionally been an ally of the British.[12] At the outset of the Revolutionary War, the Colonial government sought to secure the neutrality of the Iroquois. Although this result was not achieved, at least the Iroquois did not fight in unison against the Colonists. Because the Oneidas and Tuscaroras allied themselves with the Colonists, the Six Nations put out the council fires and permitted each nation to choose its ally independently.

After the War, the new nation sought to reward and protect its valuable ally, the Oneida Nation. The Treaty of Fort Stanwix, executed in 1784 to make peace with the Six Nations, expressly secured the Oneidas "in the possession of the lands on which they are settled." (Exh. 1).[13] A few years later, in further thanks for their help, the federal government commissioned, post facto, several Oneidas as officers in the United States Army. (Tr. 88, Exh. 11). Twice again, in treaties between the Six Nations and the United States, the federal government secured the Oneidas in the possession of their land.[14]

However, in 1788, because of increasing pressures to open up the Oneidas' land to settlement, the State of New York purchased the great majority of the Oneidas' land from them. They were left with a reservation of about 300,000 acres in the area southwest of Oneida Lake. This reservation is outlined in Exh. 7 and the parties have stipulated that the land involved in this suit lies within the boundaries of this 1788 reservation.

---

12. *See* F. Cohen, *Handbook of Federal Indian Law* 417–418 (University of New Mexico Press reprint of 1942 Ed.) (hereinafter, *Federal Indian Law*).

13. Treaty of Fort Stanwix (October 22, 1784) 7 Stat. 15

14. Treaty at Fort Harmar (January 9, 1789) 7 Stat. 33 (Exh. 3); Treaty with the Six Nations (November 11, 1794) 7 Stat. 44 (Exh. 4).

In 1790, Congress passed the first Indian Nonintercourse Act (the Act). That statute prohibited any land transactions with Indian tribes that were not executed by public treaty under the authority of the United States. 1 Stat. 137–38 (Exh. 10). In 1793, the Act was amended into substantially its present form. The gist of the Act remains the same—unless by treaty with the United States or under the authority of the United States, no purchase or grant of land from an Indian tribe "shall be of any validity." 25 U.S.C. § 177.

The 1795 Purchase

By 1795 a conflict had developed between the United States and the State of New York over the State's power to negotiate purchases of land from the Oneidas. The federal policy toward the Oneidas remained the same—the government intended to reward them for past services and to protect them from predation by the white settlers. (Exhs. 17, 19). New York, however, desired to purchase the Oneidas' land, along with the land of many other Indian nations within its borders. Secretary of War, Timothy Pickering, wrote to United States Attorney General William Bradford for an opinion on whether or not New York had the power to purchase Indian land without the intervention of the United States government. The Attorney General responded by stating the language of the Nonintercourse Act was "too express to admit of any doubt upon the question." (Exh. 22). The Act applied to New York. In his opinion Bradford did not question New York's right to land ceded to the State by treaty entered into prior to the adoption of the Constitution of the United States. However, as to the land reserved to the Oneidas under those treaties, he held that the Oneidas' rights could not be extinguished except "by a treaty holden under the authority of the United States, and in the manner prescribed by the laws of Congress." (Id.)

Pickering had been informed that New York was attempting to purchase land from the Cayuga, Onondaga and Oneida Nations. In June of 1795, he wrote to Israel Chapin,

Jr., Superintendent of the Affairs of the Six Nations, ordering him not to aid New York in these purchases. Chapin was further instructed to warn the Six Nations of the illegality of any such transactions with New York. Finally, noting that New York's Governor Clinton refused to request federal commissioners, Pickering hoped that the situation would improve when the new governor, John Jay, took office. (Exh. 24). The hope remained only a hope. In July, Jay wrote Pickering that, "on *this* occasion I think I should forbear officially to consider and decide" whether the "Act of 1 March 1793" was constitutional or whether the conduct of New York violated either the United States Constitution or the 1793 Nonintercourse Act. He observed, however, that under the New York Constitution, transactions with Indian tribes must be pursuant to acts of the Legislature; that the enabling legislation in this instance was silent "[a]s to any intervention or concurrence of the United States", nor did it "by implication direct or authorize the Governor to apply for such intervention." (Exh. 26). Jay noted that arrangements for the meeting with the Six Nations planned for later that summer were finished "before I came into office." (Id.)

Within a week, however, Jay wrote Pickering and requested the appointment of United States Commissioners to negotiate a treaty between New York and the St. Regis Indians. (Exh. 28). In a letter to President Washington, suggesting that a commissioner be appointed for the treaty with the St. Regis, Pickering pointed out New York's inconsistent policy for negotiating with Indians. The State was complying with statutory requirements for the St. Regis, but refused to do so when dealing with the Six Nations. (Exh. 29). The reasons for these differing approaches are nowhere made specific. However, Dr. Jack Campisi, a professor of anthropology and an expert on the Oneida Nations, suggested why New York acted as it had. He stated that New York perceived a difference in federal treatment of different Indian tribes. Since the Oneidas and the United States had been allies, the federal government felt bound to protect their interests. Tribes that had allied with the British received less federal protection. Consequently, New York complied with the Nonintercourse Act when negotiating with previously hostile Indians, but refused to do so when dealing with the friendly Oneidas. The State feared excessive federal protective intervention in the latter case.

In July, New York purchased the Cayuga and Oneida reservations for sums to be paid annually. The tribes were left with small parcels of land. (Exh. 31). When the New York Commissioners then moved on to the Village of Oneida, intending to purchase the Oneidas' land, Chapin travelled to Oneida hoping to dissuade the Indians from dealing with the State. (*Id.*). At Oneida, he informed the tribe of the federal government's opinion of the illegality of such a transaction. (Exh. 32). He remained there for nine days and no deal was made. After leaving Oneida, Chapin was informed that the state commissioners left two days later, having been unable to reach any agreement with the tribe. (*Id.*). Late in August, Pickering wrote Chapin and informed him that he had acted properly in warning the Oneidas of the illegality of any purchase by New York. However, Pickering then told Chapin that "having done this much, the business might there be left." (Exh. 33). Chapin was instructed to leave matters as they stood.

Despite another letter from Pickering to Governor Jay, outlining the procedure to be followed under the Nonintercourse Act of 1793 (Exh. 34), the State continued to negotiate with the Oneidas. These negotiations culminated in a sale contrary to the provisions of the Act on September 15, 1795 by the Oneidas of approximately 100,000 acres of their reservation. (Exhs. 6, 35). The papers transferring the land were signed at Albany, which was not within the boundaries of the Oneidas' aboriginal land. (Exh. 35). Although the Six Nations had met with the British at Albany, the Oneida Nation had never before executed any treaty or land transaction there. (Tr. 111a–112a).

Another irregularity in the transaction appears from the record. Ordinarily, treaties were entered into by tribal consensus (Tr. 188–89), by unanimous decision of the tribe. In this case, powers of attorney were executed enabling certain individuals, none of them chiefs, to negotiate the transaction at Albany. (Tr. 189). Also, although women were not allowed to speak at the tribal council (Tr. 190), half of those Oneidas signing the power of attorney were women. (Tr. 189). Finally, the names of the sachems and chiefs that appear on the September 15, 1795 document were not the signatures of Oneida chiefs. Rather, the signatories of the documents merely used the traditional Oneida names for their sachems and chiefs. (Tr. 192).

In the opinion of Dr. Campisi, no United States Commissioner was present in Albany when the State purchased this land from the Oneidas. (Tr. 126). Superintendent Chapin's expense account shows no expenses incurred in Albany in September of 1795. (Exh. 36). Defendants have presented no evidence demonstrating or even suggesting that a United States Commissioner was present. There is no record that Governor Jay ever requested a commissioner for this transaction. The only finding permitted by the record before me is that no United States Commissioner or other official of the federal government was present at the September 15, 1795 transaction.

Developments after 1795

After 1795, New York State continued to negotiate with the Oneidas for the purchase of their land. Between 1795 and 1846, 25 treaties were executed between the State and the Oneida Nation. Only two of these treaties were conducted under federal supervision as required by the Nonintercourse Act.[15] By 1846, the Oneidas' landholdings in New York had been diminished to a few hundred acres. (Tr. 267).

The social and economic pressures on the Oneidas naturally resulted in the alienation of their land. (Tr. 127–131). In addition,

---

15. *See United States v. Oneida Nation of New York*, 477 F.2d 939, 201 Ct.Cl. 546 (1973).

white settlers living in the areas continually encroached on the Oneidas' land. (Tr. 232–233). Land speculators were always urging the Oneidas to sell their reservations. At the same time, New York began agitating for the removal of the Oneidas and other Indians to western lands.[16] The policy of removal was not universally accepted among the Oneidas, and the problem was exacerbated by the efforts of outsiders, clergy and advisors, to urge the Oneidas to move west. (Tr. 131). The Oneida Nation was split into several factions by these pressures. As a result, by the 1840's, three distinct bands of Oneidas existed. One band stayed on the remaining Oneida reservation land in New York; one group of almost 600 had settled on about 65,000 acres in Wisconsin; and another group of about 400 had moved to Ontario, Canada.

Unfortunately, the pressures on the Oneidas to part with their land did not cease once removal had been effected. The Oneidas' meager landholdings in New York were reduced further as a result of a New York statute which divided the tribal landholdings and gave the Oneidas an option to sell their land. (Tr. 227). This option to sell, coupled with the state of extreme poverty in which they lived, more or less forced the sale of much of the remaining Indian land. The loss of land in Wisconsin was much more drastic. In 1887, the Dawes Act, or General Allotment Act, was enacted by Congress. (24 Stat. 388, February 8, 1887). This Act broke up tribal landholdings, distributed individual parcels to individual Indian families, and removed restrictions on the transfer of title.[17] Again, because of the poverty of the Oneidas, they then lost their land through sales, tax sales, or mortgage foreclosures. By the time of the depression, the extent of the Wisconsin Oneidas' landholdings had decreased from 65,000 acres to approximately 600. (Tr. 132, 203, 220).

These forces which acted to deprive the Oneidas of their land had a similar adverse impact on the social conditions of the Onei-

da Nation. After the Revolutionary War, the Oneida Nation was extremely disorganized because of the displacements which had occurred during the many years of fighting, first against the French and later against the British. (Tr. 128). The tribe was suffering from famine and widespread alcoholism. (Tr. 130). The poverty they then experienced became locked in a vicious circle with the loss of their land. These problems were complicated by the Oneidas' illiteracy. Prior to 1800, at the time the great mass of their land was lost, only a few Oneidas had even a minimal ability to understand English orally. (Tr. 129). None could read or write. This state continued through the early 1800's, during the time of removal. (Tr. 218). In fact, up through the 1950's, a translator was needed at meetings of the Oneida Nation of Wisconsin in order to explain actions of the federal government. (Tr. 225). The modest attempts to educate the Oneidas must be viewed, in retrospect, as failures. There were schools established by missionaries on the New York reservation by 1796 and on the Wisconsin land by 1907. (Tr. 264). However, these schools had little or no impact on the Oneidas' illiteracy. It was not until 1928 that the first person graduated from the eighth grade from the mission school for the Oneidas in Wisconsin. (*Id.*)

Despite these conditions of poverty and illiteracy, and although their attempts to redress grievances were totally futile, the Oneidas did protest the continuing loss of their tribal land. These efforts were not documented prior to 1909. However, expert witnesses testified that between 1840 and 1875 the Oneidas often attempted to petition the federal government. (Tr. 234). Usually, such petitioning was conducted through the Oneidas' Indian agent. On one occasion, in 1874, a group of Oneidas travelled from Wisconsin to Albany, New York and consulted with a private law firm. All of these efforts were to no avail. (Tr. 234–38). Between 1909 and 1965, the Oneidas contacted the federal government innu-

16. *Federal Indian Law* 420.

17. *Id.* at 206–17.

merable times in connection with land claims and other grievances. (*See* Exhibits 54, 55).

IV. PLAINTIFFS' CLAIM

The plaintiffs' claim is uncomplicated. The complaint alleged that from time immemorial down to the time of the American Revolution the Oneidas had owned and occupied some six million acres of land in the State of New York. The complaint also alleged that in the 1780's and 1790's various treaties had been entered into between the Oneidas and the United States confirming the Indians' right to possession of their lands until purchased by the United States [18] and that in 1790 the treaties had been implemented by federal statute, the Nonintercourse Act, 1 Stat. 137, forbidding the conveyance of Indian lands without the consent of the United States. It was then alleged that in 1788 the Oneidas had ceded five million acres to the State of New York, 300,000 acres being withheld as a reservation, and that in 1795 a portion of these reserved lands was also ceded to the State. Assertedly, the 1795 cession was without the consent of the United States and hence ineffective to terminate the Indians' right to possession under the federal treaties [19] and the applicable federal statutes. Also alleging that the 1795 cession was for an unconscionable and inadequate price and that portions of the premises were now in possession of and being used by the defendant counties, the complaint prayed for damages representing the fair rental value of the land for the period January 1, 1968, through December 31, 1969.

18. *See* notes 13 and 14 *supra*.

19. Plaintiffs claim relief under both the Treaty and the Nonintercourse Act. Since relief is afforded under the statute, it is unnecessary to decide whether the plaintiffs are afforded a claim against these defendants for the alleged treaty violation.

Oneida Indian Nation v. County of Oneida, 414 U.S. 661, 663–65, 94 S.Ct. 772, 775, 39 L.Ed.2d 73 (1974) (footnote omitted).

V. NONINTERCOURSE ACT VIOLATION

Since its enactment in 1790 to the present time, the Nonintercourse Act has not materially changed. It is now codified at 25 U.S.C. § 177. It provides:

No purchase, grant, lease, or other conveyance of lands, or of any title or claim thereto, from any Indian nation or tribe of Indians, shall be of any validity in law or equity, unless the same be made by treaty or convention entered into pursuant to the Constitution. Every person who, not being employed under the authority of the United States, attempts to negotiate such treaty or convention, directly or indirectly, or to treat with any such nation or tribe of Indians for the title or purchase of any lands by them held or claimed, is liable to a penalty of $1,000. The agent of any State who may be present at any treaty held with Indians under the authority of the United States, in the presence and with the approbation of the commissioner of the United States appointed to hold the same, may, however, propose to, and adjust with, the Indians the compensation to be made for their claim to lands within such State, which shall be extinguished by treaty.

[4] *Mashpee Tribe v. New Seabury Corp.,* 427 F.Supp. 899 (D.Mass.1977) (*Mashpee*), is an action similar to this case. The plaintiff tribe seeks a declaratory judgment establishing its right to certain land in Massachusetts allegedly obtained from it in violation of the Nonintercourse Act. In addressing a motion to dismiss the complaint, the court stated that in order to establish a prima facie case,

. . . plaintiff must show that:

1) it is or represents an Indian "tribe" within the meaning of the Act;

2) the parcels of land at issue herein are covered by the Act as tribal land;

3) the United States has never consented to the alienation of the tribal land;

4) the trust relationship between the United States and the tribe, which is established by coverage of the Act, has never been terminated or abandoned.

Id. at 902.

In considering these four factors, attention will focus principally upon the facts relating to the Oneida Indian Nation of New York.[20]

[5] The Oneida Indian Nation of New York has clearly established itself as a tribe within the meaning of the Nonintercourse Act. It is a tribe presently recognized by the Bureau of Indian Affairs.[21] The New York Oneidas still receive annuities under the 1794 Treaty with the Six Nations.[22] Furthermore, they, and the other plaintiffs as well, are the direct descendants of the Oneida Indian Nation which inhabited the area in question before and after the passage of the first Nonintercourse Act. The Act was intended to protect the Oneida Nation. *See Joint Tribunal Council of the Passamaquoddy Tribe v. Morton,* 528 F.2d 370 (1st Cir. 1975) (*Passamaquoddy*).

[6] The land involved is covered by the Act. The land purchased in 1795 was part of an area reserved for the Oneidas in an earlier treaty with New York State and occupied by them at the time of the enactment of the first Nonintercourse Act. The tract was part of the Oneidas' aboriginal land. The Supreme Court has specified that Indian title in their aboriginal land is entitled to federal protection. *Oneida Indian Nation v. County of Oneida,* 414 U.S. 661, 666–69, 94 S.Ct. 772, 39 L.Ed.2d 73 (1974). Furthermore, this land was secured to the Oneidas in three treaties with the United States, including the 1794 Treaty with the Six Nations.[23] The aboriginal home land of the Oneidas, later confirmed

in treaties with the United States Government, is certainly land covered by the Nonintercourse Act, 25 U.S.C. § 177. Therefore, a fiduciary relationship exists between the plaintiffs and the United States. *United States v. Oneida Nation of New York,* 477 F.2d 939, 201 Ct.Cl. 546 (1973).

[7] The proof clearly establishes that the United States never consented to the 1795 purchase. No United States commissioner was present in Albany when New York consummated this cession.[24] In fact, the federal agent for the Six Nations, Israel Chapin, Jr., had earlier traveled to Oneida to dissuade the Indians from dealing with New York. No evidence of any subsequent treaty or act of Congress ratifying the transaction was offered. The federal consent required by the Nonintercourse Act was not obtained before or after the fact.

[8, 9] Defendants argue that federal consent to this purchase was manifested by the subsequent conduct of the United States government. Defendants first raise the broad claim that the federal policy of removal of the Indians[25] validated the 1795 transfer. This broad argument misconceives the nature of Congressional approval required. Termination of Congressional responsibility under the Nonintercourse Act must be explicit. "[A]ny withdrawal of trust obligations by Congress would have to have been 'plain and unambiguous' to be effective." *Passamaquoddy, supra,* 528 F.2d at 380 (footnote omitted). *See also United States v. Santa Fe Pacific Railroad Co.,* 314 U.S. 339, 346, 62 S.Ct. 248, 86 L.Ed. 260 (1941). Adoption of defendants' argument would emasculate the Nonintercourse Act. The policy of removal, in and of itself, did not effect ratification. Neither did the government's alleged awareness of subsequent transactions between the Oneidas and New York State, *see United States v.*

20. Since this phase of the trial is solely to determine liability, the rights of the individual plaintiffs to share in a recovery can be left for another day.

21. Tr. 26.

22. Tr. 25–26.

23. *See* notes 13 and 14 *supra.*

24. *See* text *supra* at 12–13.

25. *See Federal Indian Law* 420.

Oneida Nation of New York, 477 F.2d 939, 201 Ct.Cl. 546 (1973), constitute a ratification of the 1795 purchase. Again, defendants can point to no "plain and unambiguous" expression of federal approval.

Defendants see in the 1838 Treaty of Buffalo Creek[26] and its treatment in *New York Indians v. United States,* 170 U.S. 1, 18 S.Ct. 531, 42 L.Ed. 927 (1898), "an explicit recognition and implicit ratification"[27] by Congress of the 1795 purchase, among others. They see a mirage rather than an oasis. The federal government's policy of removal began affecting the Oneidas shortly after 1810. Initially, some Oneidas moved to Wisconsin, where they received a large tract of land ceded by the Menominee and Winnebago tribes.[28] Other Oneidas moved to Canada.[29] The Wisconsin land with some exception was later "cede[d] and relinquish[ed] to the United States" in exchange for a large tract of land in Kansas. Treaty of Buffalo Creek, Article 1, 7 Stat. 551.

[10, 11] An examination of the Buffalo Creek Treaty and the *New York Indians* case fails to support the defendants' interpretation. On its face, the Treaty of Buffalo Creek ceded Indian rights in land in Wisconsin only; no mention was made of Oneida land in New York State. Neither is there any mention of the 1795 agreement with New York. This is a particularly significant omission in view of the strenuous efforts made by the United States through President Washington and Secretary of War Pickering to enforce compliance with the Nonintercourse Act. (*See* Exhs. 17, 24). In light of the diametrically opposed views of the Governor of New York and the Central Government as to the applicability of the Nonintercourse Act to the 1795 transaction, (*compare* Exh. 22 *with* Exh. 26), it is hardly likely that the Treaty of Buffalo Creek would have ratified the agreement implicitly instead of expressly. Had there been a desire to legitimatize a transaction theretofore regarded as a contravention of the Nonintercourse Act, the opportunity was presented without question by the Treaty of Buffalo Creek. Article 13, headed "Special Provisions for the Oneidas Residing in the State of New York", 7 Stat. 554, not only presented a logical and convenient place for such a provision, but even suggested it if the parties, in fact, had it in mind. Furthermore, there was resistance among the Oneidas to the removal policy initially,[30] and to the arrangements specified in the Treaty of Buffalo Creek. This resistance to removal was a factor that brought about the dispute resulting in the *New York Indians* case.

The difficult point in the case, in its equitable aspect, is whether the protests of the Indians and their final refusal to remove in 1846 do not estop them from claiming the benefit of the reservation made for them [in Kansas].

New York Indians, supra, 170 U.S. at 28, 18 S.Ct. at 538.[31]

---

26. Treaty of Buffalo Creek (January 15, 1838) 7 Stat. 550.

27. Defendant County of Madison's Post-Trial Memorandum 32.

28. *See Federal Indian Law* 420

29. Tr. 130–32, 163–65.

30. Tr. 130–32.

31. Defendants' assertion that the Court of Claims' opinion in *New York Indians v. United States,* 40 Ct.Cl. 448 (1905), established either federal ratification of the 1795 purchase or abandonment of the Oneidas' New York land is equally unsupportable. That opinion merely decided which Indians would participate in the award of damages for the disposition of their reservation in Kansas. The right to such damages had been established by the Supreme Court in *New York Indians v. United States,* 170 U.S. 1, 18 S.Ct. 531, 42 L.Ed. 927 (1898). The Court of Claims held that the Ontario Oneidas were entitled to share in the recovery. At no point did the court find that the New York Oneidas had abandoned their rights to their land in New York. In discussing the unsuccessful nature of the Treaty of Buffalo Creek, the Court noted that:

> None of the tribes moved or was removed to the country set apart; none of them made a demand or request for removal; some of them positively refused to remove when requested by agents and commissioners of the United States; others of them denied that they were parties to the treaty and averred that it had been procured in their names by corruption and fraud.

In a similar context, the Supreme Court refused to infer that Congress extinguish the Walapais Indians' rights in their aboriginal land when it established a new reservation for the Walapais and other Indian tribes.

We find no indication that Congress by creating that reservation intended to extinguish all of the rights which the Walapais had in their ancestral home. That Congress could have effected such an extinguishment is not doubted. But an extinguishment cannot be lightly implied in view of the avowed solicitude of the Federal Government for the welfare of its Indian wards. As stated in *Choate v. Trapp*, 224 U.S. 665, 675, [32 S.Ct. 565, 569, 56 L.Ed. 941], the rule of construction recognized without exception for over a century has been that "doubtful expressions, instead of being resolved in favor of the United States, are to be resolved in favor of a weak and defenseless people, who are wards of the nation, and dependent wholly upon its protection and good faith."

United States v. Santa Fe Pacific Railroad Co., 314 U.S. 339, 353–54, 62 S.Ct. 248, 255, 86 L.Ed. 260 (1941) (footnote omitted).

[12] The fourth element is proof that the trust relationship between the Oneidas and the United States was never terminated or abandoned.[32] The uncontradicted evidence establishes that this is so. The Oneidas are today a federally recognized Indian nation.[33] Furthermore, they continue to receive annuities under the 1794 Treaty with the Six Nations.[34] Defendants have introduced no evidence whatsoever of any plain

and unambiguous withdrawal of Congress' trust obligations. See *Passamaquoddy, supra*, 528 F.2d at 380.

A prima facie case of violation of the Nonintercourse Act, 25 U.S.C. § 177, has been established.

[13, 14] Two additional points urged by the defendants should be noted. In reliance on *United States v. Franklin County*, 50 F.Supp. 152 (N.D.N.Y.1943), defendant County of Oneida construes the Nonintercourse Act as exempting from its coverage states "having a right of preemption", such as New York. In the light of later decisions, this holding of *Franklin County* cannot be considered authoritative. "The rudimentary propositions that Indian title is a matter of federal law and can be extinguished only with federal consent shall apply in all of the states including the original 13." *Oneida Indian Nation v. County of Oneida*, 414 U.S. 661, 670, 94 S.Ct. 772, 778, 39 L.Ed.2d 73 (1974); *see also United States v. Oneida Nation of New York*, 477 F.2d 939, 943–44, 201 Ct.Cl. 546 (1973); *Seneca Indian Nation v. New York*, 397 F.Supp. 685 (W.D.N.Y.1975).

Franklin County's description of the Act as "at most regulatory, designed to prevent fraud", *Franklin County, supra*, 50 F.Supp. at 156, and that conclusion that the Act, by its terms, does not require the presence of a United States Commissioner at a treaty as "a prerequisite to its validity", *Id.*, is also urged. The plaintiffs contend that a purchase of land in violation of the act is totally void, whether the Indian nation was defrauded or whether the consideration paid for the land was inadequate.[35] The

---

New York Indians v. United States, 40 Ct.Cl. 448, 451 (1905).

32. The essential elements of a prima facie case under the Nonintercourse Act trace their ancestry to *Passamaquoddy, supra*. See *Mashpee, supra*, 427 F.Supp. at 902. Obviously, this fourth element was essential to plaintiffs' claim in *Passamaquoddy*, for the main issue there was whether a trust relationship existed between the United States and the Passamaquoddy tribe. Although I entertain doubts as to the need for proof of this element in an action brought by the tribe itself, the question is academic in this case since the trust relationship

between the United States and the Oneidas has clearly never been terminated or abandoned.

33. Tr. 26, Exh. 49.

34. Treaty with the Six Nations (November 11, 1794) 7 Stat. 44. *See* Tr. 25–26.

35. At a pre-trial conference, it was stipulated that inadequacy or lack of consideration is not relevant to either plaintiffs' claims or defendants' affirmative defenses, insofar as issues of liability are concerned. This stipulation does not extend to the damages phase of the trial. (Tr. 7).

language of the statute and cases which consider other transfers of restricted Indian land compel the conclusion that the statute renders the 1795 purchase void.

The Nonintercourse Act states that no purchase of Indian land, unless made by treaty or convention pursuant to the Constitution, "shall be of *any validity* in law or equity." 25 U.S.C. § 177 (emphasis added). Any person not employed or authorized by the United States Government who even attempts to negotiate such a purchase can be fined. *Id.* The language of Congress is plain. The statute makes no reference to overreaching or fraud or inadequate consideration. By prohibiting all unauthorized dealings with Indians, it cuts off any inquiry into the fairness of such dealings insofar as the validity of the resulting transfer is concerned.

When Indian land has been transferred contrary to the terms of Congressional enactment, the Supreme Court has not hesitated to void the transaction. In *Bunch v. Cole,* 263 U.S. 250, 44 S.Ct. 101, 68 L.Ed. 290 (1923), a Cherokee Indian leased his land in violation of Congressional restrictions. The Court held the lease void and further held that an Oklahoma statute creating a tenancy-at-will was invalid as applied to the land. In *Ewert v. Bluejacket,* 259 U.S. 129, 42 S.Ct. 442, 66 L.Ed. 858 (1922), a Quapaw Indian sold allotted land in accordance with a statute permitting alienation but prohibiting any person such as the purchaser, an Indian agent, from having "any interest or concern in trade with the Indians." Rev. Stat. § 2078. The Court held the purchase void and remanded for an accounting. 259 U.S. at 138, 42 S.Ct. 442. *See also Smith v. McCullough,* 270 U.S. 456, 46 S.Ct. 338, 70 L.Ed. 682 (1926). A recent case in the Ninth Circuit concluded that the Nonintercourse Act prohibited the Walker River Paiute Tribe from granting an easement to a railroad. *United States v. Southern Pacific Transportation Co.,* 543 F.2d 676 (9th Cir. 1976). In 1882, the railroad's predecessor negotiated with the Tribe and bought a right-of-way across its reservation without Congressional authorization. Ninety-four years later the agreement was held invalid.[36]

Although it may appear harsh to condemn an apparently good-faith use as a trespass after 90 years of acquiescence by the owners, we conclude that an even older policy of Indian law compels this result.

Id. at 699.

The result in the present case may seem equally harsh. Nevertheless, it is the result mandated by the Nonintercourse Act.

VI. ABANDONMENT

[15] Defendants argue that the plaintiffs abandoned the land involved in this suit, citing *Williams v. City of Chicago,* 242 U.S. 434, 37 S.Ct. 142, 61 L.Ed. 414 (1917). The facts of that case are instructive. In *Williams,* Pattawatomie Indians ceded their land around Lake Michigan *to the United States* and then moved west. Some fifty years later, they attempted to claim land which had originally been under Lake Michigan but had been reclaimed by the time of the suit. The Supreme Court held that the land under Lake Michigan, along with the rest of the aboriginal Pattawatomie land, had been abandoned. However, *Williams* is inapposite to the present case. The Oneida Indians never abandoned their claim to their aboriginal homeland. The small area of land they now occupy lies within the boundaries of the aboriginal land. Furthermore, they never acquiesced in the loss of their land, but have continued to protest its diminishment up until today.

VII. THE PASSAGE OF TIME HAS NOT BARRED THIS SUIT

[16, 17] The violation of the Nonintercourse Act which gave rise to this suit occurred in 1795. Plaintiffs did not commence this action until 1970, 175 years later. Defendants argue that the passage of

---

36. The Ninth Circuit also considered whether or not the railroad acquired a license for its right-of-way under various Congressional statutes granting rights-of-way to railroads. *See United States v. Southern Pacific Transportation Co.,* 543 F.2d 676 (9th Cir. 1976).

time has barred this suit; they raise the defenses of statute of limitations,[37] laches, adverse possession and bona fide purchaser for value. Despite the extraordinary period of time which has passed, the action is not barred. The suit was commenced within the time permitted by 28 U.S.C. § 2415 which governs actions brought by the United States for or on behalf of Indian tribes. This period of limitations applies also to a case such as this one, brought by Indian tribes in their own behalf. Even assuming the necessity of fashioning a federal statute of limitations, Congress has supplied the model to be followed by Section 2415.

[18] It is quite clear that state statutes of limitations and state laws of adverse possession and laches would not bar a suit brought by the United States on behalf of an Indian nation. Where the United States holds title to land in trust for Indians, adverse possession cannot run against the land. *United States v. 7,405.3 Acres of Land,* 97 F.2d 417 (4th Cir. 1938). Restrictions on the alienation of Indian land, which have their origin either in treaties or in land patents, are not weakened by the passage of time. Adverse possession and laches are no defense to a suit by the government to protect restricted land. "It has long been held that adverse possession under a state statute of limitations cannot run against Indians if the land is not alienable by them, so long as such restrictions exist." *United States v. Schwarz,* 460 F.2d 1365, 1371 (7th Cir. 1972); *see United States v. Ahtanum Irrigation District,* 236 F.2d 321 (9th Cir. 1956), *cert. denied,* 352 U.S. 988, 77 S.Ct. 386, 1 L.Ed.2d 367 (1957). In *Ahtanum,* the Ninth Circuit pointed out the impact of the Nonintercourse Act on these defenses.

And in respect to the rights of Indians in an Indian reservation, there is a special reason why the Indians' property may not be lost through adverse possession, laches or delay. This, as pointed out, in *United*

States v. 7,405.3 Acres of Land, 4 Cir., 97 F.2d 417, 422, arises out of the provisions of Title 25 U.S.C.A. § 177, R.S. § 2116, which forbids the acquisition of Indian lands or of any title or claim thereto except by treaty or convention.

United States v. Ahtanum Irrigation District, supra, 236 F.2d at 334 (footnote omitted).

[19, 20] Similarly, where individual Indians sue to rescind transfers of restricted Indian land, state defenses cannot render the transfers effective. In a suit to declare invalid a transfer of a restricted land patent, the Supreme Court held that laches was inapplicable. *Ewert v. Bluejacket,* 259 U.S. 129, 42 S.Ct. 442, 66 L.Ed. 858 (1922). Also, in an action for wrongful use and occupancy, a state statute which created a tenancy-at-will was held ineffective where Indian land had been leased in violation of Congressional restrictions. *Bunch v. Cole,* 263 U.S. 250, 44 S.Ct. 101, 68 L.Ed. 290 (1923). If a transfer of Indian land is void under federal law, *see, e. g.,* 25 U.S.C. § 177, it cannot later be made valid by operation of state law.

[21] In the instant case, aboriginal Oneida land was transferred in violation of the Nonintercourse Act, 25 U.S.C. § 177. That statute declares, without any qualification, that no purchase made in violation of the Act "shall be of any validity in law or equity." The language of Congress could not have been plainer. Although this purchase occurred in 1795, it had no validity then nor does it today. New York's statute of limitations and the doctrines of laches, adverse possession, and bona fide purchaser cannot validate this transaction.

This same conclusion has been reached by two other district courts in suits brought to regain Indian land alienated in violation of the Nonintercourse Act. *Schaghticoke Tribe of Indians v. Kent School Corp.,* 423

---

37. Defendants contend that the action is barred by two of New York's statutes of limitations: the six year statute of limitations governing actions "for which no limitation is specifically prescribed by law", *N.Y.C.P.L.R.* § 213(1)

(McKinney 1972); and the one year and ninety day statute of limitations governing actions against a county, *N.Y.Gen.Munic.Law* § 50–i (McKinney 1965).

F.Supp. 780 (D.Conn.1976); *Narragansett Tribe of Indians v. Southern Rhode Island Land Development Corp.,* 418 F.Supp. 798 (D.R.I.1976). These cases emphasize the supremacy of federal law, which forbade the transfers, over state statutes which would validate them after the fact. The court in *Narragansett* went further. It noted that the United States, as sovereign, was not subject to these defenses. *See Narragansett, supra,* 418 F.Supp. at 805 and cases cited therein. It reasoned that the Congressional interests in protecting Indian land are the same, whether the United States or the Indians are plaintiffs. Thus, the Indians were permitted to assert the sovereign's interests and the defenses based on the passage of time were held inapplicable. It would be anomalous to permit the government, as trustee for the Indians, to achieve a result more beneficial to the Indians than the Indians could, suing on their own behalf. *See Schaghticoke, supra,* 423 F.Supp. at 785.

This conclusion does not necessarily eliminate the application of any statute of limitations. 28 U.S.C. § 2415 [38] provides a federal statute of limitations for cases brought by the United States for or on behalf of a recognized tribe of American Indians. Actions relating to restricted Indian lands are barred unless brought within 11 years of the date the claim accrued. Any claims which accrued prior to July 18, 1966, the date of the statute's enactment, are deemed to have accrued on the date of enactment. Although Section 2415 does not expressly include suits brought by Indian tribes *in haec verba,* it has been so construed. *Capi-*

---

38. The relevant portions of 28 U.S.C. § 2415 provide:

(a) Subject to the provisions of section 2416 of this title, and except as otherwise provided by Congress, every action for money damages brought by the United States or an officer or agency thereof which is founded upon any contract express or implied in law or fact, shall be barred unless the complaint is filed within six years after the right of action accrues or within one year after final decisions have been rendered in applicable administrative proceedings required by contract or by law, whichever is later: *Provided,* That in the event of later partial payment or written acknowledgment of debt, the right of action shall be deemed to accrue again at the time of each such payment or acknowledgment: *Provided further,* That an action for money damages brought by the United States for or on behalf of a recognized tribe, band or group of American Indians shall not be barred unless the complaint is filed more than six years and ninety days after the right of action accrued: *Provided further,* That an action for money damages which accrued on the date of enactment of this Act in accordance with subsection (g) brought by the United States for or on behalf of a recognized tribe, band, or group of American Indians, or on behalf of an individual Indian whose land is held in trust or restricted status, shall not be barred unless the complaint is filed more than eleven years after the right of action accrued or more than two years after a final decision has been rendered in applicable administrative proceedings required by contract or by law, whichever is later.

(b) Subject to the provisions of section 2416 of this title, and except as otherwise provided by Congress, every action for mon-ey damages brought by the United States or an officer or agency thereof which is founded upon a tort shall be barred unless the complaint is filed within three years after the right of action first accrues: *Provided,* That an action to recover damages resulting from a trespass on lands of the United States; an action to recover damages resulting from fire to such lands; an action to recover for diversion of money paid under a grant program; and an action for conversion of property of the United States may be brought within six years after the right of action accrues, except that such actions for or on behalf of a recognized tribe, band or group of American Indians, including actions relating to allotted trust or restricted Indian lands, may be brought within six years and ninety days after the right of action accrues, except that such actions for or on behalf of a recognized tribe, band, or group of American Indians, including actions relating to allotted trust or restricted Indian lands, or on behalf of an individual Indian whose land is held in trust or restricted status which accrued on the date of enactment of this Act in accordance with subsection (g) may be brought within eleven years after the right of action accrues.

(c) Nothing herein shall be deemed to limit the time for bringing an action to establish the title to, or right of possession of, real or personal property.

.   .   .   .

(g) Any right of action subject to the provisions of this section which accrued prior to the date of enactment of this Act shall, for purposes of this section, be deemed to have accrued on the date of enactment of this Act.

tan Grande Band of Mission Indians v. Helix Irrigation District, 514 F.2d 465 (9th Cir.), *cert. denied,* 423 U.S. 874, 96 S.Ct. 143, 46 L.Ed.2d 106 (1975). Actually, whether the limitations of Section 2415 apply to suits brought by Indian tribes as well as the United States is irrelevant in this case. The plaintiffs' complaint was filed in 1970, well within the bar provided by the statute. *See Id.* at 472 (Miller, J., concurring).

VIII. THE UNITED STATES IS NOT AN INDISPENSABLE PARTY

[22] Defendants argue that the case must be dismissed for failure to join the United States as an indispensable party. They contend that the fiduciary relationship between the United States and the Indian nation, along with the general federal interest in Indian lands, requires that the United States be made a party to the action or that the action be dismissed. Neither Rule 19 of the Federal Rules of Civil Procedure, nor the adjudicated cases require such a result.[39] The Court of Appeals for the Tenth Circuit, faced with an almost identical situation, refused to dismiss the action. There, plaintiff Indian nations had sued to recover possession of land that was part of the tribes' communal allotment.

If we hold that the United States is an indispensable party, the Nations will be unable to prosecute a suit to establish their title to, and recover the possession and use of, their lands predicated upon an alleged cause of action which arose more than twenty years ago. On the other hand, if they are permitted to prosecute the suit, in the absence of the United States, a judgment in favor of the defendants will not bind the United States. Defendants assert that that will result in a continuing cloud upon their titles. But, that is their present situation. So long as the United States fails to commence and prosecute to final judgment, an action to establish the title of the Nations to such lands and to recover possession thereof for the Nations, the title of the defend-

ants will continue to be clouded by the possibility of the United States thereafter bringing such an action. So it comes down to this: If we hold that the United States is an indispensable party, the Nations will be unable to assert their longstanding claim to the land; and if we hold that the United States is not an indispensable party, the defendants will run the risk of the burden and expense of defending two lawsuits, even though they succeed in obtaining a judgment in their favor in the instant action.

We are of the opinion that the equities presented by the situation and the inconveniences that will result to the Nations, if they are denied the right to prosecute an action, and to the defendant, if the Nations are permitted to prosecute the action without the joinder of the United States, weigh heavily in favor of the Nations.

We conclude that a final decree determining the title and right to possession as between the Nations and the defendants would not leave the controversy in a situation inconsistent with equity and good conscience.

Choctaw and Chickasaw Nations v. Seitz, 193 F.2d 456, 460–61 (10th Cir. 1951), *cert. denied,* 343 U.S. 919, 72 S.Ct. 676, 96 L.Ed. 1332 (1952).

Two recent decisions in cases almost identical to this one, have held that the United States is not an indispensable party. *Mashpee Tribe v. New Seabury Corp.,* 427 F.Supp. 899 (D.Mass.1977); *Narragansett Tribe of Indians v. Southern Rhode Island Land Development Corp.,* 418 F.Supp. 798 (D.R.I.1976). These decisions were based on a long line of cases which have consistently held that, whenever Indian tribes or individual Indians sued to recover either tribal land or individual allotments, the United States is not an indispensable party. *Poafpybitty v. Skelly Oil Co.,* 390 U.S. 365, 88 S.Ct. 982, 19 L.Ed.2d 1238 (1968); *Fort Mojave Tribe v. Lafollette,* 478 F.2d 1016 (9th Cir. 1973); *Jackson v. Sims,* 201 F.2d 259

---

39. For an analysis of the factors to be considered in connection with Fed.R.Civ.P. 19, *see*

Prescription Plan Service Corp. v. Franco, 552 F.2d 493 (2d Cir. 1977).

(10th Cir. 1953); *Choctaw and Chickasaw Nations v. Seitz,* 193 F.2d 456 (10th Cir. 1951), *cert. denied,* 343 U.S. 919, 72 S.Ct. 676, 96 L.Ed. 1332 (1952). *See generally* 3A J. Moore, Federal Practice ¶ 19.09[8] at 2325 (2d Ed. 1974).[40]

Defendants cite cases that have reached the opposite conclusion for the general proposition that, whenever title to Indian land is involved, the United States is an indispensable party. *See Minnesota v. United States,* 305 U.S. 382, 59 S.Ct. 292, 83 L.Ed. 235 (1939); *Carlson v. Tulalip Tribes of Washington,* 510 F.2d 1337 (9th Cir. 1975); *Nicodemus v. Washington Water Power Co.,* 264 F.2d 614 (9th Cir. 1959). However, these cases all involve attempts to burden land adversely to the interests of the Indians or the United States. These cases have found the United States to be an indispensable party because the United States owns the ultimate fee title to such land, and because a judgment adverse to the Indians could impair the rights of the United States in that fee. These cases differ from the instant suit by Indian tribes to recover aboriginal land, and this important distinction has been noted by the Tenth Circuit.

> In *Choctaw and Chickasaw Nations v. Seitz,* [citation omitted] we recognized the distinction between the indispensability of the Secretary of Interior in a suit, the effect of which would alienate Indian land, and the dispensability of the Secretary in a suit, the effect of which would protect Indian land against alienation, particularly where the Secretary refused, refrained or neglected to protect the Indian's interest.

Jackson v. Sims, 201 F.2d 259, 262 (10th Cir. 1953).

Finally, defendants contend that *Joint Tribal Council of the Passamaquoddy Tribe v. Morton,* 388 F.Supp. 649 (D.Me.), *aff'd,* 528 F.2d 370 (1st Cir. 1975), compels a dismissal here. Defendants assert that *Passa-*

maquoddy requires a "*judicially*-initiated effort asking that the United States act on the plaintiffs' behalf" as "a prerequisite to any suit alleging noncompliance with the *Nonintercourse Act.*" Defendant County of Madison's Post-Trial Memorandum 9. This suggested reading of *Passamaquoddy* lacks support in the facts. It appears to be a case of the wish being father to the thought.

> Whether, even if there is a trust relationship with the Passamaquoddies, the United States has an affirmative duty to sue Maine on the Tribe's behalf is a separate issue that was not raised or decided below and which consequently we do not address.

Passamaquoddy, supra, 528 F.2d at 375. Nor was the right of the tribe to litigate without the intervention of the United States at issue because of the apparent immunity of Maine to suit. *Passamaquoddy* definitely did not require a suit against the United States as a prerequisite to a tribe's suit under the Nonintercourse Act.

Two actions similar to the instant one, both brought in the First Circuit, have found that *Passamaquoddy* did not hold the United States to be an indispensable party. *Mashpee Tribe v. New Seabury Corp.,* 427 F.Supp. 899 (D.Mass.1977); *Narragansett Tribe of Indians v. Southern Rhode Island Land Development Corp.,* 418 F.Supp. 798 (D.R.I.1976).

IX. THE STATE OF NEW YORK IS NOT AN INDISPENSABLE PARTY

[23] Defendants contend that the action must be dismissed for failure to join the State of New York as an indispensable party. Defendants argue that, as counties, they hold land only as agents of the State. They further argue that an action against the counties will be binding on the State under the law of agent and principal—thus

---

40. Nor need the United States be joined in an action against third persons by certain Indian nations to establish title to and to recover possession of land constituting part of the unallotted common domain of the nations, or

in an action by an Indian tribe to quiet title to lands claimed under a treaty with the United States.

3A *J. Moore, Federal Practice,* ¶ 19.09[8] at 2325 (2d Ed. 1974) (footnotes omitted).

making the State an indispensable party and requiring the dismissal of the suit. The first premise of this argument, however, is faulty and with that faulty foundation removed, the argument collapses.

[24] New York County Law empowers a county's Board of Supervisors to "acquire by purchase or condemnation and accept by gift real . . . property for lawful county purposes." *N. Y. County Law* § 215(3). The county is permitted to lease such property (*Id.*), build upon it (*Id.*), and "sell and convey all the right, title and interest of the county therein." *Id.* § 215(5). Nothing in the statutes limits the extent of the county's title nor specifies that the county holds property as an agent for the State. Neither do any of the cases cited by defendants state that counties in New York hold title to land as agents of the State. *Village of Kenmore v. Erie County*, 252 N.Y. 437, 169 N.E. 637 (1930) (statute requiring counties to collect taxes for villages struck down as violative of state constitutional provision forbidding counties from incurring debts); *Village of Croton-on-Hudson v. County of Westchester*, 38 A.D.2d 979, 331 N.Y.S.2d 883 (2d Dep't.), *aff'd*, 30 N.Y.2d 959, 335 N.Y.S.2d 825, 287 N.E.2d 617 (1972) (county enjoined from diverting parkland to use as a dump without legislative authorization). One case cited by defendants stated, by way of dicta, that a "county is a mere agent of the State." *County of Cayuga v. McHugh*, 4 N.Y.2d 609, 614, 176 N.Y.S.2d 643, 647, 152 N.E.2d 73, 76 (1958). However, the New York Court of Appeals added that counties, as political subdivisions, have "no power save that deputed to them by [the State Legislature]." *Id.* The language of § 215 of the County Law is clear enough—the

State has authorized counties to acquire lands, to hold title to these lands, and to use or dispose of them, within certain limits. *N. Y. County Law* § 215. *See also Cooke v. Mulligan*, 81 Misc.2d 1025, 1026–27, 367 N.Y.S.2d 204, 206 (Sup.Ct.1975).[41]

Ward v. Louisiana Wild Life and Fisheries Commission, 224 F.Supp. 252 (E.D.La. 1963), *aff'd*, 347 F.2d 234 (5th Cir. 1965), cited by defendants, is inapposite. There, the state was the record owner of the land in question. That land had originally been deeded to the Louisiana Board of Commissioners for the Protection of Birds, Game and Fish. A subsequent statute transferred the land to the State of Louisiana.

Since the defendants are the record owners of the land involved in this suit, and since they hold this land in their own right and not as agents for the State, the State need not be joined. Fed.R.Civ.P. 19(a). Complete relief can be accorded among the present parties; the State cannot be prejudiced in any way by its absence; nor does the State's absence subject any of the parties to possible multiple liabilities. Dismissal under Fed.R.Civ.P. 19(b) is not required. *Mashpee Tribe v. New Seabury Corp.*, 427 F.Supp. 899 (D.Mass.1977).

Defendants concede that the Eleventh Amendment does not insulate them from suit. They argue that the suit must be dismissed against them, however, because the State cannot be made a party defendant by reason of the Eleventh Amendment. Having already determined that it is not necessary to make the State a party defendant, it is equally unnecessary to consider any argument based on the Eleventh Amendment.[42]

---

41. All of the properties involved here had already been acquired by Albany County as the result of previously held tax sales—most, if not all, of which were conducted long before the plaintiff was elected to office. As such they must be considered county properties and the County owns them proprietorially and can continue to hold them, sell them or lease them pursuant to the provisions of County Law § 215, or otherwise dispose of them at such times and upon such terms as shall be determined by the County Legisla-

ture, with or without advertising for bids, subject only to ultimate approval by a majority vote of that body.
Cooke v. Mulligan, 81 Misc.2d 1025, 1026–27, 367 N.Y.S.2d 204, 206. (Sup.Ct.1975).

42. In any event, equity and good conscience, as in the case of the United States, would militate against dismissal. Fed.R.Civ.P. 19(b). The State is no more an indispensable party than any other person in the chain of title.

X. FORM OF THE ACTION

Casting about among the old common law forms of action for a label with which to tag the claim in this action, the defendants state, "it is difficult to characterize the nature of the plaintiffs' action." Defendant County of Madison's Post-Trial Memorandum 26. They find the most appropriate to be either the old common law "action for use and occupancy" or "an action for wrongful desseisin" or one "of trespass for mesne profits." The defendants then argue with some force that the complaint does not allege all of the essential elements required for any of these actions. *See Crawford v. Town of Hamburg*, 19 A.D.2d 100, 101, 241 N.Y.S.2d 357, 359 (4th Dep't. 1963); *Kelman v. Wilen*, 283 App.Div. 1113, 131 N.Y. S.2d 679, 680 (2d Dep't. 1954); *see generally* 28 C.J.S. *Ejectment* § 132 (1941); 91 C.J.S. *Use and Occupation* § 3 (1955). There is no need to consider the pleading question posed by this argument. As I said in the initial decision considering the jurisdictional question, "[n]o purpose would be served trying to tack a name on the cause of action asserted." *Oneida Indian Nation v. County of Oneida*, 70–CV–35, slip op. at 3 (N.D. N.Y., November 9, 1971).

[25] To start with, the precise form of this action, which would have been so important at common law, is no longer determinative of the action's outcome. Under the Federal Rules of Civil Procedure, the question is not how plaintiffs have characterized the action, but whether plaintiffs are entitled to relief. "[E]very final judgment shall grant the relief to which the party in whose favor it is rendered is entitled, even if the party has not demanded such relief in his pleadings." Fed.R.Civ.P. 54(c). *See generally* 6 *J. Moore, Federal*

Practice ¶ 54.62 (2d Ed. 1976); *10 C. Wright and A. Miller, Federal Practice and Procedure* § 2664 (1973).

[It] is of no importance at the present time to consider whether the plaintiff's remedy is by replevin, trover, money had and received, or trespass. The real question is whether, under the facts disclosed in the complaint, the plaintiff is entitled to relief. If he is, the court can apply the proper remedy, [under] Rule 54(c) . . ..

Commonwealth Trust Co. of Pittsburgh v. Reconstruction Finance Corp., 28 F.Supp. 586, 588 (W.D.Pa.1939). *See also Herzog & Straus v. GRT Corp.*, 553 F.2d 789, 791 n.2 (2d Cir. 1977).

[26] Neither can the defendants derive comfort from their contention that the plaintiffs' complaint and proof failed to meet the requirement of state law. "There being no federal statute making the statutory or decisional law of the State of New York applicable to the reservations, the controlling law remained federal law . . .." *Oneida Indian Nation, supra,* 414 U.S. at 674, 94 S.Ct. at 781. Referring to the Indian tribes' right of occupancy, the Supreme Court pointed out that such right "sometimes called Indian title and good against all but the sovereign, could be terminated only by sovereign act. . . . [T]hese tribal rights to Indian lands became the exclusive province of the federal law." *Id.* at 667, 94 S.Ct. at 777. Thus, it is of little import that the plaintiffs failed to establish the elements of a state-based cause of action. *United States v. Forness*, 125 F.2d 928 (2d Cir.), *cert. denied,* 316 U.S. 694, 62 S.Ct. 1293, 86 L.Ed. 1764 (1942) (Seneca Indian Nation suit not barred by failure to comply with state law).[43]

---

43. In *United States v. Forness*, 125 F.2d 928 (2d Cir.), *cert. denied,* 316 U.S. 694, 62 S.Ct. 1293, 86 L.Ed. 1764 (1942), the Seneca Indian Nation sued to cancel a 99 year lease of a portion of its land. Defendant lessees first argued that the suit should be dismissed since they had tendered the rent as New York law requires. The Second Circuit refused to apply New York Law. *Id.* at 932. Defendants also argued that, according to the common law, the remedy of cancellation was unavailable because plaintiffs had not made a demand for the rent. The

court rejected this argument and declined to be bound by "ancient doctrine." *Id.* at 937

It follows that we are here at liberty to apply legal rules as to landlord and tenant which comport with the Congressional intent concerning the Senecas.

Id. at 938. The Court of Appeals ultimately remanded the case to the district court for entry of judgment in favor of plaintiffs, on the condition that plaintiffs' offer for a new lease at a more reasonable rent be kept open. *Id.* at 943.

The plaintiffs have established a claim for violation of the Nonintercourse Act. Unless the act is to be rendered nugatory, it must be concluded that the plaintiffs' right of occupancy and possession to the land in question [44] was not alienated. By the deed of 1795, the State acquired no rights against the plaintiffs; consequently, its successors, the defendant counties, are in no better position.

In this phase of the trial, the only question to be determined is that of liability.[45] The extent of the liability and the manner in which the relief is to be fashioned remain for another day. *Cf. Illinois v. City of Milwaukee,* 406 U.S. 91, 92 S.Ct. 1385, 31 L.Ed.2d 712 (1972).

This Memorandum-Decision and Order shall constitute the court's findings of fact and conclusions of law. Fed.R.Civ.P. 52(a).

The court having jurisdiction of the subject matter and the parties hereto, for the reasons herein, it is

ORDERED, that the issue of liability be and it hereby is decided in favor of the plaintiffs and against the defendants; and it is further

ORDERED, ADJUDGED AND DE-CREED that the defendants be and they hereby are held liable to the plaintiffs by reason of said defendants' occupancy of the land in question during the years 1968 and 1969, all other issues to be determined in a subsequent trial.

The parties have indicated a need for, and the circumstances would seem to compel an appeal from this Order. However, the determination herein does not constitute a final judgment or a judgment which could appropriately be certified for entry as a final judgment pursuant to Rule 54(b), Fed.R.Civ.P. *Liberty Mutual Insurance Co. v. Wetzel,* 424 U.S. 737, 96 S.Ct. 1202, 47 L.Ed.2d 435 (1976); *United States v. Southern Pacific Transportation Co.,* 543 F.2d 676, 681 n.5 (9th Cir. 1976). Therefore, pursuant to 28 U.S.C. § 1292(b), I hereby

certify that in my opinion the within Order involves a controlling question of law, i. e. whether a violation of the Nonintercourse Act in 1795 gives rise to a claim against the present record owners of a portion of the involved land. I further certify that an immediate appeal from the Order may materially advance the termination of this and other litigation held in abeyance pending the determination of the issue herein. *See* Rule 5, Fed.R.App.P.

---

44. The parties have stipulated that defendants are record owners of part of the land transferred in 1795. (Tr. 6).

ONEIDA PETITION TO THE PRESIDENT
OF THE UNITED STATES,
MARCH 21, 1977

March 21 1977

The President
The White House
Washington, D.C.
    Re: Petition to the President of the United States
       from the Oneida Indians

My Dear Mr. President:

The Oneida Indians residing in New York and Canada present this Petition to you pursuant to Article 7 of the 1794 Six Nations Treaty between the United States and the Iroquois Indians. Article 7 implements the promise made in Article 2, of the 1794 Treaty, that our land will be secure, by providing that the President will take "prudent measures" to help the Oneida Nation if their lands are disturbed by white men. The specific promise made by the United States is that the Oneida Reservation as of 1794 ". . . shall remain theirs until they choose to sell the same to the people of the United States, who have the right to purchase."

THE WRONG DONE TO US

We are complaining about the illegal and fraudulent taking of our land by New York State in the period 1785–1842 in a series of about thirty separate transactions. These takings were illegal because:

(1) They were accomplished by means of state treaties which are specifically forbidden by Article VI of the Constitution;

(2) They violated the provisions of three federal treaties;

(3) They violated the provisions of the Nonintercourse Acts, or the Articles of Confederation, and thus are void at law and equity; and

(4) They were fraudulent and unconscionable (in one case, for instance, the state acquired over 5,000,000 acres of land for $5,500.00 cash and an annuity of $600.00 per year in silver, in another case the state purchased 125,000 acres at $.50 per acre and made a 600% profit on resale in two years).

199

PAST ATTEMPTS TO OBTAIN JUSTICE

The Oneida Nation, like other New York Indians, has repeatedly over the years sought justice. The law books of New York State are replete with Indian land cases; in almost every one, the New York Indians were rebuffed or defeated on some technicality. Neither New York nor the federal government has ever faced up to the problems resulting from the illegal taking of 600,000,000 acres of our land. In addition, the State has formally admitted that the acquisition of the Oneida Lands did not comply with federal law. See the amicus brief of the State before the Supreme Court in our case there.

On many occasions in the past, the Oneida Nation or its members have sought justice or help from the United States. We were ignored, turned off, or just plain misled. We have documentation of the poor advice and counsel given to us by the United States over the years. Our attorneys can make this documentation available to you; it is based on official U.S. records.

In recent years, our attorneys have made numerous petitions in our behalf to various federal personnel. The first of these, was a 1968 petition to President Johnson. These recent petitions were denied, on the ground that the Oneida Nation had a conflicting claim against the United States in the Indian Claims Commission. In a recent communication the Department of Interior has admitted this, as well as the validity of our claims.

POSSIBLE SETTLEMENT OF THE CASE
IN INDIAN CLAIMS COMMISSION

Up to now, the United States has failed to help us for the stated reason that it considered the Nonintercourse Act, 25 U.S.C. 177, to be inapplicable to acquisitions by New York State and that this position created a conflict in the Indian Claims Commission case where it was being used as a defense. This is a patently inadequate excuse since the Supreme Court has held that 25 U.S.C. 177 does apply to New York; however it allowed the United States to put off responsibility until now, when the period of limitation on part of our claim is about to expire. See 28 U.S.C. 2415.

At a March 12 meeting in New York, the Oneida Nation of New York voted to accept a settlement in the Indian Claims Commission of its monetary claims against the United States. The settlement agreement specifically provides that United States' treaty obligations and land rights are not waived. The Oneidas of Wisconsin have to approve the settlement before it becomes effective.

In the settlement agreement there is no payment by the United States for land lost after 1790. This is so there will be no claim of a cloud on an action to recover possession of our 300,000 acre Reservation in New York State.

WHY WE NEED UNITED STATES HELP NOW

Following denial of our petition in the late 1960's our counsel commenced action against Oneida and Madison Counties, New York, in respect of part of the land which they occupy in our Reservation. The District Court and the Second Circuit Court of Appeals denied jurisdiction; in 1974 the U.S. Supreme Court held there is federal court jurisdiction, 94 S. Ct. 772. A trial was held in November, 1975 and we are awaiting a decision on the merits of the 1795 taking by the State.

One may ask why it has taken so long, well over 100 years, to get within reach of justice. Part of the problem is that:

(1) The federal courts long held that an Indian Tribe out of possession of its land cannot use the federal courts to get possession back; they held this is a state matter and not under "federal question" jurisdiction;

(2) The New York courts sought to deny federal and assert state authority, but they held that an Indian tribe or nation is *not a person* who has standing to sue in New York courts.

Thus we were effectively "locked out" of the federal and state courts till the Supreme Court saw the injustice and broke the log jam in its 1974 decision in our case. Previously, we could only ask the United States for help; and the United States would not listen. It told us there was no merit to our claim.

We believe that ultimately we will prevail in our federal court action. However, we think the help of the United States is now necessary for these reasons:

(1) The statute of limitations on historic damages claims expires in July of this year. Such a claim may be the only way we can get justice and compensation from New York for the millions of acres taken from us prior to 1790. The 11th Amendment to the Constitution bars us from suing the state for damages. Only the United States can do this. Must we stand by and allow this large claim to expire?

(2) Without federal help in an action against the state, the only way we can get complete justice is by piecemeal private litigation with the landowners in the huge acreage involved. This is expensive and time consuming and may cause harm as well as expense to the non-Indian people now occupying the land. Why should we and they have to go through this when the State of New York is the real wrong-doer and the federal duty is so clear?

(3) We are on a contingent fee arrangement with our attorneys. (The retainer contract is on file with the B.I.A. and has been approved by it.) We, and our attorneys, have repeatedly pointed out to U.S. officials that intervention by the U.S. may save us legal costs. Why should we have to pay for what the U.S. is obligated to do?

(4) The action of the federal government is necessary in any event before a final resolution to our claims can be had and title cleared. See 25 U.S.C. 177. Doesn't it make sense for the U.S. to be involved now rather than later?

(5) Federal treaties are the "supreme law of the land." The 1794 treaty specifically provides for the relief we seek. President George Washington promised such aid to the Iroquois. Is the law of the United States going to be observed, or is it not?

HELP FOR THE MAINE INDIANS

We understand from current press releases that the U.S. is going to help the Maine Indians with their land claims. We are delighted with this action; the Maine Indians have a just cause.

We are aware that the Maine Indians had to bring suit against the United States to compel this action on the part of the U.S. We are also aware that nothing really happened in the Maine situation until the non-Indian occupants of the land were inconvenienced. No one in the Maine government or in the U.S. government really listened until mortgages and titles were questioned, until bonding sales were delayed, until the voters became angry at their representatives. Is this right?

The Oneida Nation has always taken the course which would cause the least injury to our non-Indian friends. We have been peaceful, lawful and reasonable; we have listened to the advice of our attorneys that the avenue of white man's law is the straightest and best one. Were we wrong about this?

Must we, like our brothers in Maine, resort to the courts to force the United States to do its legal duty?

It is unthinkable that the answer to these questions is "Yes." Please respond to us soon and let us know where we stand.

If we must bring legal action against our ally, the United States, to compel it to do its duty, we shall.

We are unwilling to stand still any longer, while the United States lets our rights expire.

SPECIFIC ACTION REQUESTED

We believe that justice for all parties can best be obtained as follows:

First. The U.S. Attorney General should notify the Attorney General of New York State that the acquisition of land by New York State from the Oneida Nation over the period 1785–1842, as much as 6,000,000 acres, was illegal under federal laws.

Second. The President should appoint a mediator or other representative pursuant to 25 U.S.C. 177 to initiate negotiations with the state and to represent the U.S. in the negotiation between the state and the Oneida Nation.

Third. Such mediator should advise the state that a federal suit will be commenced on June 1, 1977, if a satisfactory settlement has not then been reached. (The period of limitation in historic damage suits will expire on July 18, 1977.)

Fourth. If there is no settlement by June 1, 1977, the U.S. should commence legal action as follows: (a) against the state for damages in respect of the approximately 5,500,000 acres acquired prior to 1790, plus interest, less the amount of the ICC settlement; (b) against the state and its political subdivisions and agencies to eject them from land, to which we have title, or alternatively, to collect damages with interest, and the amount of fair value of the land; (c) against the state for damages, with interest, for the acquisition and patenting back to non-Indians of the balance of the Reservation land acquired by it after 1790; and (d) such other action as may be appropriate.

Fifth. We ask that the United States supply our tribal representatives with reasonable travel, out of pocket living expenses, and loss of pay for attendance at the numerous meetings that will be held during negotiations. We would expect to have three delegates from Wisconsin, three from Canada and three from New York. (Our attorneys, who pay their own expenses, will refuse to attend any negotiating meeting unless at least two authorized representatives from each branch are present thereat.) We can't pay these costs ourselves, but it is the illegal taking of our 6,000,000 acres inland empire which brings us to this situation.

Sixth. It is our request that such meetings be held in Albany, the capital of New York State.

If the above procedure does not produce a reasonable and agreeable settlement, then the U.S. will be obliged under our treaties to bring ejectment actions and damage suits in the manner currently being planned for Maine. By suggesting mediation and negotiations to speed a fair settlement, the Oneida Nation does not intend to waive any rights or claims, or remedies which it may have. Of course, we reserve the right to take appropriate legal action before April 20, if we deem advisable. Your response at our meeting may determine this.

MEETING REQUESTED

This is a matter of great importance to all parties. It is difficult to set forth all the factors in one short document. We, therefore, request a meeting with you, or with your delegate, at a very early date to discuss this petition.

We should note that the Oneida Indians in Wisconsin, The Oneida Tribe of Indians of Wisconsin, Inc., have not yet voted approval of filing a petition at this time. However, they are entitled to a share of any settlement, the same as we.

CONCLUSION

We, therefore, request that the United States fulfill its legal duty to us by: (a) appointing a mediator to negotiate with New York State in our behalf prior to April 20, 1977, and (b) committing itself in writing prior to April 20, 1977, to filing a protective suit before June 1, 1977, if settlement has not then been reached. If such actions are not taken by April 20, our attorneys will bring suit against State officials for a declaration of rights and will also sue United States officials to compel them to sue in our behalf.

We know it may seem disrespectful to impose a deadline on the President of the United States, whom we consider to be an understanding friend. If so, we apologize. However, we have been petitioning for generations, to no avail. With the period of limitation in damage suits expiring in July, we can afford to wait no longer.

May the United States keep its pledged word to us and not forget that our Warriors, and Scouts, and our contributions of grain at Valley Forge, helped sustain the United States in its fight for justice.

May the United States observe its own laws and its treaties, which are the supreme law of the land.

Very truly yours,

Dated: March 21, 1977   THE ONEIDAS OF THE THAMES (Canada)
Dated: March 21, 1977   THE ONEIDA INDIANS OF NEW YORK

APPENDIX H

ONEIDA & MADISON COUNTIES v.
ONEIDA INDIAN NATION,
UNITED STATES SUPREME COURT DECISION,
MARCH 4, 1985

rental value of land presently owned and occupied by the counties. The United States District Court for the Northern District of New York dismissed action, and the Court of Appeals, 464 F.2d 916, affirmed. The Supreme Court, 414 U.S. 661, 94 S.Ct. 772, 39 L.Ed.2d 73, reversed and remanded. On remand, the United States District Court for the Northern District of New York, Edmund Port, J., 434 F.Supp. 527, entered judgment for Indians and subsequently awarded damages, and appeals were taken. The Court of Appeals for the Second Circuit, 719 F.2d 525, affirmed on liability and indemnification but remanded for further proceedings on damages, and counties and state petitioned for review. The Supreme Court, Justice Powell, held that: (1) Indian tribes could maintain action for violation of their possessory rights based on federal common law; (2) the Nonintercourse Acts did not preempt tribes' right of action under federal common law; (3) action was not barred by limitations, laches, abatement, ratification or doctrine of nonjusticiability; and (4) counties' cross claim for indemnity from state raised question of state law and thus, since state had not waived its constitutional immunity to suit in federal court on this question, no ancillary jurisdiction existed.

Judgment affirmed in part and reversed in part.

Justice Brennan filed an opinion concurring in part and dissenting in part in which Justice Marshall joined.

Justice Stevens concurred in the judgment in part and filed an opinion dissenting in part in which Chief Justice Burger and Justices White and Rehnquist joined.

470 U.S. 226, 84 L.Ed.2d 169

₁₂₂₆COUNTY OF ONEIDA, NEW YORK, et al., Petitioners

v.

ONEIDA INDIAN NATION OF NEW YORK STATE, etc., et al.

NEW YORK, Petitioner

v.

ONEIDA INDIAN NATION OF NEW YORK STATE, etc., et al.

Nos. 83–1065, 83–1240.

Argued Oct. 1, 1984.

Decided March 4, 1985.

Rehearing Denied April 22, 1985.

See 471 U.S. 1062, 105 S.Ct. 2173.

Indian tribes sued two New York counties seeking damages representing fair

1. Indians ⟨key⟩2

With the adoption of the Federal Constitution, Indian relations became the exclusive province of federal law. U.S.C.A. Const. Art. 1, § 8, cl. 3.

2. Indians ⟨key⟩27(1)

Indian tribes could maintain federal common-law action for violation of their possessory rights in tribal land that was allegedly conveyed unlawfully in 1795.

3. States ⟜4.10

In determining whether a federal statute preempts common-law causes of action, relevant inquiry is whether statute speaks directly to question otherwise answered by federal common law.

4. Indians ⟜27(1)

The Nonintercourse Acts, which did not speak directly to the question of remedies for unlawful conveyances of Indian land, which did not establish a comprehensive remedial plan for dealing with violations of Indian property rights, and which did not address directly the problem of restoring unlawfully conveyed land to Indians, did not preempt Indian tribes' right of action under federal common law for violation of their possessory rights. Act March 1, 1793, §§ 1–3, 5–8, 10–12, 1 Stat. 329; Act May 6, 1822, § 4, 3 Stat. 683; 25 U.S.C.A. § 194.

5. Indians ⟜27(1)

Availability of suits by United States on behalf of Indian tribe does not preclude common-law actions by tribes themselves.

6. Federal Courts ⟜424

In absence of controlling federal limitations period, general rule is that state limitations period for analogous cause of action is borrowed and applied to federal claim, provided that application of state statute is consistent with underlying federal policies.

7. Indians ⟜27(4)

Under the supremacy clause, state law time bars, e.g. adverse possession and laches, do n⌐t apply of their own force to Indian land title claims.

8. Indians ⟜27(4)

Although there is no federal statute of limitations governing federal common-law actions by Indians to enforce property rights, borrowing of a state limitations period would be inconsistent with federal policy against application of state statutes of limitations in context of Indian land claims.

28 U.S.C.A. §§ 2415, 2415(c); Indian Claims Limitation Act of 1982, §§ 3–6, 5(c), 28 U.S.C.A. § 2415 note.

9. Indians ⟜27(4)

Indian tribes' federal common-law right of action for violation of their possessory right in connection with an allegedly unlawful conveyance of tribal land in 1795 was not subject to any statute of limitations. Indian Claims Limitation Act of 1982, §§ 3–6, 5(c), 28 U.S.C.A. § 2415 note; 28 U.S.C.A. §§ 2415, 2415(a, b).

10. Federal Courts ⟜461

While New York counties argued at trial that Indian tribes were guilty of laches in connection with tribes' federal common-law right of action for violation of their possessory rights in 1795, counties did not reassert this defense on appeal, and thus as a result the Court of Appeals did not rule on claim and the Supreme Court likewise declined to do so.

11. Indians ⟜27(1)

Where pertinent provision of 1793 Nonintercourse Act, like its predecessor, merely codified principle that a sovereign act was required to extinguish original title and that a conveyance without the sovereign's consent was void ab initio, and since all subsequent versions of Nonintercourse Act contained substantially same restraint on alienation of Indian lands, Indian tribes' federal common-law right of action for violation of Nonintercourse Act of 1793 did not abate when statute expired. 25 U.S.C.A. § 177; Act July 22, 1790, § 4, 1 Stat. 137; Act March 1, 1793, § 8, 1 Stat. 329.

12. Indians ⟜11

Federally approved treaties in 1793 and 1802 in which Indian tribes ceded additional land to New York did not ratify New York's unlawful purchase of Indian tribes' land where references in treaties did not demonstrate plain and unambiguous intent to extinguish title and there was no indication that either Senate or President intended by those references to ratify 1795 conveyance. Act March 1, 1793, § 1 et seq., 1 Stat. 329.

13. Constitutional Law ⬥68(1)

Congress' delegation of civil remedial authority to the President concerning Indian affairs did not mean that issue raised in Indian tribes' federal common-law action for violation of their possessory rights was a nonjusticiable political question and thus Indian tribe's claim was not barred by the political question doctrine. U.S.C.A. Const. Art. 1, § 8, cl. 3.

14. Federal Courts ⬥265

The Eleventh Amendment forecloses application of normal principles of ancillary and pendent jurisdiction when claims are pressed against the state. U.S.C.A. Const. Amend. 11.

15. Federal Courts ⬥265

Where counties' indemnification claim, whether cast as question of New York bar or federal common law, was a claim against the state for retroactive monetary relief in Indian tribes' federal common-law action brought for violation of their possessory rights, indemnification claim was barred by the Eleventh Amendment in absence of state's consent. U.S.C.A. Const. Amend. 11.

16. Federal Courts ⬥266

State's alleged violation of 1793 Intercourse Act by purchasing Indian tribes' land did not waive state's immunity to suit in federal court with respect to counties' indemnification claim and thus, since counties' cross claim for indemnity raised question of state law and state had not waived its constitutional immunity to suit in federal court on question, no ancillary jurisdiction existed over indemnification claim in suit brought by Indian tribes asserting federal common-law right of action for violation of their possessory rights. Act March 1, 1793, § 1 et seq., 1 Stat. 329.

---

* The syllabus constitutes no part of the opinion of the Court but has been prepared by the Reporter of Decisions for the convenience of the

Syllabus *

Respondent Indian Tribes (hereafter respondents) brought an action in Federal District Court against petitioner counties (hereafter petitioners), alleging that respondents' ancestors conveyed tribal land to New York State under a 1795 agreement that violated the Nonintercourse Act of 1793—which provided that no person or entity could purchase Indian land without the Federal Government's approval—and that thus the transaction was void. Respondents sought damages representing the fair rental value, for a specified 2-year period, of that part of the land presently occupied by petitioners. The District Court found petitioners liable for wrongful possession of the land in violation of the 1793 Act, awarded respondents damages, and held that New York, a third-party defendant brought into the case by petitioners' cross-claim, must indemnify petitioners for the damages owed to respondents. The Court of Appeals affirmed the liability and indemnification rulings, but remanded for further proceedings on the amount of damages.

Held:

1. Respondents have a federal common-law right of action for violation of their possessory rights. Pp. 1251–1254.

(a) The possessory rights claimed by respondents are federal rights to the lands at issue. *Oneida Indian Nation v. County of Oneida,* 414 U.S. 661, 671, 94 S.Ct. 772, 779, 39 L.Ed.2d 73. It has been implicitly assumed that Indians have a federal common-law right to sue to enforce their aboriginal land rights, and their right of occupancy need not be based on a treaty, statute, or other Government action. Pp. 1251–1252.

(b) Respondents' federal common-law right of action was not pre-empted by the Nonintercourse Acts. In determining whether a federal statute pre-empts common-law causes of action, the relevant inquiry is whether the statute speaks directly

---

reader. See *United States v. Detroit Lumber Co.,* 200 U.S. 321, 337, 26 S.Ct. 282, 287, 50 L.Ed. 499.

to the question otherwise answered by federal common law. Here, the 1793 Act did not speak directly to the question of remedies for unlawful conveyances of Indian land, and there is no indication in the legislative history that Congress intended to pre-empt common-law remedies. *Milwaukee v. Illinois,* ₍₂₂₇₎451 U.S. 304, 101 S.Ct. 1784, 68 L.Ed.2d 114 (1981), distinguished. And Congress' actions subsequent to the 1793 Act and later versions thereof demonstrate that the Acts did not pre-empt common-law remedies. Pp. 1252–1254.

2. There is no merit to any of petitioners' alleged defenses. Pp. 1254–1260.

(a) Where, as here, there is no controlling federal limitations period, the general rule is that a state limitations period for an analogous cause of action will be borrowed and applied to the federal action, provided that application of the state statute would not be inconsistent with underlying federal policies. In this litigation, the borrowing of a state limitations period would be inconsistent with the federal policy against the application of state statutes of limitations in the context of Indian claims. Pp. 1254–1256.

(b) This Court will not reach the issue of whether respondents' claims are barred by laches, where the defense was unsuccessfully asserted at trial but not reasserted on appeal and thus not ruled upon by the Court of Appeals. Pp. 1256–1257.

(c) Respondents' cause of action did not abate when the 1793 Act expired. That Act merely codified the principle that a sovereign act was required to extinguish aboriginal title and thus that a conveyance without the sovereign's consent was void *ab initio.* All subsequent versions of the Act contain substantially the same restraint on alienation of Indian lands. P. 1257.

(d) In view of the principles that treaties with Indians should be construed liberally in favor of the Indians, and that congressional intent to extinguish Indian

title must be plain and unambiguous and will not be lightly implied, the 1798 and 1802 Treaties in which respondents ceded additional land to New York are not sufficient to show that the United States ratified New York's unlawful purchase of the land in question. Pp. 1257–1259.

(e) Nor are respondents' claims barred by the political question doctrine. Congress' constitutional authority over Indian affairs does not render the claims nonjusticiable, and, *a fortiori,* Congress' delegation of authority to the President does not do so either. Nor have petitioners shown any convincing reasons for thinking that there is a need for "unquestioning adherence" to the Commissioner of Indian Affairs' declining to bring an action on respondents' behalf with respect to the claims in question. Pp. 1259–1260.

3. The courts below erred in exercising ancillary jurisdiction over petitioners' cross-claim for indemnity by the State. The cross-claim raises a question of state law, and there is no evidence that the State has waived its constitutional immunity under the Eleventh Amendment to suit in federal court on this question. Pp. 1260–1261.

719 F.2d 525 (CA2 1983), affirmed in part, reversed in part, and remanded.

₍₂₂₈₎Allan van Gestel, for petitioners in No. 83–1065.

Peter H. Schiff, Asst. Atty. Gen., Albany, N.Y., for petitioner in No. 83–1240.

Arlinda F. Locklear, Washington, D.C., for respondents.

Edwin S. Kneedler, Washington, D.C., for U.S. as amicus curiae, by special leave of Court.

₍₂₂₉₎Justice POWELL delivered the opinion of the Court.**

These cases present the question whether three Tribes of the Oneida Indians may bring a suit for damages for the occupation

** THE CHIEF JUSTICE, Justice WHITE, and Justice REHNQUIST join only Part V of this opinion.

and use of tribal land allegedly conveyed unlawfully in 1795.

I

The Oneida Indian Nation of New York, the Oneida Indian Nation of Wisconsin, and the Oneida of the Thames Band Council (the Oneidas) instituted this suit in 1970 against the Counties of Oneida and Madison, New York. The Oneidas alleged that their ancestors conveyed 100,000 acres to the State of New York under a 1795 agreement that violated the Trade and Intercourse Act of 1793 (Nonintercourse Act), 1 Stat. 329, and thus that the transaction was void. The Oneidas' complaint sought damages representing the fair rental value of that part of the land presently owned and occupied by the Counties of Oneida and Madison, for the period January 1, 1968, through December 31, 1969.

The United States District Court for the Northern District of New York initially dismissed the action on the ground that the complaint failed to state a claim arising under the laws of the United States. The United States Court of Appeals for the Second Circuit affirmed. *Oneida Indian Nation v. County of Oneida*, 464 F.2d 916 (1972). We then granted certiorari and reversed. *Oneida Indian Nation v. County of Oneida*, 414 U.S. 661, 94 S.Ct. 772, 39 L.Ed.2d 73 (1974) (*Oneida I*). We held unanimously that, at least for jurisdictional purposes, the Oneidas stated a claim for possession under federal law. *Id.*, at 675, 94 S.Ct., at 781. The case was remanded for trial.

|230On remand, the District Court trifurcated trial of the issues. In the first phase, the court found the counties liable to the Oneidas for wrongful possession of their lands. 434 F.Supp. 527 (N.D.N.Y.1977). In the second phase, it awarded the Oneidas damages in the amount of $16,694, plus interest, representing the fair rental value of the land in question for the 2-year period specified in the complaint. Finally, the District Court held that the State of New York, a third-party defendant brought into the case by the counties, must indemnify

the counties for the damages owed to the Oneidas. The Court of Appeals affirmed the trial court's rulings with respect to liability and indemnification. 719 F.2d 525 (1983). It remanded, however, for further proceedings on the amount of damages. *Id.*, at 542. The counties and the State petitioned for review of these rulings. Recognizing the importance of the Court of Appeals' decision not only for the Oneidas, but potentially for many eastern Indian land claims, we granted certiorari, 465 U.S. 1099, 104 S.Ct. 1590, 80 L.Ed.2d 123 (1984), to determine whether an Indian tribe may have a live cause of action for a violation of its possessory rights that occurred 175 years ago. We hold that the Court of Appeals correctly so ruled.

II

The respondents in these cases are the direct descendants of members of the Oneida Indian Nation, one of the six nations of the Iroquois, the most powerful Indian Tribe in the Northeast at the time of the American Revolution. See B. Graymont, The Iroquois in the American Revolution (1972) (hereinafter Graymont). From time immemorial to shortly after the Revolution, the Oneidas inhabited what is now central New York State. Their aboriginal land was approximately six million acres, extending from the Pennsylvania border to the St. Lawrence River, from the shores of Lake Ontario to the western foothills of the Adirondack Mountains. See 434 F.Supp., at 533.

|231Although most of the Iroquois sided with the British, the Oneidas actively supported the colonists in the Revolution. *Ibid.;* see also Graymont, *supra*. This assistance prevented the Iroquois from asserting a united effort against the colonists, and thus the Oneidas' support was of considerable aid. After the War, the United States recognized the importance of the Oneidas' role, and in the Treaty of Fort Stanwix, 7 Stat. 15 (Oct. 22, 1784), the National Government promised that the Oneidas would be secure "in the possession

of the lands on which they are settled." Within a short period of time, the United States twice reaffirmed this promise, in the Treaties of Fort Harmar, 7 Stat. 33 (Jan. 9, 1789), and of Canandaigua, 7 Stat. 44 (Nov. 11, 1794).[1]

During this period, the State of New York came under increasingly heavy pressure to open the Oneidas' land for settlement. Consequently, in 1788, the State entered into a "treaty" with the Indians, in which it purchased the vast majority of the Oneidas' land. The Oneidas retained a reservation of about 300,000 acres, an area that, the parties stipulated below, included the land involved in this suit.

In 1790, at the urging of President Washington and Secretary of War Knox, Congress passed the first Indian Trade and Intercourse Act, ch. 33, 1 Stat. 137. See 4 American State Papers, Indian Affairs, Vol. 1, p. 53 (1832); F. Prucha, American Indian Policy in the Formative Years 43–44 (1962). The Act prohibited the conveyance of Indian land except ⌐232where such conveyances were entered pursuant to the treaty power of the United States.[2] In 1793, Congress passed a stronger, more detailed version of the Act, providing that "no purchase or grant of lands, or of any title or claim thereto, from any Indians or nation or tribe of Indians, within the bounds of the United States, shall be of any validity in law or equity, unless the same be made by a treaty or convention entered into pursuant to the constitution ... [and] in the presence, and with the approbation of the commissioner or commissioners of the United States" appointed to supervise such transactions. 1 Stat. 330,

§ 8. Unlike the 1790 version, the new statute included criminal penalties for violation of its terms. *Ibid.*

Despite Congress' clear policy that no person or entity should purchase Indian land without the acquiescence of the Federal Government, in 1795 the State of New York began negotiations to buy the remainder of the Oneidas' land. When this fact came to the attention of Secretary of War Pickering, he warned Governor Clinton, and later Governor Jay, that New York was required by the Nonintercourse Act to request the appointment of federal commissioners to supervise any land transaction with the Oneidas. See 434 F.Supp., at 534–535. The State ignored these warnings, and in the summer of 1795 entered into an agreement with the Oneidas whereby they conveyed virtually all of their remaining land to the State for annual cash payments. *Ibid.* It is this transaction that is the basis of the Oneidas' complaint in this case.

The District Court found that the 1795 conveyance did not comply with the requirements of the Nonintercourse ⌐233Act. *Id.*, at 538–541. In particular, the court stated that "[t]he only finding permitted by the record ... is that no United States Commissioner or other official of the federal government was present at the ... transaction." *Id.*, at 535. The petitioners did not dispute this finding on appeal. Rather, they argued that the Oneidas did not have a federal common-law cause of action for this violation. Even if such an action once existed, they contended that the Nonintercourse Act pre-empted it, and that the Oneidas could not maintain a private

1. The Treaty of Fort Harmar stated that the Oneidas and the Tuscaroras were "again secured and confirmed in the possession of their respective lands." 7 Stat. 34. The Treaty of Canandaigua of 1794 provided: "The United States acknowledge the lands reserved to the Oneida, Onondaga and Cayuga Nations, in their respective treaties with the state of New York, and called their reservations, to be their property; and the United States will never claim the same, nor disturb them ... in the free use and enjoyment thereof: but the said reservations shall remain theirs, until they choose to sell the same

to the people of the United States, who have the right to purchase." 7 Stat. 45.

2. Section 4 of the 1790 Act declared that "no sale of lands made by any Indians, or any nation or tribe of Indians within the United States, shall be valid to any person or persons, or to any state, whether having the right of pre-emption to such lands or not, unless the same shall be made and duly executed at some public treaty, held under the authority of the United States." 1 Stat. 138.

cause of action for violations of the Act. Additionally, they maintained that any such cause of action was time-barred or nonjusticiable, that any cause of action under the 1793 Act had abated, and that the United States had ratified the conveyance. The Court of Appeals, with one judge dissenting, rejected these arguments. Petitioners renew these claims here; we also reject them and affirm the court's finding of liability.

III

At the outset, we are faced with petitioner counties' contention that the Oneidas have no right of action for the violation of the 1793 Act. Both the District Court and the Court of Appeals rejected this claim, finding that the Oneidas had the right to sue on two theories: first, a common-law right of action for unlawful possession; and second, an implied statutory cause of action under the Nonintercourse Act of 1793. We need not reach the latter question as we think the Indians' common-law right to sue is firmly established.

A

Federal Common Law

By the time of the Revolutionary War, several well-defined principles had been established governing the nature of a tribe's interest in its property and how those inter-

ests could be conveyed. It was accepted that Indian nations held ⌐₂₃₄"aboriginal title" to lands they had inhabited from time immemorial. See Cohen, Original Indian Title, 32 Minn.L.Rev. 28 (1947). The "doctrine of discovery" provided, however, that discovering nations held fee title to these lands, subject to the Indians' right of occupancy and use. As a consequence, no one could purchase Indian land or otherwise terminate aboriginal title without the consent of the sovereign.[3] *Oneida I*, 414 U.S., at 667, 94 S.Ct., at 777. See Clinton & Hotopp, Judicial Enforcement of the Federal Restraints on Alienation of Indian Land: The Origins of the Eastern Land Claims, 31 Me.L.Rev. 17, 19–49 (1979).

[1] With the adoption of the Constitution, Indian relations became the exclusive province of federal law. *Oneida I, supra*, 414 U.S., at 670, 94 S.Ct., at 778–779 (citing *Worcester v. Georgia*, 6 Pet. 515, 561, 8 L.Ed. 483 (1832)).[4] From the first Indian claims presented, this Court ⌐₂₃₅recognized the aboriginal rights of the Indians to their lands. The Court spoke of the "unquestioned right" of the Indians to the exclusive possession of their lands, *Cherokee Nation v. Georgia*, 5 Pet. 1, 17, 8 L.Ed. 25 (1831), and stated that the Indians' right of occupancy is "as sacred as the fee simple of the whites." *Mitchel v. United States*, 9 Pet.

---

3. This Court explained the doctrine of discovery as follows:

"[D]iscovery gave title to the government by whose subjects, or by whose authority, it was made, against all other European governments, which title might be consummated by possession.

"The exclusion of all other Europeans, necessarily gave to the nation making the discovery the sole right of acquiring the soil from the natives, and establishing settlements upon it. . . .

"The rights thus acquired being exclusive, no other power could interpose between [the discoverer and the natives].

"In the establishment of these relations, the rights of the original inhabitants were, in no instance, entirely disregarded; but were necessarily, to a considerable extent, impaired. They were admitted to be the rightful occupants of the soil, with a legal as well as just claim to retain possession of it, and to use it according to

their own discretion; but their rights to complete sovereignty, as independent nations, were necessarily diminished, and their power to dispose of the soil at their own will, to whomsoever they pleased, was denied by the original fundamental principle, that discovery gave exclusive title to those who made it." *Johnson v. McIntosh*, 8 Wheat. 543, 573–574, 5 L.Ed. 681 (1823).

4. Madison cited the National Government's inability to control trade with the Indians as one of the key deficiencies of the Articles of Confederation, and urged adoption of the Indian Commerce Clause, Art. 1, § 8, cl. 3, that granted Congress the power to regulate trade with the Indians. The Federalist No. 42, p. 284 (J. Cooke, ed. 1961). See also Clinton & Hotopp, Judicial Enforcement of the Federal Restraints on Alienation of Indian Land: The Origins of the Eastern Land Claims, 31 Me.L.Rev. 17, 23–29 (1979).

711, 746, 9 L.Ed. 283 (1835). This principle has been reaffirmed consistently. See also *Fletcher v. Peck*, 6 Cranch 87, 142–143, 3 L.Ed 162 (1810); *Johnson v. McIntosh*, 8 Wheat. 543, 5 L.Ed. 681 (1823); *Clark v. Smith*, 13 Pet. 195, 201, 10 L.Ed. 123 (1839); *Lattimer v. Poteet*, 14 Pet. 4, 10 L.Ed. 328 (1840); *Chouteau v. Molony*, 16 How. 203, 14 L.Ed. 905 (1854); *Holden v. Joy*, 17 Wall. 211, 21 L.Ed. 523 (1872). Thus, as we concluded in *Oneida I*, "the possessory right claimed [by the Oneidas] is a *federal* right to the lands at issue in this case." 414 U.S., at 671, 94 S.Ct., at 779 (emphasis in original).

[2] Numerous decisions of this Court prior to *Oneida I* recognized at least implicitly that Indians have a federal common-law right to sue to enforce their aboriginal land rights.[5] In *Johnson v. McIntosh, supra,* the Court declared invalid two private purchases of Indian land that occurred in 1773 and 1775 without the Crown's consent. Subsequently in *Marsh v. Brooks*, 8 How. 223, 232, 12 L.Ed 1056 (1850), it was held: "That an action of ejectment could be maintained on an Indian right to occupancy and use, is not open to question. This is the result of the decision in Johnson v. McIntosh." More recently, the Court held that Indians have a common-law right of action for an accounting of "all rents, issues and |236profits" against trespassers on their land. *United States v. Santa Fe Pacific R. Co.*, 314 U.S. 339, 62 S.Ct. 248, 86 L.Ed. 260 (1941).[6] Finally, the Court's opinion in *Oneida I* implicitly assumed that the Oneidas could bring a common-law action to vindicate their aboriginal rights. Citing *United States v. Santa Fe*

5. Petitioners argue that *Jaeger v. United States,* 27 Ct.Cl. 278 (1892), holds that tribes can sue only when specifically authorized to do so by Congress. *Jaeger* is clearly inapposite to this case. It applied only to the special jurisdiction of the Court of Claims and to claims against the United States.

6. See also *Fellows v. Blacksmith,* 19 How. 366, 15 L.Ed. 684 (1857) (upholding trespass action on Indian land); *Inupiat Community of the Arctic Slope v. United States,* 230 Ct.Cl. 647, 656–657, 680 F.2d 122, 128–129 (right to sue for

Pacific R. Co., supra, at 347, 62 S.Ct., at 252, we noted that the Indians' right of occupancy need not be based on treaty, statute, or other formal Government action. 414 U.S., at 668–669, 94 S.Ct., at 777–778. We stated that "absent federal statutory guidance, the governing rule of decision would be fashioned by the federal court in the mode of the common law." *Id.,* at 674, 94 S.Ct., at 781 (citing *United States v. Forness,* 125 F.2d 928 (CA2), cert. denied *sub nom. City of Salamanca v. United States,* 316 U.S. 694, 62 S.Ct. 1293, 86 L.Ed. 1764 (1942)).

In keeping with these well-established principles, we hold that the Oneidas can maintain this action for violation of their possessory rights based on federal common law.

B

Pre-emption

[3] Petitioners argue that the Nonintercourse Acts pre-empted whatever right of action the Oneidas may have had at common law, relying on our decisions in *Milwaukee v. Illinois,* 451 U.S. 304, 101 S.Ct. 1784, 68 L.Ed.2d 114 (1981) (*Milwaukee II*), and *Middlesex County Sewerage Authority v. National Sea Clammers Assn.,* 453 U.S. 1, 101 S.Ct. 2615, 69 L.Ed.2d 435 (1981). We find this view to be unpersuasive. In determining whether a federal statute pre-empts common-law causes of action, the relevant inquiry is whether |237the statute "[speaks] *directly* to [the] question" otherwise answered by federal common law. *Milwaukee II, supra,* 451 U.S., at 315, 101 S.Ct., at 1791 (emphasis added). As we stated in *Milwaukee II,*

trespass is one of rights of Indian title), cert. denied, 459 U.S. 969, 103 S.Ct. 299, 74 L.Ed.2d 281 (1982) (right to sue for trespass is one of rights of Indian title); *United States v. Southern Pacific Transportation Co.,* 543 F.2d 676 (CA9 1976) (damages available against railroad that failed to acquire lawful easement or right-of-way over Indian reservation); *Edwardsen v. Morton,* 369 F.Supp. 1359, 1371 (DC Alaska 1973) (upholding trespass action based on aboriginal title).

federal common law is used as a "necessary expedient" when Congress has not "spoken to a *particular* issue." 451 U.S., at 313–314, 101 S.Ct., at 1790–1791 (emphasis added). The Nonintercourse Act of 1793 does not speak directly to the question of remedies for unlawful conveyances of Indian land. A comparison of the 1793 Act and the statute at issue in *Milwaukee II* is instructive.

Milwaukee II raised the question whether a common-law action for the abatement of a nuisance caused by the pollution of interstate waterways survived the passage of the 1972 amendments to the Federal Water Pollution Control Act, Pub.L. 92–500, 86 Stat. 816 (FWPCA).[7] FWPCA established an elaborate system for dealing with the problem of interstate water pollution, providing for enforcement of its terms by agency action and citizens suits. See *Milwaukee II, supra,* at 325–327, 101 S.Ct., at 1796–1798. It also made available civil penalties for violations of the Act. 33 U.S.C. §§ 1319(d), 1365. The legislative history indicated that Congress intended

FWPCA to provide a comprehensive solution to the problem of interstate water pollution, as we noted in *Milwaukee II, supra,* at 317–319, 101 S.Ct., at 1792–1794.

[4] In contrast, the Nonintercourse Act of 1793 did not establish a comprehensive remedial plan for dealing with violations of Indian property rights. There is no indication in the legislative history that Congress intended to pre-empt common-law remedies.[8] Only two sections of the Act, §§ 5 and 8, |₂₃₈involve Indian lands at all.[9] The relevant clause of § 8 provides simply that "no purchase or grant of lands, or of any title or claim thereto, from any Indians or nation or tribe of Indians, within the bounds of the United States, shall be of any validity in law or equity, unless the same be made by a treaty or convention entered into pursuant to the constitution...." 1 Stat. 330. It contains no remedial provision.[10] Section 5 subjects individuals who settle on Indian lands to a fine and imprisonment, and gives the President discretionary authority to remove illegal settlers from the Indians' land.[11] |₂₃₉Thus,

---

7. Previously, in *Illinois v. City of Milwaukee,* 406 U.S. 91, 92 S.Ct. 1385, 31 L.Ed.2d 712 (1972), the Court had held that federal common law provided a cause of action for the abatement of interstate water pollution.

8. There is some contemporaneous evidence to the contrary. President Washington, at whose urging the first Acts were passed, met with Cornplanter, Chief of the Seneca Nation, shortly after the enactment of the 1790 Act. They discussed the Senecas' complaints about land transactions, and Washington assured them that the new statute would protect their interests. Washington told Cornplanter:

   "Here, then, is the security for the remainder of your lands. No State, nor person, can purchase your lands, unless at some public treaty, held under the authority of the United States....

   .   .   .   .   .

   "If ... you have any just cause of complaint against [a purchaser] and can make satisfactory proof thereof, the federal courts will be open to you for redress, as to all other persons." 4 American State papers, Indian Affairs, Vol. 1, p. 142 (1832).

9. The Act contained 15 sections. A number of these set out licensing requirements for those who wished to trade with the Indians (§§ 1, 2, 3). Several others established special requirements for purchasing horses from Indians

(§§ 6, 7). Others gave the United States courts jurisdiction over offenses under the Act (§§ 10, 11) and provided for the division of fines and forfeitures (§ 12). 1 Stat. 329–333.

10. The second clause of § 8 makes it a criminal offense to negotiate a treaty or convention for the conveyance of Indian land, except under the authority and in the presence of United States commissioners. 1 Stat. 330. It likewise makes no provision to restore illegally purchased land to the Indians.

   Petitioners make much of the fact that the 1793 Act contained criminal penalties in arguing that the Act pre-empted common-law actions. In property law, however, it is common to have criminal and civil sanctions available for infringement of property rights, and for government officials to use the police power to remove trespassers from privately owned land. See 5 R. Powell, Real Property ¶ 758 (1984).

11. The Act authorizes the President "to take such measures, as he may judge necessary, to remove from lands belonging to any Indian tribe, any citizens or inhabitants of the United States, who have made, or shall hereafter make, or attempt to make a settlement thereon." 1 Stat. 330. It imposes no obligation on the Executive to take remedial action, and apparently

the Nonintercourse Act does not address directly the problem of restoring unlawfully conveyed land to the Indians, in contrast to the specific remedial provisions contained in FWPCA. See *Milwaukee II,* 451 U.S., at 313–315, 101 S.Ct., at 1790–1791.

Significantly, Congress' action subsequent to the enactment of the 1793 statute and later versions of the Nonintercourse Act demonstrate that the Acts did not preempt common-law remedies. In 1822 Congress amended the 1802 version of the Act to provide that "in all trials about the right of property, in which Indians shall be party on one side and white persons on the other, the burden of proof shall rest upon the white person, in every case in which the Indian shall make out a presumption of title in himself from the fact of previous possession and ownership." § 4, 3 Stat. 683; see 25 U.S.C. § 194. Thus, Congress apparently contemplated suits by Indians asserting their property rights.

[5] Decisions of this Court also contradict petitioners' argument for pre-emption. Most recently, in *Wilson v. Omaha Indian Tribe,* 442 U.S. 653, 99 S.Ct. 2529, 61 L.Ed.2d 153 (1979), the Omaha Indian Tribe sued to quiet title on land that had surfaced over the years as the Missouri River changed its course. The Omahas based their claim for possession on aboriginal title. The Court construed the 1822 amendment to apply to suits brought by Indian tribes as well as individual Indians. Citing the very sections of the Act that petitioners contend pre-empt a common-law action by the Indians, the Court interpreted the

amendment to be part of the overall "design" of the Nonintercourse Acts "to protect the rights of Indians to their properties." *Id.,* at 664, 99 S.Ct., at 2536. See also *Fellows v. Blacksmith,* 19 How. 366, 15 L.Ed 684 (1857).[12]

⌊240 We recognized in *Oneida I* that the Nonintercourse Acts simply "put in statutory form what was or came to be the accepted rule—that the extinguishment of Indian title required the consent of the United States." 414 U.S., at 678, 94 S.Ct., at 782. Nothing in the statutory formulation of this rule suggests that the Indians' right to pursue common-law remedies was thereby pre-empted. Accordingly, we hold that the Oneidas' right of action under federal common law was not pre-empted by the passage of the Nonintercourse Acts.

IV

Having determined that the Oneidas have a cause of action under federal common law, we address the question whether there are defenses available to the counties. We conclude that none has merit.

A

Statute of Limitations

[6–8] There is no federal statute of limitations governing federal common-law actions by Indians to enforce property rights. In the absence of a controlling federal limitations period, the general rule is that a state limitations period for an analogous cause of action is borrowed and applied to the federal claim, provided that the application of the state statute would not be incon-

---

was intended only to give the President discretionary authority to preserve the peace.

12. Similarly, we find no support for petitioners' contention that the availability of suits by the United States on behalf of Indian tribes precludes common-law actions by the tribes themselves. See *Poafpybitty v. Skelly Oil Co.,* 390 U.S. 365, 369, 88 S.Ct. 982, 984, 19 L.Ed.2d 1238 (1968); *Creek Nation v. United States,* 318 U.S. 629, 640, 63 S.Ct. 784, 789, 87 L.Ed. 1046 (1943) (citing *Cherokee Nation v. Southern Kansas R. Co.,* 135 U.S. 641, 10 S.Ct. 965, 34 L.Ed. 295

(1890); *Cherokee Nation v. Hitchcock,* 187 U.S. 294, 23 S.Ct. 115, 47 L.Ed. 183 (1902); and *Lone Wolf v. Hitchcock,* 187 U.S. 553, 23 S.Ct. 216, 47 L.Ed. 299 (1903)). See also *Moe v. Confederated Salish & Kootenai Tribes,* 425 U.S. 463, 473, 96 S.Ct. 1634, 1641, 48 L.Ed.2d 96 (1976) ("[I]t would appear that Congress contemplated that a tribe's access to federal court to litigate a matter arising 'under the Constitution, laws, or treaties' would be at least in some respects as broad as that of the United States suing as the tribe's trustee").

sistent with underlying federal policies.[13] See [241]*Johnson v. Railway Express Agency, Inc.*, 421 U.S. 454, 465, 95 S.Ct. 1716, 1722, 44 L.Ed.2d 295 (1975). See also *Occidental Life Ins. Co. v. EEOC*, 432 U.S. 355, 367, 97 S.Ct. 2447, 2454, 53 L.Ed.2d 402 (1977). We think the borrowing of a state limitations period in these cases would be inconsistent with federal policy. Indeed, on a number of occasions Congress has made this clear with respect to Indian land claims.

In adopting the statute that gave jurisdiction over civil actions involving Indians to the New York courts, Congress included this proviso: "[N]othing herein contained shall be construed as conferring jurisdiction on the courts of the State of New York or making applicable the laws of the State of New York in civil actions involving Indian lands or claims with respect thereto which relate to transactions or events transpiring prior to September 13, 1952." 25 U.S.C. § 233. This proviso was added specifically to ensure that the New York statute of limitations would not apply to pre-1952 land claims.[14] In *Oneida I*, we relied on the legislative history of 25 U.S.C. § 233 in concluding that Indian land claims were exclusively a matter of federal law. 414 U.S., at 680–682, 94 S.Ct., at 784–785. This history also reflects congressional policy against the application of state statutes of limitations in the context of Indian land claims.

Congress recently reaffirmed this policy in addressing the question of the appropriate statute of limitations for certain claims brought by the United States on behalf of Indians. Originally enacted in 1966, this statute provided a special limitations period of 6 years and 90 days for contract and tort suits for damages brought by the United States [242]on behalf of Indians. 28 U.S.C. §§ 2415(a), (b). The statute stipulated that claims that accrued prior to its date of enactment, July 18, 1966, were deemed to have accrued on that date. § 2415(g). Section 2415(c) excluded from the limitations period all actions "to establish the title to, or right of possession of, real or personal property."

In 1972 and again in 1977, 1980, and 1982, as the statute of limitations was about to expire for pre-1966 claims, Congress extended the time within which the United States could bring suits on behalf of the Indians. The legislative history of the 1972, 1977, and 1980 amendments demonstrates that Congress did not intend § 2415 to apply to suits brought by the Indians themselves, and that it assumed that the Indians' right to sue was not otherwise subject to any statute of limitations. Both proponents and opponents of the amendments shared these views. See 123 Cong. Rec. 22167–22168 (1977) (remarks of Rep. Dicks, arguing that extension is unnecessary because the Indians can bring suit even if the statute of limitations expires for the United States); *id.*, at 22166 and 22499 (remarks of Rep. Cohen, arguing that the basic problem with the bill is its failure to limit suits brought by Indians); 126 Cong. Rec. 3289 (1980) (remarks of Sen. Melcher, reiterating with respect to the 1980 extension Rep. Dicks' argument against the 1977 extension); *id.*, at 3290 (remarks of Sen. Cohen, same); Statute of Limitations Extension: Hearing before the Senate Select Committee on Indian Affairs, 96th Cong., 1st Sess., 312–314 (1979); Statute of Limitations Extension for Indian Claims: Hear-

---

13. Under the Supremacy Clause, state-law time bars, *e.g.*, adverse possession and laches, do not apply of their own force to Indian land title claims. See *Ewert v. Bluejacket*, 259 U.S. 129, 137–138, 42 S.Ct. 442, 444, 66 L.Ed. 858 (1922); *United States v. Ahtanum Irrigation District*, 236 F.2d 321, 334 (CA9 1956), cert. denied, 352 U.S. 988, 77 S.Ct. 386, 1 L.Ed.2d 367 (1957).

14. Representative Morris, the sponsor of the proviso, stated:

"As it is now, the Indians, as we know, are wards of the Government and, therefore, the statute of limitations does not run against them as it does in the ordinary case. This [proviso] will preserve their rights so that the statute will not be running against them concerning those claims that might have arisen before the passage of this act." 96 Cong.Rec. 12460 (1950).

ings on S. 1377 before the Senate Select Committee on Indian Affairs, 95th Cong., 1st Sess., 76–77 (1977); Time Extension for Commencing Actions on Behalf of Indians: Hearing on S. 3377 and H.R. 13825 before the Subcommittee on Indian Affairs of the Senate Committee on Interior and Insular Affairs, 92d Cong., 2d Sess., 23 (1972).

With the enactment of the 1982 amendments, Congress for the first time imposed a statute of limitations on certain tort |244and contract claims for damages brought by individual Indians and Indian tribes. These amendments, enacted as the Indian Claims Limitation Act of 1982, Pub.L. 97–394, 96 Stat. 1976, note following 28 U.S.C. § 2415, established a system for the final resolution of pre-1966 claims cognizable under §§ 2415(a) and (b). The Act directed the Secretary of the Interior to compile and publish in the Federal Register a list of all Indian claims to which the statute of limitations provided in 28 U.S.C. § 2415 applied. The Act also directed that the Secretary notify those Indians who may have an interest in any such claims. The Indians were then given an opportunity to submit additional claims; these were to be compiled and published on a second list. Actions for claims subject to the limitations periods of § 2415 that appeared on neither list were barred unless commenced within 60 days of the publication of the second list. If at any time the Secretary decides not to pursue a claim on one of the lists, "*any* right of action shall be barred unless the complaint is filed within one year after the date of publication [of the notice of the Secretary's decision] in the Federal Register." Pub.L. 97–394, 96 Stat. 1978, § 5(c) (emphasis added). Thus, § 5(c)

implicitly imposed a 1-year statute of limitations within which the Indians must bring contract and tort claims that are covered by §§ 2415(a) and (b) and not listed by the Secretary. So long as a listed claim is neither acted upon nor formally rejected by the Secretary, it remains live.[15]

[9] |244The legislative history of the successive amendments to § 2415 is replete with evidence of Congress' concern that the United States had failed to live up to its responsibilities as trustee for the Indians, and that the Department of the Interior had not acted with appropriate dispatch in meeting the deadlines provided by § 2415. *E.g.,* Authorizing Indian Tribes to Bring Certain Actions on Behalf of their Members with Respect to Certain Legal Claims, and for Other Purposes, H.R.Rep. No. 97–954, p. 5 (1982). By providing a 1-year limitations period for claims that the Secretary decides not to pursue, Congress intended to give the Indians one last opportunity to file suits covered by § 2415(a) and (b) on their own behalf. Thus, we think the statutory framework adopted in 1982 presumes the existence of an Indian right of action not otherwise subject to any statute of limitations. It would be a violation of Congress' will were we to hold that a state statute of limitations period should be borrowed in these circumstances.

B

Laches

[10] The dissent argues that we should apply the equitable doctrine of laches to hold that the Oneidas' claim is barred. Although it is far from clear that this defense is available in suits such as this one,[16] we

---

15. The two lists were published in the Federal Register on March 31, 1983, and November 7, 1983, respectively. 48 Fed.Reg. 13698, 51204. The Oneidas' claims are on the first list compiled by the Secretary. *Id.,* at 13920. These claims would not be barred, however, even if they were not listed. The Oneidas commenced this suit in 1970 when no statute of limitations applied to claims brought by the Indians themselves. Additionally, if claims like the Oneidas', *i.e.,* damages actions that involve litigating the

continued vitality of aboriginal title, are construed to be suits "to establish the title to, or right of possession of, real or personal property," they would be exempt from the statute of limitations of the Indian Claims Limitations Act of 1982. The Government agrees with this view. Brief for United States as *Amicus Curiae* 24–25.

16. We note, as Justice STEVENS properly recognizes, that application of the equitable defense of laches in an action at law would be novel indeed. Moreover, the logic of the Court's hold-

do not reach this issue today. |₂₄₅While petitioners argued at trial that the Oneidas were guilty of laches, the District Court ruled against them and they did not reassert this defense on appeal. As a result, the Court of Appeals did not rule on this claim, and we likewise decline to do so.

C

Abatement

[11] Petitioners argue that any cause of action for violation of the Nonintercourse Act of 1793 abated when the statute expired. They note that Congress specifically provided that the 1793 Act would be in force "for the term of two years, and from thence to the end of the then next session of Congress, and no longer." 1 Stat. 332, § 15. They contend that the 1796 version of the Nonintercourse Act repealed the 1793 version and enacted an entirely new statute, and that under the common-law abatement doctrine in effect at the time, any cause of action for violation of the statute finally abated on the expiration of the statute.[17] We disagree.

The pertinent provision of the 1793 Act, § 8, like its predecessor, § 4 of the 1790 Act, 1 Stat. 138, merely codified the principle that a sovereign act was required to extinguish aboriginal title and thus that a conveyance without the sovereign's consent was void *ab initio*. See *supra*, at 1251, |₂₄₆and n. 3. All of the subsequent versions of the Nonintercourse Act, including that now in force, 25 U.S.C. § 177, contain substantially the same restraint on the alienation of Indian lands. In these circumstances, the precedents of this Court compel the conclusion that the Oneidas' cause of action has not abated.[18]

D

Ratification

[12] We are similarly unpersuaded by petitioners' contention that the United States has ratified the unlawful 1795 conveyances. Petitioners base this argument on federally approved treaties in 1798 and 1802 in which the Oneidas ceded additional

---

ing in *Ewert v. Bluejacket*, 259 U.S. 129, 42 S.Ct. 442, 66 L.Ed. 858 (1922), seems applicable here: "the equitable doctrine of laches, developed and designed to protect good-faith transactions against those who have slept on their rights, with knowledge and ample opportunity to assert them, cannot properly have application to give vitality to a void deed and to bar the rights of Indian wards in lands subject to statutory restrictions." *Id.*, at 138, 42 S.Ct., at 444. Additionally, this Court has indicated that extinguishment of Indian title requires a sovereign act. See, *e.g.*, *Oneida I*, 414 U.S. 661, 670, 94 S.Ct. 772, 778, 39 L.Ed.2d 73 (1974); *United States v. Candelaria*, 271 U.S. 432, 439, 46 S.Ct. 561, 562, 70 L.Ed. 1023 (1926), quoting *United States v. Sandoval*, 231 U.S. 28, 45–47, 34 S.Ct. 1, 5–6, 58 L.Ed. 107 (1913). In these circumstances, it is questionable whether laches properly could be applied. Furthermore, the statutory restraint on alienation of Indian tribal land adopted by the Nonintercourse Act of 1793 is still the law. See 25 U.S.C. § 177. This fact not only distinguishes the cases relied upon by the dissent, but also suggests that, as with the borrowing of state statutes of limitations, the application of laches would appear to be inconsistent with established federal policy. Although the issue of laches is not before us, we add these observations in response to the dissent.

17. It is questionable whether the common-law doctrine of abatement is even relevant to the statutory provision at issue in this case. The doctrine principally applies to criminal law, and provides that all prosecutions that have not proceeded to final judgment under a statute that has been repealed or has expired have abated, unless the repealing legislature provides otherwise. See *Warden v. Marrero*, 417 U.S. 653, 660, 94 S.Ct. 2532, 2536, 41 L.Ed.2d 383 (1974).

18. The reasoning of *Bear Lake and River Water Works and Irrigation Co. v. Garland*, 164 U.S. 1, 11–12, 17 S.Ct. 7, 9, 41 L.Ed. 327 (1896), is directly on point:
"Although there is a formal repeal of the old by the new statute, still there never has been a moment of time since the passage of the [old] act ... when these similar provisions have not been in force. Notwithstanding, therefore, this formal repeal, it is ... entirely correct to say that the new act should be construed as a continuation of the old...."
Accord, *Steamship Co. v. Joliffe*, 2 Wall. 450, 458, 17 L.Ed. 805 (1865); *Great Northern R. Co. v. United States*, 155 Fed. 945, 948 (CA8 1907), aff'd, 208 U.S. 452, 28 S.Ct. 313, 52 L.Ed. 567 (1908).

land to the State of New York.[19] There is a question [247] whether the 1802 treaty ever became effective.[20] Assuming it did, neither the 1798 nor the 1802 treaty qualifies as federal ratification of the 1795 conveyance.

The canons of construction applicable in Indian law are rooted in the unique trust relationship between the United States and the Indians. Thus, it is well established that treaties should be construed liberally in favor of the Indians, *Choctaw Nation v. United States*, 318 U.S. 423, 431–432, 63 S.Ct. 672, 677–678, 87 L.Ed. 877 (1943); *Choate v. Trapp*, 224 U.S. 665, 675, 32 S.Ct. 565, 569, 56 L.Ed. 941 (1912), with ambiguous provisions interpreted to their benefit, *McClanahan v. Arizona State Tax Comm'n*, 411 U.S. 164, 174, 93 S.Ct. 1257, 1263, 36 L.Ed.2d 129 (1973); *Carpenter v. Shaw*, 280 U.S. 363, 367, 50 S.Ct. 121, 122, 74 L.Ed. 478 (1930); *Winters v. United States*, 207 U.S. 564, 576–577, 28 S.Ct. 207, 211–212, 52 L.Ed. 340 (1908). "Absent explicit statutory language," *Washington v. Washington State Commercial Passenger Fishing Vessel Assn.*, 443 U.S. 658, 690, 99 S.Ct. 3055, 3077, 61 L.Ed.2d 823 (1979), this Court accordingly has refused to find that Congress has abrogated Indian treaty rights. *Menominee Tribe v. United States*, 391 U.S. 404, 88 S.Ct. 1705, 20

L.Ed.2d 697 (1968). See generally F. Cohen, Handbook of Federal Indian Law 221–225 (1982 ed.) (hereinafter F. Cohen).

The Court has applied similar canons of construction in nontreaty matters. Most importantly, the Court has held that congressional intent to extinguish Indian title must be [248] "plain and unambiguous," *United States v. Santa Fe Pacific R. Co.*, 314 U.S., at 346, 62 S.Ct., at 251, and will not be "lightly implied," *id.*, at 354, 62 S.Ct., at 255. Relying on the strong policy of the United States "from the beginning to respect the Indian right of occupancy," *id.*, at 345, 62 S.Ct., at 251 (citing *Cramer v. United States*, 261 U.S. 219, 227, 43 S.Ct. 342, 344, 67 L.Ed. 622 (1923)), the Court concluded that it "[c]ertainly" would require "plain and unambiguous action to deprive the [Indians] of the benefits of that policy," 314 U.S., at 346, 62 S.Ct., at 251. See F. Cohen.

In view of these principles, the treaties relied upon by petitioners are not sufficient to show that the United States ratified New York's unlawful purchase of the Oneidas' land. The language cited by petitioners, a reference in the 1798 treaty to "the last purchase" and one in the 1802 treaty to "land heretofore ceded," far from demonstrates a plain and unambiguous intent to extinguish Indian title. See n. 19, *su-*

---

19. The 1798 Treaty provided:
"[T]he said Indians do cede release and quit claim to the people of the State of New York forever all the lands within their reservation to the westward and southwestward of a line from the northeastern corner of lot No. 54 in *the last purchase from them* running northerly to a Button wood tree ... standing on the bank of the Oneida lake". Treaty of June 1, 1798, reproduced in Ratified Indian Treaties 1722–1869, National Archives Microfilm Publications, Microcopy No. 668 (roll 2) (emphasis added).
The 1802 Treaty provided:
"All that certain tract of land beginning at the southwest corner of the land lying along the Gennesee Road, ... and running thence along the last mentioned tract easterly to the southeast corner thereof; thence southerly, in the direction of the continuation of the east bounds of said last mentioned tract, to *other lands heretofore ceded* by the said Oneida nation of Indians to the People of the State of New York." Treaty of June 4, 1802, reproduced in 4 American State

Papers, Indian Affairs, Vol. 1, p. 664 (1832) (emphasis added).

20. Although both treaties were approved by the Senate, see 1 Journal of the Executive Proceedings of the Senate of the United States 312 (1828); *id.*, at 428, neither is contained in the compilation of "all Treaties with ... Indian tribes" compiled at Congress' direction. See J.Res. 10, 5 Stat. 799 (1845). There is evidence that President Adams signed the 1798 Treaty in the February 23, 1799, entry in his Journal of executive actions, March 1797-March 1799 ("Signed a treaty with the Oneida nation"), reproduced in The Adams Family Papers, John Adams, *Misc.* (Lib.Cong. Reel No. 194). Moreover, the 1798 Treaty was included in an 1822 compilation of treaties with the Indians that extinguished Indian title in New York. H.R. Doc. No. 74, 17th Cong., 1st Sess., 8 (1822). There is no similar evidence that the 1802 Treaty was signed by the President.

pra. There is no indication that either the Senate or the President intended by these references to ratify the 1795 conveyance. See 1 Journal of the Executive Proceedings of the Senate 273, 312, 408, 428 (1828).[21]

E

Nonjusticiability

[13] The claim also is made that the issue presented by the Oneidas' action is a nonjusticiable political question. The counties contend first that Art. 1, § 8, cl. 3, of the Constitution explicitly commits responsibility for Indian affairs to Congress.[22] Moreover, they argue that Congress has given exclusive civil remedial authority to the Executive for cases |249 such as this one, citing the Nonintercourse Acts and the 1794 Treaty of Canandaigua.[23] Thus, they say this case falls within the political question doctrine because of "a textually demonstrable constitutional commitment of the issue to a coordinate political department." *Baker v. Carr*, 369 U.S. 186, 217, 82 S.Ct. 691, 710, 7 L.Ed.2d 663 (1962). Additionally, the counties argue that the question is nonjusticiable because there is "an unusual need for unquestioning adherence to a political decision already made." *Ibid.* None of these claims is meritorious.

This Court has held specifically that Congress' plenary power in Indian affairs under Art. 1, § 8, cl. 3, does not mean that

litigation involving such matters necessarily entails nonjusticiable political questions. *Delaware Tribal Business Committee v. Weeks*, 430 U.S. 73, 83–84, 97 S.Ct. 911, 918–919, 51 L.Ed.2d 173 (1977). Accord, *United States v. Sioux Nation*, 448 U.S. 371, 413, 100 S.Ct. 2716, 2739, 65 L.Ed.2d 844 (1980). See also *Baker v. Carr, supra*, 369 U.S., at 215–217, 82 S.Ct., at 709–710. If Congress' constitutional authority over Indian affairs does not render the Oneidas' claim nonjusticiable, *a fortiori*, Congress' delegation of authority to the President does not do so either.[24]

We are also unpersuaded that petitioners have shown "an unusual need for unquestioning adherence to a political decision already made." *Baker v. Carr, supra*, at 217, 82 S.Ct., at 710. |250 The basis for their argument is the fact that in 1968, the Commissioner of Indian Affairs declined to bring an action on behalf of the Oneidas with respect to the claims asserted in these cases. The counties cite no cases in which analogous decisions provided the basis for nonjusticiability. Cf. *INS v. Chadha*, 462 U.S. 919, 103 S.Ct. 2764, 77 L.Ed.2d 317 (1983); *United States v. Nixon*, 418 U.S. 683, 94 S.Ct. 3090, 41 L.Ed.2d 1039 (1974); *Powell v. McCormack*, 395 U.S. 486, 89 S.Ct. 1944, 23 L.Ed.2d 491 (1969). Our cases suggest that such "unusual need"

---

21. The cases relied upon by petitioners likewise do not support a finding of ratification here. *Rosebud Sioux Tribe v. Kneip*, 430 U.S. 584, 97 S.Ct. 1361, 51 L.Ed.2d 660 (1977), expressly reaffirmed the principles of construction which we apply in this case. Petitioners' other cases, *e.g.*, *FPC v. Tuscarora Indian Nation*, 362 U.S. 99, 80 S.Ct. 543, 4 L.Ed.2d 584 (1960), and *Shoshone Tribe v. United States*, 299 U.S. 476, 57 S.Ct. 244, 81 L.Ed. 360 (1937), do so implicitly.

22. "The Congress shall have Power ... To regulate Commerce with foreign Nations, and among the several States, and with the Indian Tribes."

23. The counties rely on the language in the Treaty providing that "complaint shall be made by ... the Six Nations or any of them, to the President of the United States, or the Superintendant by him appointed ... and such prudent measures shall then be pursued as shall be necessary to preserve our peace and friendship

unbroken; until the legislature ... of the United States shall make other equitable provision for the purpose." Art. VII, Treaty of Canandaigua, Nov. 11, 1794, 7 Stat. 46.

24. Moreover, Congress' delegation to the President is not a "textually demonstrable *constitutional* commitment," *Baker v. Carr*, 369 U.S., at 217, 82 S.Ct., at 710 (emphasis added), but rather a statutory commitment of authority. We have held today that the Nonintercourse Acts do not pre-empt common-law causes of action by Indian tribes to enforce their property rights. The language in the Treaty of Canandaigua, see n. 23, *supra*, is likewise an insufficient basis on which to find that the Oneidas' federal common-law right of action has been pre-empted. Thus, the predicate of petitioners' argument, that Congress has delegated exclusive civil remedial authority to the President, must fail.

arises most of the time, if not always, in the area of foreign affairs. *Baker v. Carr, supra,* 369 U.S., at 211–213, 82 S.Ct., at 706–708; see also *Gilligan v. Morgan,* 413 U.S. 1, 93 S.Ct. 2440, 37 L.Ed.2d 407 (1973). Nor do the counties offer convincing reasons for thinking that there is a need for "unquestioning adherence" to the Commissioner's decision. Indeed, the fact that the Secretary of the Interior has listed the Oneidas' claims under the § 2415 procedure suggests that the Commissioner's 1968 decision was not a decision on the merits of the Oneidas' claims. See n. 15, *supra.*[25]

We conclude, therefore, that the Oneidas' claim is not barred by the political question doctrine.

V

Finally, we face the question whether the Court of Appeals correctly held that the federal courts could exercise ancillary jurisdiction over the counties' cross-claim against the State of New York for indemnification. The counties assert that this claim arises under both state and federal law. The Court of Appeals did not decide whether it was based on state or federal law. See 719 F.2d, at 542–544. It held, however, that the 1790 and 1793 Nonintercourse Acts "placed New York on notice that Congress had exercised its power to regulate commerce with the Indians. Thus, anything New York |251thereafter did with respect to Indian lands carried with it a waiver of the State's eleventh amendment immunity." *Id.,* at 543 (citing *Edelman v. Jordan,* 415 U.S. 651, 672, 94 S.Ct. 1347, 1360, 39 L.Ed.2d 662 (1974), and *Employees v. Missouri Dept. of Public Health and Welfare,* 411 U.S. 279, 283–284, 93 S.Ct. 1614, 1617–1618, 36 L.Ed.2d 251 (1973)). In essence, the Court of Appeals held that by violating a federal statute, the State consented to suit in federal court by any party on any claim, state or federal, growing out of the same nucleus of opera-

tive facts as the statutory violation. This proposition has no basis in law.

[14, 15] The counties' cross-claim for indemnification raises a classic example of ancillary jurisdiction. See *Owen Equipment & Erection Co. v. Kroger,* 437 U.S. 365, 98 S.Ct. 2396, 57 L.Ed.2d 274 (1978). The Eleventh Amendment forecloses, however, the application of normal principles of ancillary and pendent jurisdiction where claims are pressed against the State. *Pennhurst State School and Hospital v. Halderman,* 465 U.S. 89, 104 S.Ct. 900, 79 L.Ed.2d 67 (1984). As we held in *Pennhurst:* "[N]either pendent jurisdiction nor any other basis of jurisdiction may override the Eleventh Amendment. A federal court must examine each claim in a case to see if the court's jurisdiction over that claim is barred by the Eleventh Amendment." *Id.,* at 121, 104 S.Ct., at 919. The indemnification claim here, whether cast as a question of New York law or federal common law, is a claim against the State for retroactive monetary relief. In the absence of the State's consent, *id.,* at 99, 104 S.Ct., at 907 (citing *Clark v. Barnard,* 108 U.S. 436, 447, 2 S.Ct. 878, 882, 27 L.Ed. 780 (1883)), the suit is barred by the Eleventh Amendment. Thus, as the Court of Appeals recognized, whether the State has consented to waive its constitutional immunity is the critical factor in whether the federal courts properly exercised ancillary jurisdiction over the counties' claim for indemnification. *Pennhurst, supra.*

[16] The only ground the Court of Appeals and the counties offer for believing that the State has consented to suit in federal court on this claim is the fact that it violated the 1793 Nonintercourse Act by purchasing the Oneidas' land. |252The counties assert that because the Constitution specifically authorizes Congress "[t]o regulate Commerce ... with the Indian Tribes," the States necessarily consented to

---

25. We note that the Commissioner's decision was based on the fact that the same claims were then pending before the Indian Claims Commis-

sion. The Oneidas have since withdrawn their claims from the Indian Claims Commission.

suit in federal court with respect to enactments under this Clause. See *County of Monroe v. Florida,* 678 F.2d 1124 (CA2 1982) (making an analogous argument with respect to Congress' extradition power), cert. denied, 459 U.S. 1104, 103 S.Ct. 726, 74 L.Ed.2d 951 (1983); *Mills Music, Inc. v. Arizona,* 591 F.2d 1278, 1285 (CA9 1979) (making such an argument with respect to Congress' power over copyright and patents). Thus, they contend, Congress can abrogate the States' Eleventh Amendment immunity and has done so by enacting the Nonintercourse Acts. By violating the 1793 Act, the State thus waived its immunity to suit in federal court with respect to such violations.

Assuming, without deciding, that this reasoning is correct, it does not address the Eleventh Amendment problem here, for the counties' indemnification claim against the State does not arise under the 1793 Act. The counties cite no authority for their contrary view. They urge simply that the State would be unjustly enriched if the counties were forced to pay the Oneidas without indemnity from the State, and thus that the Court should "fashion a remedy" for the counties under the 1793 Act. This is an argument on the merits; it is not an argument that the indemnification claim arises under the Act. As we said in *Pennhurst,* "[a] State's constitutional interest in immunity encompasses not merely *whether* it may be sued, but *where* it may be sued." 465 U.S., at 99, 104 S.Ct., at 907 (emphasis in original). The Eleventh Amendment bar does not vary with the merits of the claims pressed against the State.

We conclude, therefore, that the counties' cross-claim for indemnity by the State raises a question of state law. We are

referred to no evidence that the State has waived its constitutional immunity to suit in federal court on this question.[26] [253]Thus, under *Pennhurst,* we hold that the federal courts erred in exercising ancillary jurisdiction over this claim.

VI

The decisions of this Court emphasize "Congress' unique obligation toward the Indians." *Morton v. Mancari,* 417 U.S. 535, 555, 94 S.Ct. 2474, 2485, 41 L.Ed.2d 290 (1974). The Government, in an *amicus curiae* brief, urged the Court to affirm the Court of Appeals. Brief for United States as *Amicus Curiae* 28. The Government recognized, as we do, the potential consequences of affirmance. It was observed, however, that "Congress has enacted legislation to extinguish Indian title and claims related thereto in other eastern States, ... and it could be expected to do the same in New York should the occasion arise." *Id.,* at 29–30. See Rhode Island Indian Claims Settlement Act, 25 U.S.C. § 1701 *et seq.;* Maine Indian Claims Settlement Act, 25 U.S.C. § 1721 *et seq.* We agree that this litigation makes abundantly clear the necessity for congressional action.

One would have thought that claims dating back for more than a century and a half would have been barred long ago. As our opinion indicates, however, neither petitioners nor we have found any applicable statute of limitations or other relevant legal basis for holding that the Oneidas' claims are barred or otherwise have been satisfied. The judgment of the Court of Appeals is affirmed with respect to the finding of liability under federal common law,[27] and reversed with respect to the

---

26. Three cases establish our approach to the test of waiver of the Eleventh Amendment. *Edelman v. Jordan,* 415 U.S. 651, 94 S.Ct. 1347, 39 L.Ed.2d 662 (1974); *Employees v. Missouri Dept. of Public Health and Welfare,* 411 U.S. 279, 93 S.Ct. 1614, 36 L.Ed.2d 251 (1973); and *Parden v. Terminal R. Co.,* 377 U.S. 184, 84 S.Ct. 1207, 12 L.Ed.2d 233 (1964). Although each of these involved waiver for purposes of suit under a federal statute, we indicated in *Pennhurst* that the same standards apply in the context of a

state statute. 465 U.S., at 99–100, 104 S.Ct., at 907–908.

27. The question whether equitable considerations should limit the relief available to the present day Oneida Indians was not addressed by the Court of Appeals or presented to this Court by petitioners. Accordingly, we express no opinion as to whether other considerations may be relevant to the final disposition of this

exercise of ancillary jurisdiction over the counties' cross-claim for indemnification. The cases are remanded to the Court of Appeals for further proceedings consistent with our decision.

It is so ordered.

Justice STEVENS concurs in the judgment with respect to No. 83–1240.

Justice BRENNAN, with whom Justice MARSHALL joins, concurring in part and dissenting in part.

I join the Court's opinion except for Part V. I dissent from Part V because I adhere to my view that the Eleventh Amendment "bars federal court suits against States only by citizens of other States," *Yeomans v. Kentucky*, 423 U.S. 983, 984, 96 S.Ct. 404, 404, 46 L.Ed.2d 309 (1975) (BRENNAN, J., dissenting). Thus, I would hold that the State of New York is not entitled to invoke the protections of that Amendment in this federal-court suit by counties of New York. See *Employees v. Missouri Dept. of Public Health and Welfare*, 411 U.S. 279, 298, 93 S.Ct. 1614, 1625, 36 L.Ed.2d 251 (1973) (BRENNAN, J., dissenting); *Edelman v. Jordan*, 415 U.S. 651, 687, 97 S.Ct. 1347, 1367, 39 L.Ed.2d 662 (1974) (BRENNAN, J., dissenting). In my view, *Hans v. Louisiana*, 134 U.S. 1, 10 S.Ct. 504, 33 L.Ed. 842 (1890), erects a limited constitutional barrier prohibiting suits against States by citizens of another State; the decision, however, "accords to nonconsenting States only a *nonconstitutional* immunity from suit by its own citizens." *Employees v. Missouri Dept. of Public Health and Welfare, supra*, 411

U.S., at 313, 93 S.Ct., at 1632 (BRENNAN, J., dissenting) (emphasis added). For scholarly discussion supporting this view, see Shapiro, Wrong Turns: The Eleventh Amendment and the *Pennhurst* Case, 98 Harv.L.Rev. 61, 68 (1984); Gibbons, The Eleventh Amendment and State Sovereign Immunity: A Reinterpretation, 83 Colum.L. Rev. 1889, 1893–1894 (1983); Field, The Eleventh Amendment and Other Sovereign Immunity Doctrines: Part One, 126 U.Pa. L.Rev. 515, 538–540, and n. 88 (1978).

Justice STEVENS, with whom THE CHIEF JUSTICE, Justice WHITE, and Justice REHNQUIST join, dissenting in No. 83–1065.

In 1790, the President of the United States notified Cornplanter, the Chief of the Senecas, that federal law would securely protect Seneca lands from acquisition by any State or person:

"If ... you have any just cause of complaint against [a purchaser] and can make satisfactory proof thereof, the federal courts will be open to you for redress, as to all other persons." 4 American State Papers, Indian Affairs, Vol. 1, p. 142 (1832).[1]

The elders of the Oneida Indian Nation received comparable notice of their capacity to maintain the federal claim that is at issue in this litigation.[2] They made no attempt to assert the claim, and their successors in interest waited 175 years before bringing suit to avoid a 1795 conveyance that the Tribe freely made, for a valuable consideration. The absence of any evidence of deception, concealment, or inter-

---

case should Congress not exercise its authority to resolve these far-reaching Indian claims.

1. Before 1875 when "Congress conferred upon the lower federal courts, for but the second time in their nearly century-old history, general federal-question jurisdiction," *Steffel v. Thompson*, 415 U.S. 452, 464, 94 S.Ct. 1209, 1218, 39 L.Ed.2d 505 (1974); Judiciary Act of March 3, 1875, 18 Stat. 470, an Indian tribe could only raise its federal land claims in this Court by appealing a state-court judgment, Judiciary Act of 1789, ch. 20, § 25, 1 Stat. 85. Until Congress made Indians United States citizens in the Act of

June 2, 1924, ch. 233, 43 Stat. 253, they were not generally considered "citizens" for the purposes of diversity jurisdiction in the lower federal courts. Nor were the tribes "foreign states" entitled to apply for original jurisdiction in this Court. *Cherokee Nation v. Georgia*, 5 Pet. 1, 8 L.Ed. 25 (1831).

2. During the negotiations leading to the 1795 treaty with New York, a federal agent informed the Tribe that no local treaty could validly transfer their interest in lands without the presence of a United States Indian Commissioner, Record Doc. No. 37, p. 122.

ference with the Tribe's right to assert a claim, together with the societal interests that always underlie statutes of repose—particularly[256] when title to real property is at stake—convince me that this claim is barred by the extraordinary passage of time. It is worthy of emphasis that this claim arose when George Washington was the President of the United States.

The Court refuses to apply any time bar to this claim, believing that to do so would be inconsistent with federal Indian policy. This Court, however, has always applied the equitable doctrine of laches when Indians or others have sought, in equity, to set aside conveyances made under a statutory or common-law incapacity to convey. Although this action is brought at law, in ejectment, there are sound reasons for recognizing that it is barred by similar principles.

In reaching a contrary conclusion, the Court relies on the legislative histories of a series of recent enactments. In my view, however, the Oneida were barred from avoiding their 1795 conveyance long before 1952, when Congress enacted the first statute that the Court relies on today. Neither that statute, nor any subsequent federal legislation, revived the Oneida's dormant claim.

I

Today's decision is an unprecedented departure from the wisdom of the common law:

"The best interests of society require that causes of action should not be deferred an unreasonable time. This remark is peculiarly applicable to land titles. Nothing so much retards the growth and prosperity of a country as

insecurity of titles to real estate. Labor is paralysed where the enjoyment of its fruits is uncertain; and litigation without limit produces ruinous consequences to individuals." *Lewis v. Marshall*, 5 Pet. 470, 477–478, 8 L.Ed. 195 (1831).

Of course, as the Court notes, there "is no federal statute of limitations governing federal common-law actions by Indians to enforce property rights." *Ante*, at 1255. However, "where Congress has not spoken but left matters for judicial determination within the general framework of familiar legal [257]principles," *Holmberg v. Armbrecht*, 327 U.S. 392, 395, 66 S.Ct. 582, 584, 90 L.Ed. 743 (1946), the settled practice has been to adopt the state law of limitations as federal law.

The Court has recognized that "State legislatures do not devise their limitations periods with national interests in mind, and it is the duty of the federal courts to assure that the importation of state law will not frustrate or interfere with the implementation of national policies." *Occidental Life Ins. Co. v. EEOC*, 432 U.S. 355, 367, 97 S.Ct. 2447, 2455, 53 L.Ed.2d 402 (1977). The Court, for example, has refused to apply state laws of limitations when a more analogous federal statute of limitations better reflects the appropriate balance between the enforcement of federal substantive policies and the historic principles of repose,[3] or when a unique federal interest in the subject matter or a paramount interest in national uniformity require the fashioning of a federal time bar in order to avoid serious conflict with federal policies or functions.[4] In applying these principles, however, the Court has always presumed that *some* principle of limitation applies to federal causes of action.[5] Thus, in *Occi-*

3. *DelCostello v. Teamsters*, 462 U.S. 151, 103 S.Ct. 2281, 76 L.Ed.2d 476 (1983); cf. *McAllister v. Magnolia Petroleum Co.*, 357 U.S. 221, 78 S.Ct. 1201, 2 L.Ed.2d 1272 (1958).

4. *Holmberg v. Armbrecht*, 327 U.S. 392, 395, 66 S.Ct. 582, 584, 90 L.Ed. 743 (1946) ("We have the duty of federal courts, sitting as national courts throughout the country, to apply their own prin-

ciples in enforcing an equitable right created by Congress").

5. In cases arising in admiralty, the Court has traditionally applied the equitable doctrine of laches. See, *e.g.*, *Gutierrez v. Waterman S.S. Corp.*, 373 U.S. 206, 215, 83 S.Ct. 1185, 1191, 10 L.Ed.2d 297 (1963). In territorial disputes arising under our original jurisdiction we have applied the doctrine of acquiescence which con-

dental Life Ins. Co., the Court concluded that Congress had intended no rigid time |258limit for EEOC enforcement actions, but the Court also recognized that federal courts have adequate power to bar an action if the defendant was "significantly handicapped in making his defense because of an inordinate EEOC delay." *Id.*, at 373, 97 S.Ct., at 2458.

Before 1966 there was no federal statute of limitations that even arguably could have supplanted a state limitation. Even the longest possibly applicable state statute of limitations would surely have barred this cause of action—which arose in 1795— many years before 1966.[6] Moreover, "[a] state statute cannot be considered 'inconsistent' with federal law merely because the statute causes the plaintiff to lose the litigation." *Robertson v. Wegmann*, 436 U.S. 584, 593, 98 S.Ct. 1991, 1996, 56 L.Ed.2d 554 (1978). Nor is the rejection of a generally applicable state law inappropriate merely because one party is an Indian tribe and the subject matter of the litigation involves tribal property. *Wilson v. Omaha Indian Tribe*, 442 U.S. 653, 673–674, 99 S.Ct. 2529, 2540–2541, 61 L.Ed.2d

153 (1979). Thus, a routine application of our practice in dealing with limitations questions would lead to the conclusion that this claim is barred by the lapse of time.

Nevertheless, there are unique considerations in cases involving Indian claims that warrant a departure from the ordinary practice. Indians have long occupied a protected status in our law, and in the 19th century they were often characterized as wards of the State.[7] At common law, conveyances of |259persons subject to similar disabilities were void. In practice, however, the common-law courts modified the wooden rules ordinarily applied to real property claims in actions at law in order to protect the ward, as far as possible, from manipulation, while at the same time avoiding the obvious inequity involved in the setting aside, at a distant date, of conveyances that had been freely made, for valuable consideration.

For example, the statute of limitations applicable to actions seeking to gain recovery of the real estate conveyed under such disabilities did not begin to run against a ward until his unique disabilities had been

firms the legal validity of a boundary line accepted for a considerable length of time by all parties as the actual boundary between two States, notwithstanding any irregularities in its legal origin. See *California v. Nevada*, 447 U.S. 125, 130–132, 100 S.Ct. 2064, 2067–2069, 65 L.Ed.2d 1 (1980); *Ohio v. Kentucky*, 410 U.S. 641, 650–651, 93 S.Ct. 1178, 1183–1184, 35 L.Ed.2d 650 (1973). Under the lost grant doctrine, "lapse of time," under carefully limited circumstances, "may cure the neglect or failure to secure the proper muniments of title," even against the United States. *United States v. Fullard-Leo*, 331 U.S. 256, 270, 67 S.Ct. 1287, 1293, 91 L.Ed. 1474 (1947).

6. While the current New York period of limitations applicable to actions "to recover real property or its possession" presently is 10 years, N.Y.Civ.Prac.Law. § 212 (McKinney 1972), the period in 1795 was 50 years, 1788 N.Y.Laws, ch. 43, p. 685.

7. See *Felix v. Patrick*, 145 U.S. 317, 330, 12 S.Ct. 862, 866, 36 L.Ed. 719 (1892) ("Whatever may have been the injustice visited upon this unfortunate race of people by their white neighbors, this court has repeatedly held them to be the wards of the nation, entitled to a special protec-

tion in its courts, and as persons 'in a state of pupilage' "); *Chouteau v. Molony*, 16 How. 203, 237–238, 14 L.Ed. 905 (1854) (Under Spanish law, "Indians, although of age, continue to enjoy the rights of minors, to avoid contracts or other sales of their property—particularly real—made without authority of the judiciary or the intervention of their legal protectors. Indians are considered as persons under legal disability . . .") (citation omitted); *Georgia & the Treaty of Indian Spring*, 2 Op.Atty.Gen. 110, 133 (1828) (Although under federal law Indians have a limited capacity to contract for the sale of their lands, "[a] limited capacity to contract is no anomaly in the law. Infants have this limited capacity to contract . . . ; beyond this limit, their contracts are void. . . . Yet it was never imagined that, because their independence or competency was not absolute and universal, but limited, that therefore their contracts *within the sphere of their competency* were to be differently construed from those of other persons"); see also *ante*, at 1255, n. 14 (opinion of the Court); *United States v. Kagama*, 118 U.S. 375, 383–384, 6 S.Ct. 1109, 1113–1114, 30 L.Ed. 228 (1886); *Cherokee Nation v. Georgia*, 5 Pet., at 17.

overcome.[8] Thus, to be faithful to these common-law principles, the application of a state statute of limitations in the context of ancient Indian claims would require flexible consideration of the development of the particular tribe's capacity to govern its own affairs.

|260Moreover, the common law developed prescription doctrines that terminated the vendor's power to avoid a void conveyance in an action in ejectment. These doctrines

could deny the ward, or those claiming under him, a cause of action in ejectment even before the running of the applicable statute of limitations. Although these doctrines were often based on theories of implied ratification, they were most often enforced in circumstances indicating undue or prejudicial delay.[9]

|261I believe that the equitable doctrine of laches,[10] with its focus on legitimate re-

8. See 2 W. Blackstone, Commentaries *291–*292; 2 J. Kent, Commentaries on American Law 248–249 (8th ed. 1854); 5 G. Thompson, Real Property § 2556 (1979); 6 G. Thompson, Real Property § 2947 (1962); cf. *Schrimpscher v. Stockton,* 183 U.S. 290, 296, 22 S.Ct. 107, 110, 46 L.Ed. 203 (1902) ("Conceding, but without deciding, that so long as Indians maintain their tribal relations they are not chargeable with laches or failure to assert their claims within the time prescribed by statutes, ... they would lose this immunity when their relations with their tribe were dissolved by accepting allotments of lands in severalty").

9. In *Brazee v. Schofield,* 124 U.S. 495, 8 S.Ct. 604, 31 L.Ed. 484 (1888), the Court rejected the claim in ejectment of a person seeking to avoid a conveyance made by a minor during his infancy:

"For eleven years after [the minor] became of age he made no objection to the proceedings, or by any act indicated his intention to disaffirm the sale or deed ...; and [only then] he gave to the grantors of the [plaintiffs] a deed of his interest in the ... claim. In the meantime, the property had greatly increased in value by the improvements put upon it by the purchaser.... Under these circumstances, ... the long acquiescence of the minor, after he became of age, in the proceedings had for the sale of his property, was equivalent to an express affirmance of them, even were they affected with such irregularities as, upon his prompt application after becoming of age, would have justified the court in setting them aside." *Id.,* at 504–505, 8 S.Ct., at 608–609.

See also *Irvine v. Irvine,* 9 Wall. 617, 19 L.Ed. 800 (1870); *Tucker v. Moreland,* 10 Pet. 58, 9 L.Ed. 345 (1836). See generally 1 L. Jones, Real Property §§ 24–26 (1896); 1 J. Kent, Commentaries on American Law 252–255 (8th ed. 1854); 1 R. Powell, Real Property ¶ 125, p. 483 (1984); 6 G. Thompson, Real Property § 2946, pp. 30–31; § 2951, pp. 63–64 (1962); cf. 2 J. Pomeroy, Equity Jurisprudence § 965 (1886).

Similar doctrines have been applied in the Indian area. For example, in *United States v. Santa Fe Pacific R. Co.,* 314 U.S. 339, 62 S.Ct. 248, 86 L.Ed. 260 (1941) the Court held that the acceptance by the Walapais Indians of reserva-

tion lands "must be regarded in law as the equivalent of a release of any tribal rights which they may have had in lands outside the reservation. They were in substance acquiescing in the penetration of white settlers on condition that permanent provision was made for them too. In view of this historical setting, it cannot now be fairly implied that tribal rights of the Walapais in lands outside the reservation were preserved.... Hence, acquiescence in that arrangement must be deemed to have been a relinquishment of tribal rights in lands outside the reservation and notoriously claimed by others." *Id.,* at 358, 62 S.Ct., at 257. See also *Mitchel v. United States,* 9 Pet. 711, 746, 9 L.Ed. 283 (1835) ("*Indian possession or occupation was considered with reference to their habits and modes of life;* their hunting-grounds were as much in their actual possession as the cleared fields of the whites; and their rights to its exclusive enjoyment in their own way, and for their own purposes were as much respected, *until they abandoned them,* made a cession to the government, or an authorized sale to individuals. *In either case their right became extinct* ...") (emphasis added); *Williams v. City of Chicago,* 242 U.S. 434, 437, 37 S.Ct. 142, 144, 61 L.Ed. 414 (1917) ("If in any view [the Pottawatomie Nation] ever held possession of the property here in question, *we know historically that this was abandoned long ago* and that for more than a half century [the tribe] has not even pretended to occupy either the shores or waters of Lake Michigan within the confines of Illinois") (emphasis added). Cf. H.R.Doc. 1590, 63d Cong., 3d Sess., 11 (1915) (The Oneida sold most of their lands to the State, and divided the remaining lands in severalty; "as a tribe these Indians are known no more in that State").

10. In their petition for certiorari, the counties raised the general question of what federal time bar should apply to this litigation in asking the Court to decide "Whether, in any case, respondent's claim is barred because it was not brought until 175 years after the conveyance." Pet. for Cert. of Counties, Question 2. The possibility that laches might apply to the claim is fairly included within that question. The laches question was fully litigated in the trial court—

liance and inexcusable delay, best reflects the limitation principles that would have governed this ancient claim at common law—without requiring a historian's inquiry into the archaic limitation doctrines that would have governed the claims at any specific time in the preceding two centuries. Of course, the application of a traditional equitable₂₆₂ defense in an action at law is something of a novelty. But this novel development in litigation involving Indian claims arose in order to benefit a special class of litigants, and it remains true that an equitable defense to the instant claim is less harsh than a straightforward application of the limitations rule dictated by our usual practice. At least equal to the maxim that equity follows the law is the truth that common-law real property principles were often tempered by equitable considerations—as the rules limiting a ward's power to avoid an unlawful conveyance demonstrate.[11]

As the Court recognizes, the instant action arises under the federal common law, not under any congressional enactment, and in this context the Court would not risk frustrating the will of the Legislature[12] by applying this familiar doctrine of equity. The merger of law and equity in one federal court[13] is, of course, primarily procedural. Considering the hybrid nature of these claims and the evolving character of the common law, however, I believe that the

application of laches as a limitation principle governing ancient Indian claims will promote uniformity of result in law and at equity, maintain the proper measure of flexibility to protect the legitimate interests of the tribes, while at the same time honoring the historic wisdom in the value of repose.

⌐₂₆₃II

Three decisions of this Court illustrate the application of the doctrine of laches to actions seeking to set aside conveyances made in violation of federal law. In *Ewert v. Bluejacket*, 259 U.S. 129, 42 S.Ct. 442, 66 L.Ed. 858 (1922), the Court stated that "the equitable doctrine of laches ... cannot properly have application to give vitality to a void deed and to bar the rights of Indian wards in lands subject to statutory restrictions." *Id.*, at 138, 42 S.Ct., at 444. A close examination of the *Ewert* case, however, indicates that the Court *applied* the doctrine of laches, but rejected relief for the defendant *in the circumstances of the case.*

In 1909, Ewert, a federal Indian agent, obtained a conveyance of allotted lands from the heirs of an Indian in violation of a statutory prohibition against federal officers engaging in trade with Indians. In 1916, the heirs brought an action, in equity, seeking to set aside the conveyance. The

the testimony of four of the six witnesses appearing on the Oneida's behalf in the liability phase of the trial was presented solely to avoid the obvious defense of laches. Record Doc. No. 37, pp. 196–276. The Court of Appeals' rejection of delay-based defenses, 719 F.2d 525, 538 (CA2 1983), will remain the law of the Circuit until it is reversed by this Court, and will no doubt apply to the numerous Indian claims pending in the lower courts, see cases cited in Brief for Respondent Counties in No. 83–1240, p. 10, and n. 8. Discussion of the applicability of equitable limitations or laches appears in the briefs, Reply Brief for Petitioner Counties in No. 83–1065, pp. 19–20; Brief for United States as *Amicus Curiae* 33–40; Brief for City of Escondido et al. as *Amici Curiae* 21–29, and occurred at oral argument. Tr. of Oral Arg. 61–65.

11. In fact, the idea that the State should protect persons suffering from disabilities who had no

other lawful protector probably arose at equity where the Chancery Courts exercised the prerogatives of the King as *parens patriae*, 3 J. Story, Equity Jurisprudence § 1748 (14th ed. 1918), and applied theories of constructive fraud, 2 J. Pomeroy, Equity Jurisprudence § 943 (1886).

12. In deference to the doctrine of the separation of powers, the Court has been circumspect in adopting principles of equity in the context of enforcing federal statutes. See generally *Weinberger v. Romero-Barcelo*, 456 U.S. 305, 102 S.Ct. 1798, 72 L.Ed.2d 91 (1982); *TVA v. Hill*, 437 U.S. 153, 98 S.Ct. 2279, 57 L.Ed.2d 117 (1978); *Hecht Co. v. Bowles*, 321 U.S. 321, 64 S.Ct. 587, 88 L.Ed. 754 (1944); Plater, Statutory Violations and Equitable Discretion, 70 Calif.L.Rev. 524, 592 (1982).

13. *E.g.,* Fed.Rules Civ.Proc. 1, 2.

Court of Appeals held that the heirs had the burden of disproving laches because they had brought their action outside the applicable state statute of limitations, and concluded that they had not satisfied this burden. "The adult plaintiffs were free to make conveyance of this land, even though they were Indians, and [since] their tribal relations had been severed, [they] were chargeable with the same diligence as white people in discovering and pursuing their legal remedies. [*Felix v. Patrick*, 145 U.S. 317, 12 S.Ct. 862, 36 L.Ed. 719 (1892)]; [*Schrimpscher v. Stockton*, 183 U.S. 290, 22 S.Ct. 107, 46 L.Ed. 203 (1902)]." *Bluejacket v. Ewert*, 265 Fed. 823, 829 (CA8 1920).

On appeal, this Court held that the plaintiffs' action was not barred by the doctrine of laches, noting that "[Ewert] still holds the legal title to the land." 259 U.S., at 138, 42 S.Ct., at 444. The Court principally relied on the doctrine that "an [unlawful] act ... is void and confers no right *upon the wrongdoer.*" *Waskey v. Hammer*, 223 U.S. 85, 94, 32 S.Ct. 187, 189, 56 L.Ed. 359 (1912) (emphasis added). On the facts of *Ewert*, the Court found that the ⌊264plaintiffs' burden of disproving laches was easily met, but the Court might well have reached a different conclusion in *Ewert* if the conveyance had not been so recent, if the defendant had not been as blameworthy, or if the character of the property had changed dramatically in the interim.

My interpretation of *Ewert* is illustrated by this Court's prior decision in *Felix v. Patrick*, 145 U.S. 317, 12 S.Ct. 862, 36 L.Ed. 719 (1892). In that case, the Court applied the doctrine of laches to bar an action by the heirs of an Indian to establish a constructive trust over lands that had been conveyed by her in violation of a federal statutory restriction. The action to set aside the unlawful transfer was brought 28 years after the transaction, and in the intervening time, "[t]hat which was wild land thirty years ago is now intersected by streets, subdivided into blocks and lots, and largely occupied by persons who have bought upon the strength of Patrick's title, and have erected buildings of a permanent character upon their purchases." *Id.*, at 334, 12 S.Ct., at 868.

The Court recognized that the long passage of time, the change in the character of the property, the transfer of some of the property to third parties, the absence of any obvious inadequacy in the consideration received in the original transaction, and Patrick's lack of direct participation in the original transfer all supported a charge of laches against the plaintiffs. In addition, the Court noted that "[t]he decree prayed for in this case, if granted, would offer a distinct encouragement to the purchase of similar claims, which doubtless exist in abundance through the Western Territories, ... and would result in the unsettlement of large numbers of titles upon which the owners have rested in assured security for nearly a generation." *Id.*, at 335, 12 S.Ct., at 868.

Nor is *Felix* the only application of these principles in a similar context. In *Wetzel v. Minnesota Railway Transfer Co.*, 169 U.S. 237, 18 S.Ct. 307, 42 L.Ed. 730 (1898), the children of a deceased Mexican War veteran received a warrant for 160 acres of land under a federal statute that prohibited any alienation of the property without the approval of the proper state probate court. The ⌊265children's guardian sold their share in the warrant without seeking the approval of the proper court. Forty-four years after the conveyance, the children brought an action, in equity, seeking to establish a constructive trust over the 160 acres—now located in a well-developed area of St. Paul, Minnesota. The Court held that the action was barred by laches relying on *Felix v. Patrick*, and noting that the property had been completely developed and had greatly increased in value. The Court also observed that title had passed to persons who were no doubt ignorant of the defect in title.

The Court also noted the relevance of the length of the delay:

"While the fact that the complainants were ignorant of the defect in the title and were without means to prosecute an investigation into the facts may properly be considered by the court, it does not mitigate the hardship to the defendants of unsettling these titles. *If the complainant may put forward these excuses for delay after thirty years, there is no reason why they may not allege the same as an excuse after a lapse of sixty. The truth is, there must be some limit of time within which these excuses shall be available, or titles might forever be insecure.* The interests of public order and tranquillity demand that parties shall acquaint themselves with their rights within a reasonable time, and although this time may be extended by their actual ignorance, or want of means, it is by no means illimitable." 169 U.S., at 241, 18 S.Ct., at 309 (emphasis added).

Ewert, Felix, and *Wetzel* establish beyond doubt that it is quite consistent with federal policy to apply the doctrine of laches to limit a vendor's power to avoid a conveyance violating a federal restriction on alienation.

III

As in *Felix* and *Wetzel,* the land conveyed by the Oneida in 1795 has been converted from wilderness to cities, towns, ₁₂₆₆villages, and farms. The 872 acres of land involved in the instant action include the principal transportation arteries in the region, and other vital public facilities owned by the Counties of Oneida and Madison.[14] The counties and the private property owners affected by the litigation, without proven notice of the defect in title caused by the State of New York's failure to comply with the federal statute, have erected costly improvements on the property in reliance on the validity of their title. Even if the counties are considered for some purposes to be the alter ego of the State, it is surely a fiction to argue that they are in any way responsible for their predicament,[15] or that their taxpayers, who will ultimately bear the burden of the judgment in this case, are in any way culpable for New York's violation of federal law in 1795.

As the Court holds, *ante,* at 1251–1252, there was no *legal* impediment to the maintenance of this cause of action at any time after 1795. Although the mere passage of time, without other inequity in the prosecution of the claim, does not support a finding of laches in the ordinary case, *e.g., Holmberg v. Armbrecht,* 327 U.S., at 396, 66 S.Ct., at 584, in cases of *gross* laches the passage of a great length of time creates a nearly insurmountable burden on the plaintiffs to disprove the obvious defense of laches.[16] As Justice Story noted for the

14. Partial Findings of Fact and Conclusions of Law (Oct. 5, 1981), App. 148a–153a.

15. *Id.,* at 151a ("The counties of Madison and Oneida, New York, were not in existence in 1795 at the time of the transaction complained of in this action. No evidence has been presented to show that the Counties ... acted other than in good faith when they came into possession of the County Land in the claim area subsequent to 1795 and prior to January 1, 1968").

16. See, *e.g., French Republic v. Saratoga Vichy Spring Co.,* 191 U.S. 427, 436–437, 24 S.Ct. 145, 146–147, 48 L.Ed. 247 (1903) (25-year delay); *Clarke v. Boorman's Executors,* 18 Wall. 493, 509, 21 L.Ed. 904 (1874) (40-year delay); *Badger v. Badger,* 2 Wall. 87, 94–95, 17 L.Ed. 836 (1864) (28-year delay); *Wagner v. Baird,* 7 How. 234, 258–259, 12 L.Ed. 681 (1849) (46-year delay); *Bowman v. Wathen,* 1 How. 189, 195, 11 L.Ed. 97 (1843) (38-year delay); *Piatt v. Vattier,* 9 Pet. 405, 416–417, 9 L.Ed. 173 (1835) (30-year delay);

see also 3 J. Story, Commentaries on Equity Jurisprudence 553 (1918) ("Courts of Equity act sometimes by analogy to the law, and sometimes act upon their own inherent doctrine of discouraging for the peace of society antiquated demands by refusing to interfere where there has been gross laches in prosecuting rights, or long and unreasonable acquiescence in the assertion of adverse rights"); cf. *Saratoga Vichy Spring Co. v. Lehman,* 625 F.2d 1037, 1041 (CA2 1980) (69-year delay); *Anheuser-Busch, Inc. v. Du Bois Brewing Co.,* 175 F.2d 370, 374 (CA3 1949) (in hypothetical lapse of 100 years "highly dubious" whether plaintiff could prevail), cert. denied, 339 U.S. 934, 70 S.Ct. 664, 94 L.Ed. 1353 (1950).

In deciding territorial disputes arising under this Court's original jurisdiction, similar principles have frequently been applied:
"No human transactions are unaffected by time. Its influence is seen on all things subject to change. And this is peculiarly the case in re-

Court in *Prevost v. Gratz*, 6 Wheat. 481, 504–505, 5 L.Ed. 311 (1821):

|267 "[G]eneral presumptions are raised by the law upon subjects of which there is no record or written instrument, not because there are the means of belief or disbelief, but because mankind, judging of matters of antiquity from the infirmity and necessity of their situation must, for the preservation of their property and rights, have recourse to some general principle, to take the place of individual and specific belief, which can hold only as to matters within our own time, upon which a conclusion can be formed from particular and individual knowledge." *Id.*, at 504–505.

Given their burden of explaining nearly two centuries of delay in the prosecution of this claim, and considering the |268legitimate reliance interests of the counties and the other property owners whose title is derived from the 1795 conveyance, the Oneida have not adequately justified their delay.

Of course, the traditional rule was "that 'the conduct of Indians is not to be measured by the same standard which we apply to the conduct of other people.' But

their very analogy to persons under guardianship suggests a limitation to their pupilage, since the utmost term of disability of an infant is but 21 years, and it is very rare that the relations of guardian and ward under any circumstances, even those of lunacy, are maintained for a longer period than this." *Felix v. Patrick*, 145 U.S., at 330–331, 12 S.Ct., at 866 (quoting *The Kansas Indians*, 5 Wall. 737, 758, 18 L.Ed. 667 (1867)). In this case, the testimony at trial indicates that the Oneida people have independently held land derived from tribal allotments at least since the Dawes Act of 1887,[17] and probably earlier in the State of New York.[18] They have received formal schooling at least since 1796 in New York, and have gradually become literate in the English language.[19] They have developed a sophisticated system of tribal government,[20] and at various times in the past 175 years, have petitioned the Government for the redress of grievances, or sent commissions to confer with their brethren.[21]

|269In all the years after the 1795 conveyance—until the years leading up to this litigation—the Oneida made few efforts to raise this specific grievance against the State of New York and the landowners

---

gard to matters which rest in memory, and which consequently fade with the lapse of time, and fall with the lives of individuals. For the security of rights, whether of states or individuals, long possession under a claim of title is protected." *Rhode Island v. Massachusetts*, 4 How. 591, 639, 11 L.Ed. 1116 (1846). See also *California v. Nevada*, 447 U.S., at 132, 100 S.Ct., at 2068 ("If Nevada felt that those lines were inaccurate and operated to deprive it of territory lawfully within its jurisdiction the time to object was when the surveys were conducted, not a century later"); *Ohio v. Kentucky*, 410 U.S., at 648–651, 93 S.Ct., at 1182–1184; *Indiana v. Kentucky*, 136 U.S. 479, 509–510, 10 S.Ct. 1051, 1053–1054, 34 L.Ed. 329 (1890).

17. General Allotment Act, 24 Stat. 388.

18. Record Doc. No. 37, p. 227.

19. *Id.*, at 210, 264. In 1948, the Secretary of the Wisconsin Oneida testified before a Senate Subcommittee that nearly all of the members of the Tribe could speak English fluently, although a few of the older members of the Tribe could not read and write. Hearings on S. 1683 before a

105 S.Ct.—32

Subcommittee of the Senate Committee on Interior and Insular Affairs, 80th Cong., 2d Sess., 41 (1948). At least into the 1950's, however, translators were required at general meetings to explain complicated actions of the Federal Government. Record Doc. No. 37, p. 225.

20. The Wisconsin Oneida, for example, have been incorporated since 1937, *id.*, at 207, 211–212, with a Constitution, bylaws, and a governing "Business Committee" which is elected by the tribal members. *Id.*, at 211–212. See also *id.*, at 37–41.

21. In 1874, for example, a party of Wisconsin Oneida traveled to Albany, New York, to confer with a private law firm and members of the New York Tribe about viable alternatives of protest against the Federal Government. *Id.*, at 237–238. The record contains numerous petitions and letters from the Tribe and tribal members in this century seeking the Government's assistance in resolving miscellaneous problems concerning treaty rights, real property ownership, and Government entitlement programs. See Record Ex. Nos. 54, 55.

holding under the State's title.[22] Claims to lands in New York most often were only made in connection with generalized grievances concerning the Tribe's treatment at the hands of the United States Government.[23] Although the Oneida plainly knew or should have known that they had conveyed their lands to the State of New York in violation of federal law, and that they might have some cause for redress, they inexplicably delayed filing a lawsuit on their claim until 175 years after the conveyance was made. Finally, "[t]here is no evidence that any of the plaintiffs or their predecessors ever refused or returned any of the payments received for the purported sale of land pursuant to the Treaty of 1795."[24]

|270The Oneida have not met their formidable burden of disproving unjustifiable delay to the prejudice of others. In my opinion their cause of action is barred by the doctrine of laches. The remedy for the ancient wrong established at trial should be

22. See, e.g., Record Ex. No. 54 (1909 correspondence).

23. Although there was much anger, resentment, and bitterness among the Oneida in the 19th century concerning their treatment by the United States, "conditions were being protested, but there was no specification of this particular treaty in the protest." Record Doc. No. 37, p. 248. No specific action was taken to enforce this claim in a court of law until 1951 when the Oneida filed a petition against the United States before the Indian Claims Commission seeking judgment against the United States, as trustee, for the fair market value of the Oneida lands sold to the State of New York since the 18th century. See App. 43a.

24. Partial Conclusions of Law, App. 152a. There is also a serious question whether the Oneida did not abandon their claim to the aboriginal lands in New York when they accepted the Treaty of Buffalo Creek of 1838, which ceded most of the Tribe's lands in Wisconsin to the United States in exchange for a new reservation in the Indian Territory. The Treaty provided that the new reservation lands were to provide "a permanent home for all the New York Indians, now residing in the State of New York, or in Wisconsin, or elsewhere in the United States, who have no permanent homes." 7 Stat. 551, Art. 2. "These proceedings, by which these tribes divested themselves of their title to lands in New York, indicate an intention on the part,

provided by Congress, not by judges seeking to rewrite history at this late date.

IV

The Oneida argue that the legislative histories of a series of congressional enactments, beginning in 1952, persuasively establish that their claims have never been barred. This argument has serious flaws, not the least, being that whatever Congress said in 1952 or 1966 is extremely weak authority for the status of the common law in 1795, or for a considerable period thereafter. Believing, as I do, that the Oneida's claim was barred by the doctrine of laches or by a related common-law doctrine[25] long before 1952, it is quite clear that the statutes discussed by the Court did not revive it.

First, and most obviously, the principal statute relied on by the Court, by its very terms, only applies to claims brought *by the United States* on behalf of Indians or Indian tribes.[26] This|271action, of course, is

both of the Government and the Indians, that they should take immediate possession of the tracts set apart for them in Kansas." *New York Indians v. United States,* 170 U.S. 1, 21, 18 S.Ct. 531, 535, 42 L.Ed. 927 (1898). Cf. *United States v. Santa Fe R. Co.,* 314 U.S., at 358, 62 S.Ct., at 257; n. 9, 62 S.Ct., at 257, *supra.*

25. See n. 9, *supra.*

26. For example, the relevant portion of 28 U.S.C. § 2415(b) provides:
"That an action to recover damages resulting from a trespass on lands of the United States; ... may be brought within six years after the right of action accrues, except that *such* actions *for or on behalf of a recognized tribe, band, or group of American Indians,* ... which accrued [prior to the date of enactment of this Act but under subsection (g) are deemed to have accrued on the date of enactment of this Act] may be brought on or before sixty days after the date of the publication of the list required by ... the Indian Claims Act of 1982: Provided, That, for *those* claims that are on either of the two lists published pursuant to the Indian Claims Act of 1982, *any* right of action shall be barred unless the complaint is filed within (1) one year after the Secretary of the Interior has published in the Federal Register a notice rejecting such claim ..." (emphasis added).
The Court relies on the word *"any"* in the final clause of the statute and construes this as

brought by an Indian Tribe *on its own behalf.*

Secondly, neither the statutes themselves,[27] nor the legislative discussions that preceded their enactment,[28] provide |_272_any indication of an intent to *revive* already barred claims.[29] Quite the contrary, they merely indicate a congressional intent to preserve the status quo with respect to ancient claims that might already be barred, and to establish a procedure for making sure that the claims would not survive eternally.

Congress, for the most part, has been quite clear when it decides to revive causes

of action that might be barred or to deny any time limitation for a private cause of action.[30] When the will of Congress is as lacking in clarity as it is in this case, we should be wary of attributing to it the intention of reviving ancient claims that will upset long-settled expectations. In divining the intent of Congress concerning the applicable limitation on a cause of action, Chief Justice Marshall once noted that "it deserves some consideration," that in the absence of an applicable limitation, "those actions might, in many cases, be brought at any distance of time. This would be utterly repugnant to the genius

implicitly providing a federal statute of limitations for causes of action brought by Indian tribes *on their own behalf,* notwithstanding the unmistakable references throughout the statute and its legislative history to claims brought by the United States *on behalf of Indians.* See, *e.g.,* H.R.Rep. No. 96–807, p. 2 (1980), U.S.Code Cong. & Admin.News 1980, pp. 206, 207; H.R. Rep. No. 92–1267, pp. 2–3 (1972); S.Rep. No. 1328, 89th Cong., 2d Sess., 8–9 (1966), U.S.Code Cong. & Admin.News 1966, pp. 2502, 2510–2511; 126 Cong.Rec. 3289 (1980) (remarks of Sen. Melcher); *id.,* at 3290 (remarks of Sen. Cohen); *id.,* at 5745 (remarks of Rep. Clausen); 123 Cong.Rec. 22499 (1977) (remarks of Rep. Cohen); *id.,* at 22507 (remarks of Rep. Dicks); *id.,* at 22509 (remarks of Rep. Studds); *id.,* at 22510 (remarks of Rep. Udall); *ibid.* (remarks of Rep. Yates). Even if the Court's construction were correct, it does not establish that Congress intended to *revive* previously barred causes of action.

27. Each of the statutes is phrased in a form indicating an intention to preserve the law as it existed on the date of passage. See, *e.g.,* 25 U.S.C. § 233 ("*[N]othing herein contained shall be construed* as conferring jurisdiction on the courts of the State of New York or making applicable the laws of the State of New York in civil actions involving Indian lands or claims with respect thereto which relate to transactions or events transpiring prior to September 13, 1952") (emphasis added); 28 U.S.C. § 2415(c) ("*[N]othing herein shall be deemed* to limit the time for bringing an action to establish the title to, or right of possession of, real or personal property") (emphasis added).

28. The comments of Representative Morris concerning the meaning of the proviso contained in 25 U.S.C. § 233, reflect an intent to "*preserve* their rights," 96 Cong.Rec. 12460 (1950). The proviso was designed to preserve an "impartial" federal forum for resolving pre-existing Indian land claims and to ensure that federal law

would be applied in deciding them. See *Oneida Indian Nation v. County of Oneida,* 414 U.S. 661, 680–682, 94 S.Ct. 772, 784–785, 39 L.Ed.2d 73 (1974). The application of laches as a federal doctrine of limitation in a federal forum is entirely consistent with this view.

As for § 2415 and its various amendments since 1966, the record is barren of any reference to revival. At most, Congress was of the view that nothing in § 2415 would "preclude" actions by the tribes themselves. See, *e.g.,* 123 Cong. Rec. 22499 (1977) (remarks of Rep. Cohen). It may very well be that in view of the hospitable treatment that these ancient claims received in the lower federal courts, some Members of Congress may have *assumed* that there was no time bar to such actions. In the absence of legislation, however, the assumptions of individual Congressmen about the status of the common law are not enacted into positive law. In enacting the Indian Claims Limitation Act of 1982, Pub.L. 97–394, 96 Stat. 1976, note following 28 U.S.C. § 2415, Congress simply provided a *procedure* for exhausting the Federal Government's responsibility, as trustee, for prosecuting meritorious claims—leaving this Court ultimately to decide whether claims brought by the tribes themselves were still alive.

29. Indeed, if the statutes had that effect, the Court would have to resolve the question of their constitutionality. Cf. *Stewart v. Keyes,* 295 U.S. 403, 417, 55 S.Ct. 807, 813, 79 L.Ed. 1507 (1935).

30. *E.g.,* 25 U.S.C. § 640d–17(b) ("Neither laches nor the statute of limitations shall constitute a defense to any action authorized by this subchapter for existing claims if commenced within two years from December, 22, 1974"); § 653 ("If any claim or claims be submitted to said courts, they shall settle the equitable rights therein, notwithstanding lapse of time or statutes of limitation"); see also *New York Indians v. United States,* 170 U.S., at 35, 18 S.Ct., at 541.

of our laws." *Adams v. Woods*, 2 Cranch 336, 341, 2 L.Ed. 297 (1805). The Court |₂₇₃today prefers to impute to Congress the intent of rewarding those whom "Abraham Lincoln once described with scorn [as sitting] in the basements of courthouses combing property records to upset established titles." *Arizona v. California*, 460 U.S. 605, 620, 103 S.Ct. 1382, 1392, 75 L.Ed.2d 318 (1983). The more appropriate presumption in this case is that Congress intended to honor legitimate expectations in the ownership of real property and not to disturb them.

V

The Framers recognized that no one ought be condemned for his forefathers' misdeeds—even when the crime is a most grave offense against the Republic.[31] The Court today ignores that principle in fashioning a common-law remedy for the Oneida Nation that allows the Tribe to avoid its 1795 conveyance 175 years after it was made. This decision upsets long-settled expectations in the ownership of real property in the Counties of Oneida and Madison, New York, and the disruption it is sure to cause will confirm the common-law wisdom that ancient claims are best left in repose. The Court, no doubt, believes that it is undoing a grave historical injustice, but in doing so it has caused another, which only Congress may now rectify.

I respectfully dissent.

---

31. U.S. Const. Art. III, § 3, cl. 2 ("no Attainder of Treason shall work Corruption of Blood, or Forfeiture except during the Life of the person attainted"). Cf. *Adams v. Woods,* 2 Cranch 336, 341, 2 L.Ed. 297 (1805) ("In a country where not even treason can be prosecuted after a lapse of three years, it could scarcely be supposed that an individual would remain for ever liable to a pecuniary forfeiture").

INDEX